THE ROUG

FLORENCE

Forthcoming travel guides include

The Algarve • The Bahamas • Cambodia
Caribbean Islands • Costa Brava
New York Restaurants • Rocky Mountains • Zanzibar

Forthcoming reference guides include

Children's Books • Chronicle: China (pocket history)
Online Travel • Weather

Rough Guides online

www.roughguides.com

Rough Guide Credits

Text editor: Helena Smith
Series editor: Mark Ellingham
Production: Helen Ostick and Katie Pringle
Cartography: Maxine Repath
Proofreading: Antonia Hebbert

Publishing Information

This second edition published January 2002
by Rough Guides Ltd,
62–70 Shorts Gardens, London, WC2H 9AH

Distributed by the Penguin Group:

Penguin Books Ltd, 80 Strand, London WC2R ORL.
Penguin Putnam, Inc. 375 Hudson Street, New York 10014, USA
Penguin Books Australia Ltd, 487 Maroondah Highway,
PO Box 257, Ringwood, Victoria 3134, Australia
Penguin Books Canada Ltd, 10 Alcorn Avenue,
Toronto, Ontario, Canada M4V 1E4
Penguin Books (NZ) Ltd,
182–190 Wairau Road, Auckland 10, New Zealand

Typeset in Bembo and Helvetica to an original design by Henry Iles.
Printed in Spain by Graphy Cems.

© Tim Jepson and Jonathan Buckley
384pp, includes index
A catalogue record for this book is available from the British Library.

ISBN 1-85828-728-6

THE ROUGH GUIDE TO

FLORENCE

by Tim Jepson
and Jonathan Buckley

with additional contributions by
James McConnachie

ROUGH
GUIDES

We set out to do something different when the first Rough Guide was published in 1982. Mark Ellingham, just out of university, was travelling in Greece. He brought along the popular guides of the day, but found they were all lacking in some way. They were either strong on ruins and museums but went on for pages without mentioning a beach or taverna. Or they were so conscious of the need to save money that they lost sight of Greece's cultural and historical significance. Also, none of the books told him anything about Greece's contemporary life – its politics, its culture, its people, and how they lived.

So with no job in prospect, Mark decided to write his own guidebook, one which aimed to provide practical information that was second to none, detailing the best beaches and the hottest clubs and restaurants, while also giving hard-hitting accounts of every sight, both famous and obscure, and providing up-to-the-minute information on contemporary culture. It was a guide that encouraged independent travellers to find the best of Greece, and was a great success, getting shortlisted for the Thomas Cook travel guide award, and encouraging Mark, along with three friends, to expand the series.

The Rough Guide list grew rapidly and the letters flooded in, indicating a much broader readership than had been anticipated, but one which uniformly appreciated the Rough Guide mix of practical detail and humour, irreverence and enthusiasm. Things haven't changed. The same four friends who began the series are still the caretakers of the Rough Guide mission today: to provide the most reliable, up-to-date and entertaining information to independent-minded travellers of all ages, on all budgets.

We now publish more than 150 titles and have offices in London and New York. The travel guides are written and researched by a dedicated team of more than 100 authors, based in Britain, Europe, the USA and Australia. We have also created a unique series of phrasebooks to accompany the travel series, along with an acclaimed series of music guides, and a best-selling pocket guide to the Internet and World Wide Web. We also publish comprehensive travel information on our Web site: **www.roughguides.com**

Help us update

We've gone to a lot of trouble to ensure that this Rough Guide is as up to date and accurate as possible. However, things do change. All suggestions, comments and corrections are much appreciated, and we'll send a copy of the next edition (or any other Rough Guide if you prefer) for the best letters.

Please mark letters "Rough Guide Florence Update" and send to:

Rough Guides, 62–70 Shorts Gardens, London, WC2H 9AH, or Rough Guides, 4th Floor, 345 Hudson St, New York NY 10014.

Or send email to: mail@roughguides.co.uk

Acknowledgements

The authors would like to thank: Claudia Attucci, Oliva Rucellai, Titi and Claudio Magagnoli, Giulia Bartolozzi, Giovanni Paternò di Roccaromana, Massimo Marcolim and the staff at the Palazzo Vecchio, Sacha Kolev, Harriet Jaine and Alice Hunt. Thanks to the readers who wrote to us with comments: Hilary Brindley, Suzanne Dell'Orto, Janet Goldman, Christine Headley, Annalisa Henderson, Guy and Helen Joosten, Ann and Bernard Kirwan, Michael Lilley, Jenifer and Alex Morton, M. Pickford, Kevin Ryan and William Scheinman.

CONTENTS

CONTENTS

MAPS AND PLANS

Colour map section (back of book)

Introduction

Florence (Firenze) has long been celebrated as Italy's most captivating city: Stendhal staggered around its streets in a perpetual stupor of delight; the Brownings sighed over its idyllic charms; and E.M. Forster's *A Room with a View* portrayed it as the great southern antidote to the sterility of Anglo-Saxon life. For Shelley, the Tuscan capital was simply the "most beautiful city I have ever seen."

Today Florence lives up to the myth in its first, resounding impressions, most notably in the Piazza del Duomo, with the multicoloured **Duomo** rising behind the marble-clad **Baptistery**. Wander from there down towards the River Arno and the attraction still holds – beyond the **Piazza della Signoria**, site of the immense **Palazzo Vecchio**, the water is spanned by the shop-laden medieval **Ponte Vecchio**, with the gorgeous church of **San Miniato al Monte** glistening on the hill behind it.

Yet after registering these marvellous sights, it's hard to stave off a sense of disappointment, at least as far as the city's physical appearance is concerned. Away from the beaten track, much of Florence is a city of narrow streets and dour, fortress-like houses, of unfinished buildings and character-less squares. Restorers' scaffolding is endemic, and almost incessant traffic provides all the usual city stresses. Just roaming the streets is a pleasure in Venice, Rome, Verona – but not in Florence.

The fact is, the best of Florence is to be seen indoors. Under the rule of the **Medici** family – the greatest patrons of Renaissance Europe – Florence's artists and thinkers were instigators of the shift from the medieval to the modern world-view, and the churches, galleries and museums of this city are the places to get to grips with their extraordinary achievement.

1. TUSCANY

The development of the Renaissance can be plotted stage by stage in the vast picture collection of the **Uffizi**, and charted in the sculpture of the **Bargello**, the **Museo dell'Opera del Duomo** and the church of **Orsanmichele**. Equally revelatory are the fabulously decorated chapels of **Santa Croce** and **Santa Maria Novella** – the city's key churches – forerunners of such astonishing creations as Masaccio's frescoes at the **Cappella Brancacci**, Fra' Angelico's serene paintings in the monks' cells at the **Museo di San Marco** and Andrea del Sarto's work at **Santissima Annunziata**.

The Renaissance emphasis on harmony and rational design is expressed with unrivalled eloquence in Brunelleschi's interiors of **San Lorenzo**, **Santo Spirito** and the **Cappella dei Pazzi**. The bizarre architecture and sculptures of San Lorenzo's **Sagrestia Nuova** and the marble statuary of the **Accademia** – home of the *David* – display the full genius of **Michelangelo**, the dominant creative figure of sixteenth-century Italy. Every quarter of Florence can boast a church or collection worth an extended call, and the enormous **Palazzo Pitti** contains half a dozen museums, including an art gallery that would be the envy of any city.

To enjoy a visit fully it's best to ration yourself to a couple of big sights each day, and spend the rest of your hours or days exploring the **quieter** peripheral spots, such as the **Giardino di Boboli** behind the Palazzo Pitti. You could head out to the pretty hill-town of **Fiesole**, just outside Florence, or – if you've time for an hour or so on a bus or train – make an excursion to one of Florence's great medieval rivals, **Siena** and **Pisa**.

Allow some time, too, to involve yourself in the life of the city. Though Florence might seem a little sedate on the surface, its university – and the presence of large numbers of language- and art-schools – guarantees a fair range of

nightlife. The city has some excellent **restaurants** and enjoyable **café–bars** amid the tourist joints, as well as the biggest and liveliest **markets** in Tuscany, and plenty of browsable, high–quality **shops**.

When to visit

Summer is not the best time to visit: the heat, and the log jam of tour groups, make viewing the major attractions a purgatorial experience – a two-hour queue for the Uffizi is not unusual. It's also worth noting that many restaurants, and some hotels, are closed throughout August. To enjoy your visit to the full, go there shortly **before Easter** or in **late autumn**, when the crowds become bearable and the city resumes its normal life. If you stay on for Easter itself, you

	F°		C°		RAINFALL	
	AVERAGE DAILY		AVERAGE DAILY		AVERAGE MONTHLY	
	MAX	MIN	MAX	MIN	IN	MM
Jan	48	36	9	2	2.5	63
Feb	52	37	11	3	2.6	65
March	54	40	14	5	2.4	61
April	66	46	19	8	2.4	61
May	71	54	23	12	2.8	70
June	80	58	27	15	2.2	56
July	86	66	30	18	1.4	35
Aug	84	62	29	17	1.8	47
Sept	78	58	26	15	2.8	70
Oct	68	52	20	11	3.7	94
Nov	54	44	14	7	4.4	110
Dec	52	39	11	4	3.7	93

can witness the **Scoppio del Carro** – the spectacular deto-
nation of a cartload of fireworks in the Piazza del Duomo.
Not that there's any shortage of **special events** during the
rest of the year, from the high-art festivities of the **Maggio
Musicale** to the licensed bedlam of the **Calcio Storico**, a
series of rough-and-tumble football matches played in sixteenth-century costume during the last week of June.

THE GUIDE

THE GUIDE

Introducing the city

Florence is an easy city to find your way around. Most of the main sights lie north of the **Arno**, the river which bisects the city from west to east. A handful are scattered in the district to the south, an area known as the **Oltrarno**. In both cases distances between sights are easily manageable on foot.

North of the river the city hinges around two main piazzas, **Piazza del Duomo** and **Piazza della Signoria**, and their connecting street, Via dei Calzaiuoli. Here you'll find some of the big set-piece sights – the Duomo (cathedral), Baptistery and Uffizi gallery – as well as attractions such as the Palazzo Vecchio and the Museo dell'Opera (the cathedral museum).

Away from these pivotal squares lie less well defined areas at the four points of the compass. To the east is a tangle of streets around the **Bargello** sculpture gallery, vaguely united by their Dantesque associations, and beyond that an appealing district which goes by the name of the great church at its heart, **Santa Croce**. To the north is the **San Lorenzo** quarter, visited primarily for its markets, church and the Michelangelo sculptures in the Cappelle Medicee. Further north, the **San Marco** area has two key sights: the Museo di San Marco, a monastery filled with paintings by Fra' Angelico, and the Accademia, home to Michelangelo's

David. Immediately west, the streets around the medieval church of **Orsanmichele** hide some low-key attractions among clusters of designer shops. Further north and west, near the railway station, lies a less prepossessing area redeemed by the monastic church of **Santa Maria Novella**.

South of the river, in the **Oltrarno**, the city has a different feel altogether: quieter, less visited, and a touch more pleasant to explore for its own sake. The central area, just across the Ponte Vecchio, centres on the huge **Palazzo Pitti**, with its major picture gallery and the formal Boboli gardens behind. To the west are two important churches and their equally well known squares: **Santo Spirito**'s piazza is the focus of a bustling and youthful little neighbourhood, while **Santa Maria del Carmine** is home to the Cappella Brancacci and its famous fresco cycle. Only the sights of **eastern Oltrarno** – an area which climbs up towards San Miniato al Monte, Florence's prettiest church with Florence's prettiest view – are far enough away to tempt you towards public transport.

Arrival

Central Florence is a compact area, and **arriving** by bus or train – or by bus or taxi from Peretola airport – will bring you right into the heart of it. Those arriving by car will find things less convenient: the city centre is a traffic-free zone, and parking is severely restricted.

BY AIR

Florence is served by three **airports**. The routine approach is to fly to Pisa and take a train, but the small city airport at

Peretola, just 5km northwest of the city centre, is increasingly popular, as is flying via Bologna.

Pisa airport

Most scheduled and charter flights use Pisa's **Galileo Galilei airport** (℡055.216.076 or ℡050.500.707; ⓦwww.pisa-airport.com), 95km west of Florence. Direct trains leave roughly every hour from a platform at the far left end of the airport concourse, 150m from arrivals. Journey time is an hour. Tickets (€4.40) can be bought from the **tourist office** (daily 8.45am–7.30pm; ℡055.503.700) at the opposite end of the airport concourse – turn right as you exit the arrivals gate. For the return journey, there's a check-in desk for most airlines found 200m down platform 5 at Florence's Santa Maria Novella station (daily 7am–5pm). But bags must be checked in thirty minutes before the departure of the train, and you won't save yourself much walking by taking advantage of the service, which costs €2.60. Check that the train runs through to Pisa Aeroporto – some go no further than Pisa Centrale station, in the city itself. The first train leaves at 8.49am and the last at 8.10pm, and there's a single train that runs after midnight; if you're arriving late (or very early), consider the ten-minute taxi ride to Pisa Centrale, from where there is a fuller service to Florence.

Peretola airport

Increasing numbers of international air services use Florence's **Peretola** (Amerigo Vespucci) airport (℡055.373.498, ⓦwww.safnet.it). The airport has a small **tourist office** in arrivals (daily 8.30am–10.30pm; ℡055.315.874).

  SITA buses (℡055.241.721) provide roughly hourly shuttles to and from the airport from outside the arrivals area: the first bus into the city is 9.15am (last 11.05pm), the first out to the airport at 8.15am (last 7.30pm). Tickets (€3.10) can be bought on board. In Florence buses arrive and depart from the main bus terminal on Via di Santa Caterina da Siena (Map 3, C6) just west of Santa Maria Novella train station. A taxi costs about €15. The journey by bus or taxi takes between fifteen and thirty minutes, depending on traffic.

Bologna airport

A few airlines use **Bologna** – about the same distance from Florence as Pisa – as a gateway airport for the city. Aerobus shuttles depart every twenty minutes between 7.30am and 11.30pm from outside Terminal A (Arrivi) to Bologna's main train station (journey time about 25min). Tickets can be bought on the bus or at the airport *tabaccaio*. From the station, regular trains reach Florence's Santa Maria Novella station in about an hour. Note that a supplement (*supplemento*) is payable on Intercity (IC) and Eurostar trains.

BY TRAIN

Trains from Pisa airport and elsewhere arrive at Florence's main central station **Santa Maria Novella**, or Firenze SMN (Map 3, D5). It's located just north of the church and square of Santa Maria Novella, a couple of blocks west of the Duomo (cathedral). The station has an information office just outside (see p.8), an accommodation service (see p.213) and left-luggage facilities. For information on trains call free ☏8488.88088. Keep a close eye on your bags at all times – the station's a prime target for thieves and pickpockets. Also avoid the concourse's various taxi and hotel touts: use only licensed cabs on the rank outside and, if you're stuck for a bed, use the station's official accommodation service (see p.213).

    Orientation from the station is straightforward – it's just ten minutes' walk from Santa Maria Novella to the central Piazza del Duomo (**Map 2, G3**). Cross the busy station square (a rather insalubrious subway-cum-shopping centre avoids the worst of the bus traffic) and leave by Via de'Panzani, in the far left corner, opposite the church. This street bends left into Via de' Cerretani and so to the Duomo. The great majority of the major sights are within a few minutes of the Duomo area.

Travelling by train from Pisa or Bologna, be sure to validate your ticket in one of the orange machines on the platform.

BY CAR

Driving into central Florence isn't a great idea. Although the traffic's nowhere near as bad as in Rome, parking and security problems are both formidable. Only residents are allowed to park on the streets in the centre, though a few expensive hotels offer parking. Otherwise you'll have to leave your car in one of the main peripheral car parks.

North of the Arno, **car parks** nearest the centre are: underneath the train station; Fortezza da Basso; Mercato Centrale; and along the Arno at Lungarno Amerigo Vespucci, Lungarno delle Grazie and Lungarno della Zecca Vecchia. South of the river the best options are Lungarno Torrigiani, Piazza del Carmine, and Piazza Cestello. You can also find parking spaces alongside the city's main ring roads (the *Viali*). All these places are greatly oversubscribed; the best bet, with the most space, is probably Fortezza da Basso (**Map 3, C1/2**).

BY BUS

Half a dozen **bus** companies run to Florence from various

parts of Tuscany. The main operator is SITA
(☎055.214.721, ⓦwww.sita-on-line.it), which has a terminal just round the corner from the train station, at Via di
Santa Caterina da Siena (**Map 3, C6**). All the other companies have offices near the station.

**The telephone code for Florence is 055, and must be used
with all numbers whether you're calling from outside or
within the city, and from abroad too.**

Information

For information about Florence's sights and events, the
main **tourist office** is at Via Cavour 1r (**Map 3, G5**) just
north of the Duomo (March–Oct Mon–Sat 8.15am–
7.15pm, Sun 8.30am–1.30pm; ☎055.290.832/3,
ⓕ055.276.0383). There's also a quieter office (**Map 2, L8**),
run by the town council, just off Piazza Santa Croce at
Borgo Santa Croce 29r (Mon–Sat 9am–7pm, Sun
9am–1pm; ☎055.234.0444, ⓕ055.226.4524). The most
convenient office for those arriving by bus or train is right
outside the train station in Piazza della Stazione (**Map 3,
D5**) – it's just to the right of the church on the far side of
the large square (Mon–Sat 8.30am–7pm, Sun
8.30am–1.30pm; ☎055.212.245, ⓕ055.238.1226). In winter, the Santa Croce and Piazza della Stazione offices stay
open but keep shorter hours.

All three provide an adequate **map** and various leaflets,
including a sheet with updated opening hours and entrance
charges, which can be handy at **festival times** when some
attractions extend their hours – or close altogether. The

FLORENCE ON THE INTERNET

Firenze online

Ⓦwww.fionline.it/turismo/wel_eng.htm

Classy if commercially oriented site from one of Florence's main service providers, with information on art, music, theatre, cinema, shopping – and even finding a job.

Tourist information

Ⓦwww.firenze.turismo.toscana.it

An official tourist office site (there are many), with an English-language option. Useful for information on forthcoming exhibitions and hotel listings.

Firenze.net

Ⓦwww.english.firenze.net

Smart, stylish website of "Florence's first town net", packed with city info and links. You can even take a virtual reality tour of the Uffizi courtyard, the Ponte Vecchio and other sights.

Uffizi Gallery

Ⓦwww.uffizi.firenze.it

The official website of the Uffizi, with images of the paintings, historical notes, news, virtual reality tours of some rooms and an index of artists.

Virtual Uffizi

Ⓦwww.televisual.net/uffizi/indice/html

The best produced virtual tour of the gallery, with images of every painting in the collection. A cross-referenced index of artists and subjects has useful thumbnail images and helps locate individual paintings in Florence.

Your Way to Florence

Ⓦwww.arca.net/florence.htm

The most comprehensive site with news plus information on transport, accommodation and opening hours.

FLORENCE ON THE INTERNET

THE EURO

Italy is one of twelve European Union countries which have changed over to a single currency, the euro (€). Euro notes and coins were issued on January 1, 2002, with lire remaining in place for cash transactions, at a fixed rate of 1936.27 lire to 1 euro, until they are scrapped entirely on February 28, 2002. After this date you will still be able to exchange your lire in banks.

All prices in this book are given in euros, correct at the time of going to press. There will no doubt be some rounding off – and, more probably, up – of prices in the first few months after the introduction of the euro. Notes will be issued in **denominations** of 5, 10, 20, 50, 100, 200 and 500 euro, and coins in denominations of 1, 2, 5, 10, 20 and 50 cents and 1 and 2 euro.

office at Via Cavour also handles information on the whole Florence province. None of these offices will book accommodation – see p.295 for the agencies that do. Another excellent source of information is *Firenze Spettacolo* (€1.60), a monthly, mostly bilingual listings magazine available from most bookshops and larger news-stands.

City transport

Within the historic centre, **walking** is generally the most efficient way of getting around. All the main sights except for San Miniato are easily accessible on foot. **Cars** have been banned, or at least discouraged, from most of the areas covered in this book (north of the Arno, at least). This has dramatically reduced the pollution, noise and danger, but watch out for rogue drivers, the almost silent electric buses and *motorini* – Florence claims to have more scooters per head than anywhere else in Europe. **Buses** are quick and efficient, and **taxis** inexpensive by European standards.

BUSES

The city's orange **buses** are run by ATAF (freephone ☎800.424.500, ⓦwww.ataf.net). Tickets are valid for sixty minutes (€0.80), three hours (€1.30), 24 hours (€3.10), two days (€4.10), three days (€5.70) or seven days (€9.80). They can be bought from shops and stalls displaying the ATAF sign, and from automatic machines all over Florence. The same outlets and machines also sell a **Biglietto Multiplo**, which gives you four sixty-minute tickets for €3 and 24-hour passes for €3.10. Tickets cannot be bought on buses. They must be stamped in a machine on board and there's a hefty on-the-spot fine for any passenger without a validated ticket. All tickets should be validated at the start of the first journey.

Small **electric buses** serve four of the most useful bus routes. Bus #A runs from the station right through the historic centre, passing close by the Duomo and Signoria, then heading east just north of Santa Croce; #B follows the north bank of the Arno; while #C descends from Piazza San Marco, heading south past Santa Croce and across the Ponte delle Grazie on its way to Via Bardi. These three buses follow similar routes on their return journeys. Bus #D leaves the station and crosses the river at Ponte Vespucci; from here it becomes a handy Oltrarno bus, running right along the south bank of the river and, on the return journey, jinking up past Palazzo Pitti, Santo Spirito and the Carmine church on its way back to the Ponte Vespucci.

Most ordinary, polluting buses serve **outlying areas**. Buses #14 and #23, however, connect the station, Duomo

●

and Santa Croce. And bus #11 makes a useful circuit: from Piazza Santa Maria Novella, near the station, it briefly crosses the river, making a short loop through central Oltrarno; it then heads back past the Duomo before heading out to Piazza San Marco (and beyond), and returning to Santa Maria Novella via the Duomo. Most other city bus routes originate at or pass by the train station and either Piazza del Duomo or Piazza San Marco. Buses #12 (anticlockwise) and #13 (clockwise) make a giant loop of the city on both sides of the river. ATAF offices hand out a well designed free map.

TAXIS

Taxis are white with yellow trim. It's difficult to flag down a cab on the street but there are plenty of central ranks: key locations include the station, Piazza della Repubblica, Piazza del Duomo, Piazza Santa Maria Novella, Piazza San Marco, Piazza Santa Croce and Piazza Santa Trìnita. You can also call a "radio taxi" on ☎055.4242, 055.4798 or 055.4390. If you do, you'll be given the car's code name – usually a town, city or country – and its number, both of which are emblazoned on the cab. Being Florence, there's even a scooter taxi firm (☎055.353.333). Italians tend not to order cabs far in advance – simply call up a few minutes before you need a car.

Owner-drivers are generally honest (but avoid touts) and all rides are **metered**; expect to pay €5–8 for a short hop within the centre. Supplements on the metered fare are payable between 10pm and 6am (€2.60), all day on Sunday and public holidays (€2.30), for journeys outside the city limits (to Fiesole, for example) and for each piece of luggage placed in the boot (€0.60). There's no extra fee for calling a cab but it will arrive with a small sum on the meter – which is switched on from the moment the taxi begins the journey to pick you up.

Piazza del Duomo

Most first-time visitors to Florence make a bee-line for **Piazza del Duomo**, drawn by the splendours of the **Duomo** and the adjacent **Baptistery**. The initial sight of this ensemble still comes as a jolt, the red, green and white patterned marble of the exteriors making a startling contrast with the dun-toned buildings around. The Duomo is unmissable: the interior forms a minor artistic treasure trove, while the *cupola*, or **dome** – one of the most astounding achievements in European architecture – provides a platform for awesomely romantic views over the city to the hazy Tuscan hills beyond.

After seeing the cathedral, you can escape the crowds by climbing the **Campanile**, the Duomo's detached bell-tower, which offers another breathtaking panorama. Then walk to the cathedral's rear for the **Museo dell'Opera del Duomo**, a repository for works of art removed over the centuries from the Duomo, Baptistery and Campanile. With pieces by Donatello, Michelangelo and many others, it's the city's second-ranking sculpture collection after the Bargello.

Inevitably, the bravura buildings at Florence's heart are hemmed in by a less elevating scene: the Piazza del Duomo is the prime honeypot for uniformed tour groups, schoolchildren and hawkers of cheap sunglasses (they'll ask for around €15), and there are few cafés from which to admire the view.

THE DUOMO

Map 2, D1. Piazza del Duomo. Mon–Wed, Fri & Sat 10am–5pm, Thurs 10am–3.30pm, Sun 1.30–4.45pm; free.

Some time in the seventh century the seat of the Bishop of Florence was transferred from San Lorenzo to Santa Reparata, a sixth-century church which stood on the site of the present-day **Duomo**, or **Santa Maria del Fiore**. Later generations modified this older church until 1294, when Florence's ruling priorate was stung into action by the magnificence of newly commissioned cathedrals in Pisa and Siena. Their own cathedral, they lamented, was too "crudely built and too small for such a city".

A suitably immodest plan to remedy this shortcoming was ordered from Arnolfo di Cambio, who drafted a scheme to create the largest church in the Roman Catholic world and "surpass anything of its kind produced by the Greeks and Romans in the times of their greatest power". Progress on the project faltered after Arnolfo's death in 1302, picking up again between 1331 and 1334 under the guiding hand of Giotto. By 1380 Francesco Talenti and a string of mostly jobbing architects had brought the nave to completion. By 1418 the tribunes (apses) and the dome's supporting drum were also completed. Only the dome itself – no small matter – remained unfinished (see p.22).

The exterior

Parts of the Duomo's **exterior** date back to Arnolfo's era, but most of the overblown and pernickety main **facade** is a nineteenth-century simulacrum of a Gothic front. The original facade, which was never more than quarter-finished, was pulled down in 1587 on the orders of Ferdinand I. A competition to produce a new facade proved fruitless, and for three centuries the cathedral remained faceless. After Florence became capital of the newly unified Italy in 1865, however, no fewer than 92 plans were submitted. The winning entry, by the otherwise obscure Emilio de Fabris, was completed in 1887. To its credit, the new frontage at least retained the same colour scheme and materials used elsewhere, most notably the marble, which was quarried from three different sources – white from Carrara, red from Maremma and green from Prato.

The cathedral's south (right) side is the oldest part of the exterior – both its side portals deserve a glance – but the most attractive adornment is the **Porta della Mandorla** (C), on the other side. This takes its name from the almond-shaped frame (or *mandorla*) that contains the pollution-streaked relief of *The Assumption of the Virgin* (1414–21), sculpted by Nanni di Banco; the lunette features a mosaic of the *Annunciation* (1491) to a design by Ghirlandaio. The two heads in profile either side of the gable may be early works by Donatello.

The interior

The Duomo's **interior** is the converse of the exterior – a vast, uncluttered enclosure of bare masonry. Its ambience is more that of a great assembly hall than a devotional building, and yet its apparently barren walls hold a far greater accumulation of treasures than at first appears (see plan, pp.16–17). The interior also has two worthwhile mini-excursions: an ascent of the **dome** (see p.20) and a descent into **Santa Reparata**, the remains of the earlier church (or churches) on the site.

THE DUOMO

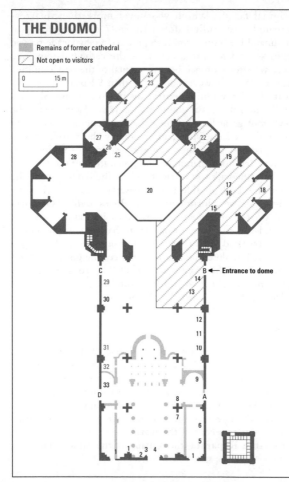

THE DUOMO

- Remains of former cathedral
- Not open to visitors

0   15 m

24
23

27
26
25

28

22
21

19

20

17
16

18

15

C

29

30

31

32

33

D

A

8
7

6

5

1

1 2 3 4

9

10

11

12

13

14

B ← Entrance to dome

1 Stained glass: St Stephen (left), Assumption (centre) and St Lawrence (right), Lorenzo Ghiberti
2 Tomb of Antonio d'Orso, bishop of Florence (1323), Tino da Camaino
3 Mosaic: Coronation of the Virgin (1300), attrib. Gaddo Gaddi
4 Clock (1443) – decoration, Paolo Uccello
5 Tondo: Bust of Brunelleschi (1447), Andrea Cavalcanti
6 Bust: Giotto at Work (1490), Benedetto da Maiano
7 Gothic water stoup (1380), attrib. Urbano da Cortona
8 Entrance and steps to Santa Reparata
9 Painting: St Bartholomew Enthroned (1408), Rossello di Jacopo Franchi
10 Painted sepulchral monument: Fra Luigi Marsili (1439), Bicci di Lorenzo
11 Statue: Isaiah (1427), Bernardo Ciuffagni
12 Painted sepulchral monument: Archbishop Pietro Corsino of Florence (1422), Bicci di Lorenzo
13 Stained glass: Six Saints (1395), Agnolo Gaddi
14 Bust: Marsilino Ficino (1521), philosopher friend of Cosimo I, holding a copy of Plato's works
15 Eight statues of the apostles (1547–72) against the pillars of the octagon
16 Tribune: each tribune has five chapels; each chapel has two levels of stained glass, most by Lorenzo Ghiberti
17 Frescoes below windows of west and east tribunes: Saints (1440), attrib. Bicci di Lorenzo
18 Altar, attrib. Michelozzo
19 Fresco fragment: Madonna del Popolo (thirteenth-century), attrib. Giotto
20 Dome fresco cycle: The Last Judgement (1572–79), Giorgio Vasari and Federico Zuccari
21 Enamelled terracotta (above door): Ascension (1450), Luca della Robbia
22 Sagrestia Vecchia (Old Sacristy)
23 Bronze reliquary (1432–42) of St Zenobius (below altar), Lorenzo Ghiberti
24 Candle-holders: Two Angels (1450), Luca della Robbia
25 Enamelled terracotta: Resurrection (1444), Luca della Robbia
26 Bronze doors (1446–67), Luca della Robbia and Michelozzo
27 Sagrestia Nuova (New Sacristy): intarsia (inlaid wood, 1436–45), Benedetto and Giuliano da Maiano
28 Former site of Michelangelo's Pietà, currently in the Museo dell'Opera
29 Painting: Dante explaining the Divine Comedy (1465), Domenico di Michelino
30 Fresco: SS. Cosmas and Damian (1429), Bicci di Lorenzo; two windows by Agnolo Gaddi
31 Equestrian portrait: Sir John Hawkwood (1436), Paolo Uccello
32 Equestrian portrait: Niccolò da Tolentino (1456), Andrea del Castagno
33 Bust: Antonio Squarcialupi (former cathedral organist, 1490), Benedetto da Maiano

The Exterior
A Porta del Campanile
B Porta dei Canoncini: sculpture (1395–99), Lorenzo d'Ambrogio
C Porta della Mandorla: sculpture, Nanni di Banco and Donatello
D The Prophet Joshua (1415), Nanni di Bartolo; the head is by Donatello

---

Works of special note are highlighted in green in the text
and on the plan on p.16–17

Monuments and paintings

The interior's most conspicuous decorations are a pair of memorials to *condottieri* (mercenary commanders). Paolo Uccello's monument to Sir John Hawkwood (31) created in 1436, is often cited as the epitome of Florentine mean-spiritedness; according to local folklore – unsupported by any evidence – the mercenary captain of Florence's army was promised a proper equestrian statue as his memorial, then was posthumously fobbed off with this trompe l'oeil version. Perhaps the slight was deserved. Before being employed by Florence, Hawkwood and his White Company had marauded their way through Tuscany, holding entire cities to ransom under threat of ransack. The monument features a strange shift of perspective, with the pedestal depicted from a different angle from what's on it; it's known that Uccello was ordered to repaint the horse and rider, presumably because he'd shown them from the same point of view as the base, which must have displayed the horse's belly and not much else. Look back at the entrance wall and you'll see another Uccello contribution to the interior – a clock (4) adorned with four rather abstracted Evangelists. It uses the old *hora italica*, common in Italy until the eighteenth century, when the 24th hour of the day ended at sunset.

Andrea del Castagno's monument to Niccolò da Tolentino (32), created twenty years later, is clearly derived from Uccello's fresco, but has an aggressive edge that's typical of this artist. Just beyond the horsemen, Domenico di Michelino's Dante Explaining the Divine Comedy (29) (1465) gave Brunelleschi's dome – then only recently completed, the brick drum still to receive its marble cladding – a place only marginally less prominent than the mountain of Purgatory. Dante stands outside the walls, a symbol of his exile from Florence.

- -
For more on Dante's life and work, see p.84.
- -

Judged by mere size, the major work of art in the Duomo is the fresco of **The Last Judgement (20)** (1572–79) which fills much of the interior of the dome. At the time of its execution, however, a substantial body of opinion thought Vasari and Zuccari's combined effort did nothing but deface Brunelleschi's masterpiece, and quite a few people today would have preferred the painting to have been stripped away rather than cleaned up.

The sacristies

Just short of a barrier a pair of glass doors allow you to look into the **Sagrestia Nuova (27)**, closed to visitors, where the lavish panelling is inlaid with beautiful intarsia work (1436–45) by Benedetto and Giuliano Maiano, notably a delicate trompe l'oeil *Annunciation* in the centre of the wall facing the door. The relief of the *Resurrection* (1442) above the entrance is by Luca della Robbia: much imitated by later artists, it was Luca's first important commission in the enamelled terracotta for which he became famous. The stunning **sacristy door** (1445–69) was his only work (with Michelozzo) in bronze. It was in this sacristy that Lorenzo de' Medici famously took refuge in 1478 after his brother Giuliano had been mortally stabbed on the altar steps by the Pazzi conspirators (see p.28–29) – the bulk of della Robbia's recently installed doors protected him from his would-be assassins. Small portraits on the handles commemorate the brothers.

Across the way, della Robbia's *Ascension* (1450) can be

THE DUOMO

19

seen above the door of the Sagrestia Vecchia (22); it was once accompanied by Donatello's sublime *cantoria*, or choir-loft, now in the Museo dell'Opera (see p.33). Luca della Robbia's equally mesmeric *cantoria*, in the same museum, occupied a matching position above the Sagrestia Nuova.

Santa Reparata

Mon–Sat 10am–5pm; €2.60.

In the 1960s remnants of the Duomo's predecessor, **Santa Reparata (8)**, were uncovered underneath the west end of the nave. The remains are extensive, as the nave of the Duomo was built, on the same alignment, several feet above that of the old church, which was thus not fully demol-ished. Subsequent excavations have revealed a complicated jigsaw of Roman, paleochristian and Romanesque remains, plus fragments of mosaic and fourteenth-century frescoes. The explanatory diagrams tend to intensify the confusion: to make sense of it all, you'll have to keep referring to the colour-coded model in the farthest recess of the crypt. In 1972, further digging revealed **Brunelleschi's tomb**, an unassuming marble slab so simple that it had lain forgotten under the south aisle. The tombstone's present position is hardly any more glorious (it can be seen, without paying, through a grille at the foot of the steps), but the architect does at least have the honour of being one of the only Florentines to be buried in the Duomo itself.

The dome

Mon–Fri 8.30am–6.20pm, Sat 8.30am–5pm (first Sat of every month 8.30am–3.20pm); €5.20.

Climbing the **dome** (see box overleaf) is an unmissable experience, both for the views from the top and for the insights it offers into Brunelleschi's engineering genius. Be prepared for the queue that usually stretches from the entrance, on the south flank of the nave; it does however move fairly briskly. Also be ready for the 463 lung-busting steps. And if you suffer from claustrophobia, note that the climb involves some very confined spaces.

After an initial ascent, you emerge onto a narrow gallery that runs around the interior of the dome, with a dizzying view down onto the maze-patterned pavement of the nave. It's also the best vantage point from which to inspect the seven **stained-glass roundels**, designed by Uccello, Ghiberti, Castagno and Donatello, below Vasari's *Last Judgement* fresco (see p.19). Beyond the gallery, you enter the more cramped confines of the dome itself. As you clamber up between the inner and outer shells, you can observe many ingenious features of Brunelleschi's construction: the ribs and arches, the herringbone brickwork, the wooden struts that support the outer shell – even the hooks and holes left for future generations of repairers. From the white marble lantern that crowns the dome, the views across the city are breathtaking.

The Campanile

Map 2, D2. Piazza del Duomo. Daily 8.30am–6.50pm; €5.20.

The **Campanile** – the cathedral's bell-tower – was begun in 1334 by Giotto during his period as official city architect and *capo maestro* (head of works) in charge of the Duomo. By the time of his death three years later, the base, the first of five eventual levels, had been completed. Andrea Pisano, fresh from creating the Baptistery's south doors (see p.25), then continued construction of the second storey (1337–42), probably in accordance with Giotto's plans. Work was rounded off by Francesco Talenti, who rectified deficiencies in Giotto's original calculations in the process – the base's original walls teetered on the brink of collapse until he doubled their thickness. When completed the

THE DUOMO

●

21

BRUNELLESCHI'S DOME

Since Arnolfo di Cambio's scale model of the Duomo collapsed under its own weight some time in the fourteenth century, nobody has been sure quite how he intended to crown his achievement. In 1367 Neri di Fioraventi proposed the construction of a magnificent **cupola** (dome) that was to span nearly 43m, broader than the dome of Rome's Pantheon, which had remained the world's largest for 1300 years, and rise from a base some 55m above the floor of the nave – taller than the highest vaulting of any Gothic cathedral. Just as radical was Fioraventi's decision to dispense with flying buttresses, regarded as ugly vestiges of the Gothic barbarism of enemy states such as France and Milan.

There was just one problem – nobody had worked out how to build the thing. Medieval domes were usually built on wooden "centring", a network of timbers that held the stone in place until the mortar was set. In the case of the Duomo, the cost would have been prohibitive, the weight of stone too great (the entire dome is thought to weigh some 33,000 tonnes) and in any event there was no sufficient source of wood. A committee of the masons' guild was set up to solve the dilemma. One idea was to build the dome from pumice. Another, according to Vasari, was to support the dome on a vast mound of earth that would be seeded with thousands of coins; when the dome was finished, the mound would be cleared by inviting Florence's citizens to excavate the money.

After years of bickering the project was thrown open to competition. A goldsmith and clockmaker called **Filippo Brunelleschi** presented the winning scheme, defeating Ghiberti in the process – revenge of sorts for Ghiberti's triumph seventeen years earlier in the competition to design the Baptistery doors (see p.27). Doom-mongers, Ghiberti among them, criticized Brunelleschi at every turn, eventually forcing the authorities to employ both rivals. An exasperated Brunelleschi feigned illness and resigned. Ghiberti, left to his own devices, found himself flummoxed, and in 1423 Brunelleschi was invited to become the dome's sole "inventor and chief director".

Experts long doubted that the dome could have been built without centring, but during the excavations of the 1970s, the mystery was largely solved. The key to Brunelleschi's success lay in the construction of two shells, each concealing a lattice of stone beams that allowed the octagonal dome to be built as if it was a stack of concentric circles, thereby creating a much stronger structure. And as the dome curved upward and inward, this lattice was filled with lightweight bricks laid in a herringbone pattern that prevented the higher sections from falling inward. Brunelleschi's relentless inventiveness extended to a new hoist with a reverse gear, a new type of crane, individually designed bricks and even a boat for transporting marble that was so ungainly it was nicknamed *Il Badalone* (the monster).

The dome's completion was marked by the **consecration** of the cathedral on March 25, 1436 – Annunciation Day, and the Florentine New Year – in a ceremony conducted by the pope. Even then, the topmost piece, the lantern, remained unfinished, with many people convinced the dome could support no further weight. But once again Brunelleschi won the day, beginning work on the dome's final stage in 1446, just a few months before his death. The whole thing was finally completed in the late 1460s, when the cross and gilded ball, both cast by Verrocchio, were hoisted into place.

Today it is still the largest masonry dome in the world. Only the gallery around the base remains incomplete – abandoned with only one face finished after Michelangelo compared it to "cages for crickets". This one criticism aside, Michelangelo was awestruck: gazing on the cupola he is supposed to have said: *"Come te non voglio, meglio di te non posso"* – "Similar to you I will not, better than you I cannot."

BRUNELLESCHI'S DOME

●

bell-tower reached 84.7 metres, well over the limit set by the city in 1324 for civic towers, the building of which had long been a means of expressing aristocratic or mercantile power.

These days a climb to the summit is one of the highlights of any Florentine trip, though first it's worth taking in the tower's decorative **sculptures and reliefs** (most are now copies, but you can get a closer look at the age-blackened originals in the Museo dell'Opera del Duomo – see p.33). As it moved up the tower, the decoration was intended to mirror humankind's progress from original sin to a state of divine grace, a progress facilitated by manual labour, the arts and the sacraments, and guided by the influence of the planets and the cardinal and theological virtues.

Thus the first storey is studded with two rows of bas-reliefs; the lower register, in hexagonal frames – some designed by Giotto, but all executed by Pisano and pupils – illustrates the *Creation, Art and Works of Man*. In the diamond-shaped panels of the upper register are allegories of the *Seven Planets* (then believed to influence human lives), *Seven Sacraments* (which sanctify human existence) and *Seven Virtues* (which shape human behaviour). A century or so later Luca della Robbia added the *Five Liberal Arts* – which shape the human spirit – on the north face: Grammar, Philosophy, Music, Arithmetic and Astrology. Further works in the second-storey niches by Pisano were eventually replaced by Donatello and Nanni di Bartolo's figures of the *Prophets*, *Sibyls*, *Patriarchs* and *Kings* (1415–36).

The parapet at the top of the tower is a less lofty but in many ways more satisfying viewpoint than the cathedral dome, if only because the view takes in the Duomo itself. Be warned, though, that there are 414 steps to the summit. George Eliot made the ascent in 1861, finding it "a very sublime getting upstairs indeed" and her "muscles much astonished at the unusual exercise".

THE BAPTISTERY

Map 2, C1. Piazza San Giovanni. Mon–Sat noon–6.30pm; Sun 8.30am–1.30pm; €2.60.

Florence's octagonal **Baptistery** stands immediately west of the Duomo, overlooked – but not overshadowed – by the cathedral, whose geometrically patterned marble cladding mirrors that of the smaller, older building. Generally thought to date from the sixth or seventh century, the Baptistery is the oldest building in Florence, first documented in 897, when it was recorded as the city's cathedral before Santa Reparata. Though its origins lie buried in the Dark Ages, no building better illustrates the special relationship between Florence and the Roman world.

The Florentines were always conscious of their **Roman ancestry**, and for centuries believed that the Baptistery was a converted Roman temple to Mars, originally built to celebrate the defeat of Fiesole and the city's foundation. This belief was bolstered by the interior's ancient granite columns, probably taken from the city's old Roman Capitol (other columns from this site found their way to San Miniato). Further proof was apparently provided by traces of an ancient pavement mosaic, remains now thought to belong to an old Roman bakery. But if the building itself is not Roman, its exterior marble cladding – applied in a Romanesque reworking between about 1059 and 1128 – is clearly Classical in inspiration, while its most famous embellishments, the gilded **bronze doors**, mark the emergence of a more scholarly, self-conscious interest in the art of the ancient world.

The south doors

Responsibility for the Baptistery's improvement and upkeep lay with the *Arte di Calimala*, the most powerful of

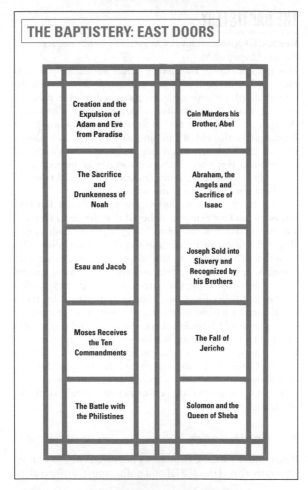

THE BAPTISTERY: EAST DOORS

Creation and the Expulsion of Adam and Eve from Paradise

Cain Murders his Brother, Abel

The Sacrifice and Drunkenness of Noah

Abraham, the Angels and Sacrifice of Isaac

Esau and Jacob

Joseph Sold into Slavery and Recognized by his Brothers

Moses Receives the Ten Commandments

The Fall of Jericho

The Battle with the Philistines

Solomon and the Queen of Sheba

THE BAPTISTERY

Florence's guilds. It was they who initiated the building's eleventh-century Romanesque revamp, and they who in the 1320s turned their attention to the exterior, and in particular to the question of a suitably **majestic entrance**. In this they were stung to action by arch-rival Pisa, whose cathedral was not only famous for its bronze portals, but whose craftsmen had recently completed some celebrated **bronze doors** for the great cathedral at Monreale in Sicily.

The arrival of Andrea Pisano in Florence in 1330 offered the chance of similar glories. Within three months the Pisan sculptor had created wax models for what would become the Baptistery's south doors (1330–36). Over the next eight years the models were cast in bronze, probably with the assistance of Venetian bell-makers, then Italy's most accomplished bronzesmiths. Twenty of the doors' 28 panels, installed in 1339, form a narrative on the life of St John the Baptist, patron saint of Florence and the Baptistery's dedicatee: the lowest eight reliefs depict *Humility* and the *Cardinal and Theological Virtues*. The bronze frame (1452–62) is the work of Vittorio Ghiberti, son of the more famous Lorenzo (see below and p.344). The bronze figures above the portal of the Baptist, Salome and executioner are late-sixteenth-century additions.

The north doors

Some sixty years of financial and political turmoil, and the ravages of the Black Death, prevented further work on the Baptistery's other entrances until 1401. That year a competition was held to design a new set of doors, each of the six main entrants being asked to create a panel showing the Sacrifice of Isaac. The doors were to be a votive offering, a gift to God to celebrate the passing of a plague epidemic.

The judges found themselves equally impressed by the work of two young goldsmiths, Brunelleschi and **Lorenzo**

THE PAZZI CONSPIRACY

Florence's murkiest act of **treachery** had its roots in the election in 1472 of Sixtus IV, a pope who distributed favours with a largesse remarkable even by the standards of the day. Six of his nephews were made cardinals, one of them, the uncouth Girolamo Riario – probably actually his son – coming in for particularly preferential treatment.

Sixtus intended Riario to take over the north Italian town of Imola as a base for papal expansion. Short of funds, the pope approached Lorenzo de' Medici for a loan, only to be rebuffed – Imola was too close to Milan and Bologna to be allowed to fall into papal hands. Enraged by the snub, and by Lorenzo's refusal to recognize his nominee, Francesco Salviati, as Archbishop of Pisa, Sixtus turned to the Medici's leading Florentine rivals, the **Pazzi**. By 1477, Riario, Salviati and Francesco de' Pazzi turned to a mercenary called Montesecco for military muscle. He made his co-operation in any plot conditional on papal blessing, a benediction that was readily obtained. Jacopo de' Pazzi, the family's wizened god-father, was also won over, even though one of his nephews was married to Lorenzo's sister.

Eventually it was decided to murder Lorenzo and his brother Giuliano while they attended Mass in the cathedral. The date set was Sunday, April 26, 1478. Since Montesecco refused "to add sacrilege to murder", Lorenzo's murder was delegated to two embittered priests, Maffei and Bagnone. Giuliano would be dispatched by Francesco de' Pazzi and Bernardo Baroncelli, a violent Pazzi side-kick deeply in debt to the fami-

Ghiberti (both winning entries are displayed in the Bargello). Unable to choose between the pair, it appears that the judges suggested the two work in tandem. Brunelleschi replied that if he couldn't do the job alone he wasn't interested – whereupon the contract was handed to Ghiberti, leaving his rival to

ly. Salviati, meanwhile, accompanied by an armed troop, was to seize control of the Palazzo della Signoria.

It all went wrong. Giuliano was killed in a crazed frenzy, his skull shattered and his body rent with nineteen stab wounds. Lorenzo escaped, wounded, to the sacristy, where he and his supporters barricaded themselves behind its heavy bronze doors. Across the city, Salviati was separated from his troops by the newly installed secret doors in the Signoria, and arrested.

A furious mob dispensed summary justice: Salviati's troops were massacred to a man, while Salviati and Francesco de' Pazzi were hanged from a window of the Signoria. Poliziano, the eminent humanist, noted that "as the Archbishop rolled and struggled at the end of his rope, his eyes goggling in his head, he fixed his teeth into Francesco de' Pazzi's naked body." Maffei and Bagnone, the bungling priests, were castrated and hanged. Baroncelli fled to Constantinople but was extradited and executed. Montesecco was tortured, but granted a soldier's execution in the Bargello.

Jacopo's end was the most sordid. Having escaped Florence, he was recaptured, tortured, stripped naked, and hanged alongside the decomposing Salviati. He was then buried in Santa Croce, but his corpse was exhumed by the mob, dragged through the streets and propped up outside the Pazzi palace; there, his rotting head was used as door-knocker. Eventually the putrefying body was thrown in the Arno, fished out, flogged, hanged again by a gang of children, and finally cast back into the river.

stomp off to study architecture in Rome. Ghiberti, barely 20 years old, was to devote much of the next 25 years to this one project, albeit in the company of distinguished assistants such as Masolino, Donatello and Paolo Uccello. His fame rests almost entirely on the extraordinary result.

THE PAZZI CONSPIRACY

For more on Ghiberti, see p.344.

The **north doors** (1403–24) he created show a new naturalism and classicized sense of composition, copying Pisano's 28-panel arrangement while transcending its traditional Gothic approach: the upper twenty panels depict *Scenes from the New Testament*, while the eight lower panels describe the *Four Evangelists* and *Four Doctors of the Church*.

The east doors

The north doors, while extraordinary, are as nothing to the sublime **east doors** (1425–52), ordered from Ghiberti as soon as the first set was finished. The artist would spend some 27 years on the new project, work which he pursued, in his own words, "with the greatest diligence and greatest love".

The doors have just ten panels, a departure from both previous sets of doors, while their enclosing squares abandon the Gothic diamond or quatrefoil frame. Unprecedented in the subtlety of their carving, the **Old Testament scenes** – the Creation, the Ten Commandments, the Sacrifice of Isaac and so on – are a primer of early Renaissance art, using rigorous perspective, gesture and sophisticated groupings to intensify the drama of each scene. Ghiberti's power of compression and detail is such that several narratives are often woven into a single scene (see plan on p.26). The sculptor has also included an understandably self-satisfied self-portrait in the frame of the left-hand door: his is the fourth head from the top of the right-hand band – the bald chap with the smirk. The other 23 medallions portray various of Ghiberti's artistic contemporaries, while the 24 statuettes depict the Prophets and Sibyls. The gorgeous golden doors now in place are reproductions, as the original panels have been restored and exhibited, to great effect, in the Museo dell'Opera.

- -

The east doors of the Baptistery have long been known as "The Gates of Paradise", supposedly because Michelangelo once remarked that they were so beautiful they deserved to be the portals of heaven.

- -

The columns

The pair of pitted **marble columns** to the side of the east doors were presented by the city of Pisa in the twelfth century, and would have been slotted into the walls had they not turned out to be too weak to bear any substantial weight. The story goes that when the Pisans set off to attack Mallorca in 1117 they were so fearful of a raid by the city of Lucca in their absence that they begged the Florentines to watch over their city. In gratitude, on their return they made Florence a gift of the two pillars, part of the booty seized during the Mallorcan raid. However, the columns were deemed to have magic powers too valuable to be left to the Florentines – their polished surfaces were meant to foretell acts of treason – and the Pisans are said to have deliberately ruined and weakened the pillars by baking them in embers.

Another marble column, just north of the Baptistery, is decorated with bronze branches and leaves to commemorate the miracle of January 429 brought about by the body of St Zenobius, Florence's first bishop; as the corpse was being carried from San Lorenzo into Santa Reparata it brushed against a barren elm here, which thereupon sprang into leaf.

THE BAPTISTERY

The interior

The Baptistery **interior** is stunning, with its black and white marble cladding and miscellany of ancient columns below a blazing **mosaic ceiling**. Mosaics were not a Florentine speciality – in the centuries to come they would give way to fresco, but in the thirteenth century they were the predominant decorative medium. Encouraged by the interest surrounding the restoration of mosaics then taking place in the early Christian basilicas of Rome and Ravenna, the city was keen to match its rivals – principally Venice.

The earliest mosaics (1225) lie above the square apse, or *scarsella*, and depict the Virgin and John the Baptist. Above them a wheel of prophets encircles the Lamb of God. The main vault is dominated by a vast figure of Christ in Judgement, flanked by depictions of Paradise and Hell to left and right respectively. Just to the left of the monstrous, man-eating Lucifer, the poet Virgil (in a white cloak) can be seen leading Dante (in black) through the Inferno. The figures were a later insertion, added after the poet's death during something of a frenzy of belated recognition. The other five sections of the octagonal ceiling depict Biblical scenes, beginning above the north doors with the Creation, and proceeding through the stories of Joseph and John the Baptist towards the Crucifixion and Resurrection, seen above the south doors.

The interior's semi-abstract mosaic pavement also dates from the thirteenth century. The empty octagon at its centre marks the spot once occupied by the huge font in which every child born in the city during the previous twelve months would be baptized on March 25 (New Year's Day in the old Florentine calendar). When a child was born, a coloured bean was dropped into an urn in the Baptistery: black for a boy, white for a girl, a system which, among other things, allowed the birth rate to be calculated.

To the right of the altar lies the **tomb of Baldassare Cossa**, the schismatic Pope John XXIII, who was deposed in 1415 and died in Florence in 1419. At the time of his death he was a guest of his financial adviser and close friend, Giovanni di Bicci de' Medici, the man who established the Medici at the political forefront of Florence. It was through Pope John that Giovanni became chief banker to the Papal Curia, a deal that laid the foundations of the Medici fortune: for years over half the Medici's profits would come from just two Rome-based banks.

That Pope John achieved a place in Florence's Holy of Holies was certainly not due to his piousness. At his deposition he was accused of heresy, murder and the seduction of over two hundred women in Bologna during his sojourn in the city as papal representative. The monument, draped by an illusionistic marble canopy, is the work of Donatello and his pupil Michelozzo.

MUSEO DELL'OPERA DEL DUOMO

Map 2, G1. Piazza del Duomo 9. Mon–Sat: April–Oct 9am–6.50pm, Sun 8.30/9–1/2pm; Nov–March 9am–6.20pm, Sun 8.30/9–1/2pm; €5.20.

Since 1296 the cathedral has had a special body responsible for its upkeep – the Opera del Duomo, literally the "Work of the Duomo". Since the early fifteenth century its home was the building behind the east end of the cathedral; since 1891 this same building has housed the **Museo dell'Opera del Duomo**, the repository of the most precious and fragile works of art from the duomo, Baptistery and Campanile. As an overview of the sculpture of Florence the museum is second only to the Bargello – it's also far easier to take in on a single visit.

The ground floor

The museum reopened in 2000 after a lengthy and controversial **restoration**. Gone are tired, dusty rooms and in their place is a smart, open-plan arrangement of broad corridors, mezzanine floors, and lots of state-of-the-art displays. Exhibits are now well labelled, with good English translations – the essay-length descriptions which open each room and display area are especially illuminating.

The museum's **courtyard**, just off the ticket hall, is thick with historical associations, despite its ultra-modern makeover: it was here that much of Michelangelo's *David* was sculpted. The court is now the site of one of the city's finest displays of sculpture, since all eight of **Ghiberti's** panels from the east doors of the Baptistery were finally brought together following restoration (see p.30), while looming over the court is the graceful *Baptism of Christ* (1502-5), by Sansovino and assistants, which originally stood above the east doors.

Beyond the ticket office are pieces of **Roman sculpture** removed from the Baptistery, including a superb second-century sarcophagus carved with the story of Orestes. Beyond this opens a room devoted to Gothic sculpture from the Baptistery – mostly works by Tino da Camaino – and beyond this is a series of larger figures from the 1330s and 1380s removed from the Porta del Campanile in 1990.

These are little more than a modest introduction to the meat of the ground floor's exhibits, which begin in earnest in a large hall devoted to the original sculptures of the cathedral's west front. Foremost among these are works by the cathedral's first architect, **Arnolfo di Cambio** (and his workshop), including an eerily glassy-eyed *Madonna and Child*; all were rescued from Arnolfo's quarter-finished cathedral facade, pulled down by Ferdinand I in 1587.

Equally striking is the sculptor's vase-carrying figure of *St Reparata*, one of Florence's patron saints, a work long thought to be of Greek or Roman origin. Also noteworthy is the ram-rod straight statue of *Boniface VIII* (in comedy hat), one of the most unpleasant of all medieval popes. Along the entrance wall are four seated figures of the Evangelists, also wrenched from the facade: Nanni di Banco's St Luke and **Donatello**'s St John are particularly fine.

The room off the far end of the hall features a sequence of **marble reliefs** (1547–72), by Bacio Bandinelli and Giovanni Bandini, part of an unfinished sequence of 300 panels proposed for the choir of the cathedral. Also here is a collection of paintings from a series of altars in the cathedral, all torn from their original home in 1838 as they were considered "futile ornaments" and an affront to the Gothic severity of the building. One of the most eye-catching is Giovanni di Biondo's triptych portraying episodes from the Martyrdom of St Sebastian: study the smaller predella panels for some of the more hair-raising events in the saint's life, notably a violent cudgelling and the panel in which he is tipped head-first into a well.

The adjoining modern **octagonal chapel** features an assembly of reliquaries which contain, among other saintly remains, the jaw of Saint Jerome and the index finger of John the Baptist. From here a vaulted gallery leads to the museum's main stairs – note the marker on the right-hand wall indicating the water level in the building after the 1966 flood. It's easy to miss the room off to the right of the **Lapidarium** (a collection of modest works in stone), which contains items removed from the cathedral's Porta della Mandorla, including a lovely terracotta *Creation of Eve* (1410) attributed to Donatello.

First floor

Up the stairs on the mezzanine level is **Michelangelo**'s anguished **Pietà** (1550–53), moved from the cathedral as recently as 1981 while restoration of the dome was in progress, but probably fated to stay. This is one of the sculptor's last works, carved when he was almost 80, and was intended for his own tomb – Vasari records that the face of Nicodemus is a self-portrait. Dissatisfied with the quality of the marble, Michelangelo mutilated the group by hammering off the left leg and arm of Christ; his pupil Tiberio Calcagni restored the arm, then finished off the figure of Mary Magdalene, turning her into a whey-faced supporting player.

Although he's represented on the lower floor, it's upstairs that **Donatello**, the greatest of Michelangelo's precursors, really comes to the fore. Room I, at the top of the stairs, features his breathtaking **Cantoria**, or choir-loft (1433–9), with its playground of boisterous *putti*. Facing the latter is another almost equally staggering *cantoria* (1431–8), the first-known major commission of the young Luca della Robbia; the earnest musicians embody the text from Psalm 33 inscribed on the frame: "Praise the Lord with harp. Sing unto Him with the psaltery and instrument of ten strings."

Both lofts – actually used as supports for organ lofts rather than singing galleries – were dismantled and removed from their position above the cathedral's old and new sacristies in 1688 (see pp.19–20). The occasion was the ill-fated marriage of Violante Beatrice of Bavaria to Ferdinand de' Medici, the doomed and hopelessly ineffectual heir of Cosimo III. The ceremony gave the cathedral authorities the excuse to decorate the cathedral in a more fitting "modern" style. The ensuing clear-out left the *cantorie* languishing in dusty storage for some two centuries.

Room II, beyond the *cantorie*, is filled with bas-reliefs of Andrea Pisano, Luca della Robbia and pupils, removed from the **Campanile** between 1965 and 1967. Though darkened with age, their allegorical panels remain both striking and intelligible, depicting the spiritual refinement of humanity through labour, the arts and, ultimately, the virtues and sacraments (see p.24 for more details). The display faithfully reproduces the reliefs' original arrangement, the key panels being the hexagonal reliefs of the lower order, all of which – save for the last five by Luca della Robbia (1437–9) – were the work of Pisano (c. 1348–50), probably to original designs by Giotto.

Of the figures that Donatello carved for the Campanile, the most powerful here is that of the prophet Habbakuk, the intensity of whose gaze is said to have prompted the sculptor to seize it and yell "Speak, speak!" Donatello was apparently also responsible for the statue's nickname, Lo Zuccone – the pumpkin – after its bald head. The figure is one of sixteen ranged around the walls, which also include *Four Prophets* (1348–50) and *Two Sybils* (1342–1348) attributed to Andrea Pisano, and *The Sacrifice of Isaac* (1421), a collaboration between Nanni di Bartolo and Donatello.

The opposite pole of Donatello's temperament, in the form of his gaunt wooden figure of Mary Magdalene (1453–5), confronts you on entering Room III. It was removed from the Baptistery, as was the extraordinary altar-front at the far end of the room, a dazzling meditation in repoussé and cast silver on the life of St John the Baptist. Begun in 1366, the piece was completed in 1480, the culmination of a century of labour by, among others, Michelozzo (responsible for the central figure of *John the Baptist*), Antonio del Pollaiuolo (the *Birth of Jesus* on the left side) and Verrocchio (the *Decapitation* to the right). The sublime silver Cross (1457–59) atop the altar is by Pollaiuolo and assistants.

MUSEO DELL'OPERA DEL DUOMO

37

Ranged around the walls are fabrics, copes and other religious vestments, plus another selection of reliquaries – look out for the arm of St Philip and one of St John the Baptist's fingers. Among the former are 27 sublimely worked **needlework panels** – former vestments and altar panels from the Baptistery – produced between 1466 and 1487 by French, Flemish and Florentine artists, including members of the Arte di Calimala (one of the key textile guilds) working to designs by Antonio del Pollaiuolo. Not surprisingly, given their provenance, they portray scenes from the life of the Baptist, one of Florence's patrons and the Baptistery's dedicatee.

A corridor at the end of Room II leads past a mock-up of Brunelleschi's building site, complete with broken bricks, wooden scaffolding and some of the tools that were used to build the dome, many invented specifically for the purpose by the architect himself. More arresting is Brunelleschi's **death mask**, which almost – but not quite – looks out of the window at the dome just across the way.

The sequence of rooms beyond displays various proposals for completing the balcony of the drum below the cupola (see p.23) and the duomo's west front, including models created by Michelangelo, Giuliano da Maiano, Giambologna, Antonio da Sangallo, Andrea Sansovino and other leading architects. The wooden model of the **cathedral lantern** is presumed to have been made by Brunelleschi as part of his winning proposal for the design of the lantern in 1436. The final room, just off the main staircase, shows plans submitted to the three competitions held in the 1860s, when Florence was briefly capital of Italy and the question of the facade standing "ignominious in faded stucco", as George Eliot put it, once more became pressing. They mostly provoke relief that none came to fruition, while Emilio de Fabris's winning design of 1876 is mostly remarkable for how little it differs from the other nineteenth-century Gothic pastiches.

Piazza della Signoria

After visiting Piazza del Duomo it takes a considerable effort of will not to join the surge of people on Via dei Calzaiuoli bound for **Piazza della Signoria**, the second of Florence's major set-piece piazzas. Where Piazza del Duomo provided – and provides – the focus for the city's religious preoccupations, the Piazza della Signoria has always been the centre of its secular life. Yet though it sets the stage for Florence's main civic palace, the grand **Palazzo Vecchio**, too many of its buildings are bland nineteenth-century affairs.

This said, the square is irresistible as a public forum, if something of a zoo during busy holiday periods. People have long gathered here for entertainment and political rallies. Tempers often became frayed, and in 1343 one inflammatory meeting ended with a man being eaten by a mob. At other times wild boar and lions were released to provide public entertainment. On one occasion, stallions were loosed among a group of mares, producing, in the words of one chronicler, "the most marvellous entertainment for girls to behold". Wheeled traffic was excluded as early as

1385 (cars are still banned), while begging, prostitution and gambling were also prohibited (begging, at least, is still in evidence).

Florence's artistic heritage is very much in evidence in the piazza: the square, and Orcagna's graceful **Loggia della Signoria** that forms its south side, are filled with public statuary by Michelangelo, Donatello, Benvenuto Cellini and other leading lights of the Florentine Renaissance. The city's less well known contribution to scientific endeavour – it was here that Galileo found refuge from the Inquisition – receives its due in the **Museo di Storia della Scienza**, an excellent history of science museum tucked away behind the Uffizi.

THE PIAZZA

Map 2, D6–E6.

For so important a square, the history of the **Piazza della Signoria** is one of oddly haphazard and piecemeal development. Originally the area belonged to the Uberti family, leading members of the city's Ghibelline faction. When the Ghibellines were defeated in 1268, the land and buildings on it were confiscated and allowed to fall into ruin, supposedly as a lasting memorial to Ghibelline treachery. In time, part of the area was paved, a further act of humiliation designed to prevent the Uberti – exiled from the city – from ever raising another building within its precincts. The alleged reluctance of the city authorities to encroach on this "tainted" land partly explains the asymmetrical shape of the square and the Palazzo Vecchio.

The piazza began its formal life in 1307, when a small area was laid out to provide a setting for the Palazzo Vecchio, then known as the Palazzo dei Priori. All efforts to enlarge it over the next hundred years – a job subcontracted to the Opera del Duomo, the city's largest construction company – were hampered by work on the palace and Loggia della Signoria (see p.43). Contemporary accounts talk of decades when the area was little more than a rubble-filled building site – it was eventually paved in 1385. Further dramatic restructuring occurred during Cosimo I's megalomaniacal reordering of the Uffizi around 1560. More alterations followed in 1871, when the medieval Loggia dei Pisani was demolished, opening up much of the square's present-day westward sweep. By this time, some of the square's most salient features – its statues – were already firmly in place.

Savonarola's famous "bonfires of the vanities" (see p.132) took place in the piazza. On May 23, 1498, the hellfire preacher was consigned to the flames himself, on the very same spot – now marked by a plaque near the fountain.

The statues

Florence's political volatility is encapsulated by the Piazza della Signoria's peculiar array of **statuary**, most of which was arranged in the sixteenth century to accentuate the axis of the Uffizi. From left to right, the line-up starts with Giambologna's equestrian statue of **Cosimo I** (1587–94), the only such equestrian bronze figure produced in the late Renaissance. An echo of the famous Marcus Aurelius statue in Rome, an ancient work, it was designed to draw parallels between the power of medieval Florence (and thus Cosimo) and the glory of Imperial Rome. Three bas-reliefs at the base portray key events in Cosimo's career: becoming duke of Florence (1537); the conquest of Siena (1555); and acquiring the title Grand Duke of Tuscany (1569) from Pius V.

Next comes Ammannati's fatuous **Neptune Fountain** (1565–75), a tribute to Cosimo's prowess as a naval commander. Neptune himself is a lumpen lout, who provoked Michelangelo to coin the rhyming put-down – "Ammannato, Ammannato, che bel marmo hai rovinato" (...what a fine piece of marble you've ruined); Ammannati doesn't seem to have been too embarrassed, though in a late phase of piety he did come to regret the lasciviousness of the figures round the base, created with the assistance of Giambologna and other junior sculptors. Florentine superstition has it that Neptune wanders around the piazza when struck by the light of a full moon.

After a copy of Donatello's **Marzocco** (1418–20), the original of which is in the Bargello, comes a copy of the same sculptor's **Judith and Holofernes** (1456–60). The latter freezes the action at the moment Judith's arm begins its scything stroke – a dramatic conception that no other sculptor of the period would have attempted. Commissioned by Cosimo de' Medici, this statue originally doubled as a fountain in the Palazzo Medici, but was removed to the Piazza della Signoria after the expulsion of the family in 1495, and displayed as an emblem of vanquished tyranny; a new inscription on the base reinforced the message for those too obtuse to get it. The original is in the Palazzo Vecchio.

Michelangelo's **David**, at first intended for the Duomo, was also installed here as a declaration of civic solidarity by the Florentine Republic (see p.44); the statue is now cooped up in the Accademia. Conceived as partner piece to the *David* is Bandinelli's **Hercules and Cacus** (1534), designed as a personal emblem of Cosimo I, a symbol of Florentine fortitude, and the vanquishing of domestic enemies. The marble might well have ended up as something more inspiring. In the late 1520s, when the Florentines were once again busy tearing the Medici emblem from every building on which it had been stuck, Michelangelo offered to carve a monumental figure of Samson to celebrate the Republic's latest victory over tyranny; other demands on the artist's time put paid to this project, and the stone passed to Bandinelli, who duly vented his mediocrity on it.

A year later Bandinelli carved one of the two figures outside the Palazzo Vecchio – the other is another sixteenth-century work – the identity of which is unknown: both figures served as posts for a chain across the palace entrance.

When Bandinelli's Hercules was first unveiled, Benvenuto Cellini described the musclebound figure as looking like "a sackful of melons".

Loggia della Signoria

The square's grace note, the **Loggia della Signoria**, was begun in 1376, prompted by that year's heavy rains, which had washed out Florence's entire calendar of public ceremonies. It was completed in 1382, serving as a dais for city dignitaries, a forum for meeting foreign emissaries (including Britain's Elizabeth II in 1961), and a platform for the swearing-in of public officials. Its alternative name, the Loggia dei Lanzi, comes from Cosimo I's bodyguard of Swiss lancers, who were garrisoned nearby; its third name, the Loggia dell'Orcagna, derives from the idea that Orcagna (Andrea del Cione) may have had a hand in its original design.

Although Donatello's *Judith and Holofernes* was placed here as early as 1506 (see p.42), it was only in the late eighteenth century that the loggia became exclusively a showcase for melodramatic sculpture. In the corner nearest the Palazzo Vecchio usually stands a figure that has become one of the iconic images of the Renaissance, Benvenuto Cellini's **Perseus** (1545). However, it's currently being restored inside the Uffizi (in a special area open to the public) and may well be permanently replaced by a copy. Made for Cosimo I, the statue symbolizes the triumph of firm Grand Ducal rule over the monstrous indiscipline of all other forms of government.

THE FLORENTINE REPUBLIC

Florence's medieval history was one of almost incessant unrest, a state Dante graphically compared to a sick man forever shifting his position in bed. Yet between 1293 and 1534 – bar the odd ruction – the city maintained a **republican constitution** and well defined institutions that should have ensured centuries of peace and prosperity.

The nucleus of this structure was formed by the city's **merchants** and **guilds**, who covertly controlled Florence as early as the twelfth century. The two groups formalized their influence during an eleven-year period of quasi-democratic rule known as the **Primo Popolo** (1248–59). During the **Secondo Popolo** (1284), the leading guilds, the Arti Maggiori, introduced the **Ordinamenti della Giustizia** (1293), a written constitution that entrenched mercantile power still further and was to be the basis of Florence's government for the next two hundred and fifty years.

The rulers of this much-vaunted republic were drawn exclusively from the ranks of guild members over the age of 30. Candidates were chosen in a public ceremony held every two months, the short tenure being designed to prevent individuals or cliques amassing too much power. The names of selected guild members were placed in eight leather bags (borse) kept in the sacristy of Santa Croce. Those picked from the bags duly became the **Priori** (or Signori), forming a government called the **Signoria**, usually comprising nine men from the Arti Maggiori. Once elected, the Priori moved into the Palazzo della Signoria, where they were expected to stay, virtually incommunicado, for their period of office.

The traumatic process of the statue's creation is vividly described in Cellini's rip-roaring and self-serving autobiography. The project seemed doomed – many had believed it impossible from the outset – when the sculptor retired to

The Signoria was headed by the **Gonfaloniere**, or the "standard bearer", and consulted two elected councils or Collegi – the Dodici Buonomini (Twelve Citizens) and Sedici Gonfalonieri (Sixteen Standard Bearers). It could also call on special committees to deal with specific crises – The Ten of War, the Eight of Security, the Six of Commerce, and so on. Permanent officials included the chancellor, a post once held by Machiavelli, and the Podestà, a chief magistrate brought in from outside as an independent arbitrator.

In times of extreme crisis such as the Pazzi Conspiracy (see p.28), all male citizens over the age of 14 were summoned to a **Parlemento** in Piazza della Signoria by the tolling of the Palazzo Vecchio's famous bell, known as the *Vacca* (cow) after its deep bovine tone. When a two-thirds quorum was reached, the people were asked to approve a **Balìa**, a committee delegated to deal with the situation as it saw fit.

This looked good on paper, but in practice it was far from democratic. The lowliest workers, the **Popolo Minuto**, were excluded, as were the **Grandi**, or aristocracy. And despite the *Signoria*'s apparently random selection process, political cliques had few problems ensuring that only the names of their supporters found their way into the *borse*. If a rogue candidate slipped through the net, a *Parlemento* was summoned and the ensuing *Balìa* would ensure that the offending nominee was quietly replaced by a more pliable candidate. It was by such means that the city's great mercantile dynasties – the Peruzzi, the Albizzi, the Strozzi, and the Medici – retained their power even when not technically in office.

THE FLORENTINE REPUBLIC

bed with a fever in the middle of casting and then the
foundry in Cellini's house caught fire. Worse was to follow,
for as the inferno raged, the molten bronze began to solidi-
fy too early, a situation that was only salvaged when the
ever-resourceful hero saved the day by flinging all his
pewter plates into the mixture. When the bronze cooled
the figure was revealed as complete save for three toes,
which were added later.

The Latin inscription on the right wall of the loggia describes
how Florence adopted the modern calendar in 1750; before
that, New Year was celebrated on March 25, the date of the
Incarnation of Christ.

Equally attention-seeking is Giambologna's last work, to
the right, **The Rape of the Sabine** (1583), conjured from
the largest piece of sculptural marble ever seen in Florence,
and the epitome of the Mannerist obsession with spiralling
forms. The sculptor supposedly intended the piece merely
as a study of old age, male strength and female beauty: the
present name was coined later. The figures along the back
wall are Roman works, traditionally believed to portray
Roman empresses, while of the three central statues only
one – Giambologna's **Hercules Slaying the Centaur**
(1599) – deserves its place. The seven figures in the span-
drels between the arches above depict the Virtues
(1384–89), all carved to designs by Agnolo Gaddi save the
head of *Faith*, which was replaced by Donatello when the
original crashed to the ground.

THE PALAZZO VECCHIO

Map 2, E7. Piazza dell Signoria. Mon–Wed, Fri & Sat 9am–6.15pm,
Thurs & Sun 9am–1pm; summer late opening Mon & Fri until
10.15pm; €5.70; ⓦwww.nuovopalazzovecchio.org.

Florence's fortress-like town hall, the **Palazzo Vecchio**, was begun as the Palazzo dei Priori in the last year of the thirteenth century. It was home first to the *Priori* or *Signoria*, the highest tier of the city's republican government. Local folklore has it that the eccentric plan was not devised by the original architect (thought to be Arnolfo di Cambio), but is rather a product of factional division – the Guelph government refusing to encroach on land previously owned by the Ghibellines.

Changes in the Florentine constitution over the years entailed alterations to the layout of the palace, the most radical coming in 1540, when Cosimo I moved his retinue here from the Palazzo Medici and grafted a huge extension onto the rear. The Medici remained in residence for only nine years before moving to the Palazzo Pitti, largely, it seems, at the insistence of Cosimo's wife, Eleanor of Toledo. The "old" (*vecchio*) palace, which they left to their son, Francesco, then acquired its present name. Between 1865 and 1871, during Florence's brief tenure as capital of a newly united Italy, the palace housed the country's parliament and foreign ministry.

As for the sights, much of the palace's decoration comprises a relentless eulogy to Cosimo and his relations; the propaganda is made tolerable by some of the palace's examples of **Mannerist art** – among the finest pieces produced by that ultra-sophisticated and self-regarding movement. There are also frescoes by **Domenico Ghirlandaio** and some outstanding sculptures, not least works by **Michelangelo** and **Donatello**.

It's also possible to visit some of the more hidden and curious parts of the palace on hour-long guided tours known as **Percorsi Segreti** (Secret Routes, see p.54). What you actually see – private rooms, a secret staircase, the attic of the great hall – is of variable interest, although the guides are local, enthusiastic and well informed. Children

THE PALAZZO VECCHIO

get a better deal at the innovative new **Museo dei Ragazzi** (Kids' Museum, see p.56), as their tours are led by costumed actors. There isn't an actual museum as such, but rather a programme of lively educational workshops held in various rooms around the Palazzo Vecchio. The museum's office is immediately behind the main Palazzo Vecchio ticket office, in a small room just off the pillared court.

Courtyard and first floor

Work on the palace's beautiful inner **courtyard** was begun by Michelozzo in 1453. The decoration was largely added by Vasari, court architect from 1555 until his death in 1574, on the occasion of Francesco de' Medici's marriage to Johanna of Austria in 1565. The bride's origin explains the otherwise puzzling presence of cities belonging to the Habsburg Empire amid the wall's painted townscapes. Vasari also designed the central fountain, though the winsome putto and dolphin (1476) at its crown are the work of Verrocchio (the present statues are copies – the originals are on the Terrazzo di Giunone on the palace's second floor). Vasari was also let loose on the **monumental staircase** (1), a far more satisfying affair which leads to the palace's first floor (different routes to the first floor are sometimes used for visitors).

Vasari was given fuller rein in the huge **Salone del Cinquecento** at the top of the stairs, where tickets are checked. It was originally built in 1495 as the meeting hall for the *Consiglio Maggiore* (Great Council), the ruling assembly of the penultimate republic. The chamber might have had one of Italy's most remarkable decorative schemes: Leonardo da Vinci and Michelangelo were employed to paint frescoes on opposite sides of the room, but Leonardo's work, *The Battle of Anghiari,* was abandoned (or destroyed) after his experimental technique went wrong, while

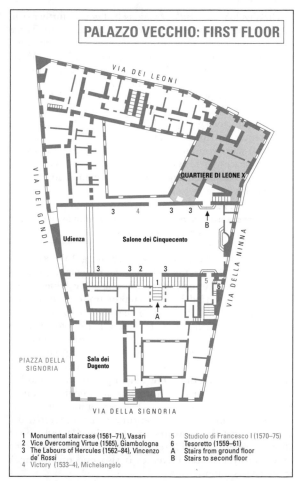

PALAZZO VECCHIO: FIRST FLOOR

VIA DEI LEONI

VIA DEI GONDI

QUARTIERE DI LEONE X

Udienza

Salone dei Cinquecento

VIA DELLA NINNA

B

A

PIAZZA DELLA SIGNORIA

Sala dei Dugento

VIA DELLA SIGNORIA

1. Monumental staircase (1561–71), Vasari
2. Vice Overcoming Virtue (1565), Giambologna
3. The Labours of Hercules (1562–84), Vincenzo de' Rossi
4. Victory (1533–4), Michelangelo
5. Studiolo di Francesco I (1570–75)
6. Tesoretto (1559–61)
A. Stairs from ground floor
B. Stairs to second floor

THE PALAZZO VECCHIO

49

Michelangelo's *The Battle of Cascina* had got no further than a fragmentary cartoon when he was summoned to Rome by Pope Julius II in 1506. Instead the hall received six drearily bombastic murals (1563–65) – painted either by Vasari or under his direction – illustrating Florentine military triumphs over Pisa (1496–1509) and Siena (1554–55).

The ceiling's 39 panels, again by Vasari, celebrate the *Apotheosis of Cosimo I* (centre), a scene surrounded by the crests of the city's guilds and further paeans to the prowess of Florence and the Medici. One of the Percorsi Segreti (see p.54) takes you into the attic above the roof, an extraordinary space where it's possible to see how Vasari pulled off the trick of suspending such a large ceiling without visible supports.

Works of special note are highlighted in green in the text and on the plans on pp.49 & 52.

The sculptural highlight is **Michelangelo's Victory (4)**, almost opposite the entrance door, depicting Genius slaying Might. Carved for the tomb of Pope Julius II, the statue was converted by the sculptor from a female to a male figure. It was donated to the Medici by the artist's nephew, then installed here by Vasari in 1565 to celebrate Cosimo's defeat of the Sienese ten years earlier. Directly opposite, on the entrance wall, is the original plaster model of a companion piece for the Victory, Giambologna's **Virtue Overcoming Vice (2)**, another artistic metaphor for Florentine military might – this time Florence's victory over Pisa. The remaining statues, the masterpiece of sixteenth-century artist Vincenzo de' Rossi, portray the **Labours of Hercules (3)** and are yet another example of Florentine heroic propaganda: the innocuously classical Hercules is also one of Florence's many civic symbols.

A roped-off door allows a glimpse of the most bizarre room in the building – the **Studiolo di Francesco I (5)**. Created by Vasari towards the end of his career and decorated by no fewer than thirty Mannerist artists (1570–74), this windowless cell was created as a retreat for the introverted son of Cosimo and Eleanor. Each of the miniature bronzes and nearly all the paintings reflect Francesco's interest in the sciences and alchemy: the entrance wall pictures illustrate the theme of "Earth", while the others, reading clockwise, signify "Water", "Air" and "Fire". The outstanding paintings are the two which don't fit the scheme: Bronzino's portraits of the occupant's parents, facing each other across the room. The oval paintings on the panels at the base hinted at the presence of Francesco's most treasured knick-knacks, which were once concealed in the compartments behind; the wooden structure is actually a nineteenth-century recreation, though the paintings are original. Another Percorso Segreto (see p.54) allows you inside the *studiolo*, then through one of the hidden doors and up a secret little staircase to the *studiolino* or **Teseretto (6)**, Cosimo's tiny private study, which was built ten years before the *studiolo*. The frescoed ceiling depicts the liberal arts.

Much of the rest of the first floor is still used by council officials, though if the seven rooms of the Quartiere di Leone X and **Sala dei Dugento** are open (they rarely are), don't miss the opportunity. The latter, in particular, is outstanding: Benedetto and Giuliano da Maiano, excellent sculptors both, were responsible for the design (1472–77) and for the fine wooden ceiling; the tapestries (1546–53) were created to designs by Bronzino, Pontormo and others.

The second floor

Steps lead from the Salone to the **second floor**, passing an intriguing fireworks fresco (1558) showing Piazza della

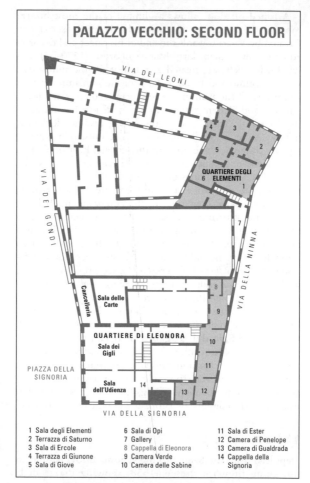

PALAZZO VECCHIO: SECOND FLOOR

VIA DEI LEONI

VIA DEI GONDI

QUARTIERE DEGLI ELEMENTI

VIA DELLA NINNA

Cancelleria

Sala delle Carte

QUARTIERE DI ELEONORA

Sala dei Gigli

PIAZZA DELLA SIGNORIA

Sala dell'Udienza

VIA DELLA SIGNORIA

1 Sala degli Elementi
2 Terrazza di Saturno
3 Sala di Ercole
4 Terrazza di Giunone
5 Sala di Giove

6 Sala di Opi
7 Gallery
8 Cappella di Eleonora
9 Camera Verde
10 Camera delle Sabine

11 Sala di Ester
12 Camera di Penelope
13 Camera di Gualdrada
14 Cappella della Signoria

Signoria during the celebrations for the feast of St John the Baptist. Turn left at the top of the stairs and you enter the **Quartiere degli Elementi**, one of the floor's three distinct suites of rooms. All five salons here are slavishly devoted to a different member of the Medici clan. Persevere, though, if only to enjoy the city **views** from the Terrazza di Saturno and Verrocchio's original Putto and Dolphin statue on the Terrazzo di Giunone.

Return to the stairs and head straight on and you cross a gallery with views down into the Salone. Immediately afterwards come the six rooms of the **Quartiere di Eleonora di Toledo**, the private apartments of Cosimo I's wife. Star turn here is the tiny and exquisite **Cappella di Eleonora** (8), superbly and vividly decorated by Bronzino in the 1540s; it seems that the artist used a novel and time-consuming technique to give these wall paintings the same glassy surface as his canvases, executing a first draft in fresco and then glazing it with a layer of tempera. The wall paintings describe scenes from the Life of Moses, episodes probably intended to draw parallels with the life of Cosimo. In the *Annunciation* on the back wall Bronzino is said to have used Cosimo and Eleanor's eldest daughter as the model for the Virgin.

Those who find all this Mannerist stuff unhealthily airless can take refuge in the more summery rooms which follow. The **Sala dell'Udienza**, originally the audience chamber of the Republic, boasts a stunning gilt-coffered ceiling by Giuliano da Maiano. The Mannerists reassert themselves with a vast fresco sequence (1545–48) by Cecchino Salviati, a cycle widely considered to be this artist's most accomplished work.

Giuliano was also responsible, with his brother Benedetto, for the intarsia work on the doors and the lovely doorway that leads into the **Sala dei Gigli**, a room that takes its name from the lilies (*gigli*) that adorn most of its

THE PALAZZO VECCHIO

surfaces – not the red lilies that form the city's emblem, incidentally, but the golden *fleur de lys* of the king of France, with whom Florence was then on amiable terms. The room has another splendid ceiling by the Maiano brothers, and a wall frescoed by Domenico Ghirlandaio with *SS Zenobius, Stephen and Lorenzo* (1481–85) and lunettes portraying *Six Heroes of Ancient Rome*. The undoubted highlight here, however, is Donatello's original **Judith and Holofernes** (1455–60), removed from Piazza della Signoria.

Two small rooms are attached to the Sala dei Gigli: the **Cancelleria**, once Machiavelli's office and now containing a bust and portrait of the often-maligned political thinker, and the lovely **Sala delle Carte**, formerly the Guardaroba, or wardrobe, the repository of Cosimo's state finery. Now it is decorated with 57 maps painted in 1563 by the court astronomer Fra' Ignazio Danti, depicting what was then the entire known world. One of the maps, in the far right-hand corner, conceals a door to another hidden staircase.

A door leads out from the second floor onto the broad balcony of the Palazzo Vecchio's **tower**. The views are superb, if not as good as those enjoyed from the cell in the body of the tower above, which was known ironically as the Alberghinetto (Little Hotel); such troublemakers as Cosimo de' Medici and Savonarola were once imprisoned here.

The final section of the museum, just before the exit, is something of an afterthought, and is wanly devoted to second-rate pictures once owned by the American collector Loeser.

Percorsi Segreti

Guided tours Mon–Sat; €6.70, includes ticket to Palazzo Vecchio.

The so-called "Secret Passageways" may not be quite as clandestine as their name suggests, but they certainly allow access to parts of the Palazzo Vecchio that are normally off limits. Most visually impressive is the trip up through the palace and into the **Attic of the Salone del Cinquecento**. From the vantage point of a balcony high above the hall, the guide describes the complex way in which Vasari created such a huge space within the medieval structure, and explains the allegorical meaning of the paintings. You are then led up into the vast attic itself: two sets of trusses – a forest of pungent timber – independently support the roof above and the ceiling below. Some of the beams are over 20m long.

Less magnificent, but still worth it for the guides' commentary, is the route leading from the street outside up through the secret **Stairway of the Duke of Athens**. The doorway was knocked through the exterior wall of the Palazzo in 1342 as an emergency escape route for the Duke, who briefly took up the reins of power here. He never in fact used the staircase, but only because his fall from grace came rather sooner than he had imagined. Another route leads into the impressive Studiolo and **Tesoretto**, described above, and further *percorsi* are planned, depending on the success of the existing tours.

All three tours last roughly an hour and the **ticket** includes entry to the palace itself; you can do further tours for €2.60. How many tours are given in English rather depends on how many people are asking, and when: during quieter periods it's likely that you'll have a guide to yourself, but in high season and at weekends it's worth booking in advance at the main ticket office (☏055.276.8224). On weekdays, guides take one party on each Percorso Segreto both mornings (9.30am, 10.30am & 11.30am) and afternoons (3.30pm, 4.30pm & 5.30pm). On Saturday all three tours run concurrently, leaving hourly from 10am, and at least one every hour should be in English.

THE PALAZZO VECCHIO

Museo dei Ragazzi

Workshops 9am–1pm & 3–7pm; €6.70, includes ticket to Palazzo Vecchio; Ⓦwww.museoragazzi.it.

Most children will be glad to hear that the **Museo dei Ragazzi** is anything but a traditional museum, though there is a whiff of the classroom about the five "interactive workshops" held in rooms dotted around the palace. These are aimed more at local *ragazzi* than visitors' children, but some classes are held in English, usually at weekends, and groups of ten or more can request them in advance (ask at the office in the Palazzo Vecchio or call ☎055.276.8224). The workshops are, on the whole, extremely well thought out. It's quite possible to leave the children behind for ninety minutes, and take a tour of the palace – or perhaps have a well earned drink in the piazza outside – but adults are welcome to attend.

Most satisfying is probably "**Clothing and the Body**". Guides lead the group through a secret door in the Sala delle Carte (see p.54) and down to a vaulted space dominated by a four-poster bed in which an actress playing Eleonora di Toledo lies sleeping. Her maid enters and gets her mistress washed, combed, primped and ready for the day – Eleonora ends up dressed exactly as in Bronzino's portrait in the Uffizi (see p.69). Meanwhile, their gossipy conversation, joined by Duke Cosimo and his servant, leads into a discussion that compares clothing and attitudes to the body now and in the Renaissance. Even when the actresses are speaking Italian, English-speaking guides are on hand to translate.

"**Architecture of the Palazzo**" takes place high up behind the Salone del Cinquecento, in a room with fabulous views. After being shown the remnants of thirteenth-century arches, bricked into an exposed wall, the children create, walk upon – and, inevitably, destroy – a load-bearing arch made from special bricks, and reconstruct a model of the Palazzo Vecchio in order to see how it was built. "**The Magic of Lenses**" allows you to play with various lenses, learn about optical effects and then put together a basic telescope. From the basement classroom it's up to the balcony of the palace to test out designs perfected by Galileo, among others. More scientific still is "**Horror Vacui?**" – (nature) abhors a vacuum – which reproduces the experiments of the Florentine mathematician Torricelli, who proved the existence of atmospheric pressure. As with all the classes, it's not as dry as it might sound, as the guides make a good job of enlivening the subject. A **playroom** for younger children also has a gently educational bent.

In league with other museums in the city, the Museo dei Ragazzi also runs **Encounters**, guided tours led by costumed actors that are aimed at both children and adults. Vasari himself leads a tour of the Palazzo Vecchio, Galileo explains his radical inventions in the Museo di Storia della Scienza (see below) and Suleiman the Magnificent takes a group of captured Christians round his armoury in the Museo Stibbert (on the outskirts of the city and not discussed in this guide; ask at the tourist office for more information). During the school holidays, at least one tour is normally held in English every day; call ☎055.276.8224 to book.

MUSEO DI STORIA DELLA SCIENZA

Map 2, E9. Piazza dei Giudici 1. Mon & Wed–Fri 9.30am–4.30pm, Tues & Sat 9.30am–12.30pm; €6.20.

Long after Florence had declined from its artistic apogee, the intellectual reputation of the city was maintained by its scientists, many of them directly encouraged by the ruling Medici-Lorraine dynasty. Two of the latter, Grand Duke Ferdinando II and his brother Leopoldo, both of whom studied with Galileo, founded a scientific academy at the Pitti in 1657. Called the Accademia del Cimento (Academy of Experiment), its motto was "Try and try again." The instruments made and acquired by this academy are the core of the city's excellent history of science museum, the **Museo di Storia della Scienza**. It is one of those taking part in the Museo dei Ragazzi's excellent "Encounters" guided tours (see p.57).

A modern and well organized affair, the museum has benefited from a major overhaul over the last few years: the exhibits now take up two upper floors, with a large research library on the lowest floor. Each room is devoted to a particular branch of science or technology. Lists of the exhibits in English are handed out to visitors on each floor, providing a full background to some of the more extraordinary items.

The first eleven exhibition rooms feature some marvellous **measuring instruments**, notably a selection of beautiful Arab astrolabes. There's also a massive armillary sphere made for Ferdinando I to provide a visual demonstration of the supposed veracity of the earth-centred Ptolemaic system, and the fallacy of Copernicus's heliocentric universe. Galileo's original instruments are on show here, such as the lens with which he discovered the four moons of Jupiter, which he tactfully named the Medicean planets. On this floor you'll also find the museum's equivalent of a religious relic – a bone from one of Galileo's fingers. Other cases display items belonging to Michelangelo, and objects such as ancient quadrants and calculating machines that have the beauty of works of art. The most impressive of several fascinating rooms is Room 7, filled with dozens of gorgeous globes and old maps.

On the floor above there are all kinds of **scientific and mechanical equipment**, some – such as a perpetual motion machine – from the quasi-magical realms of scientific endeavour. Room 12 sets the tone, with dozens of wonderful old clocks and timepieces. There are also a couple of remarkable outsized exhibits: the huge lens made for Cosimo III, with which Faraday and Davy managed to ignite a diamond by focusing the rays of the sun, and the enormous lodestone given by Galileo to Ferdinando II. Other rooms feature pharmaceutical and chemical apparatus.

The best is saved for last: a **medical section** full of alarming surgical instruments and horrifying anatomical wax models for teaching obstetrics: expectant mothers should give these a wide berth. Room 19 concludes with the contents of a medieval pharmacy, displaying such unlikely cure-alls as *Sangue del Drago* (Dragon's Blood) and *Confetti di Seme Santo* (Confections of Blessed Seed).

MUSEO DI STORIA DELLA SCIENZA

Galleria degli Uffizi

lorence can prompt an over-eagerness to reach for superlatives; in the case of the **Galleria degli Uffizi** (Map 2, D8), superlative is simply the bare truth: this is the finest picture gallery in Italy. So many masterpieces are collected here that it's not even possible to skate over the surface in a single visit; it makes sense to limit your initial tour to the first fifteen rooms, where the Florentine Renaissance works are concentrated, and to explore the rest another time – Gibbon visited fourteen times on a single trip to Florence. The map opposite gives an idea of where some of the highlights are to be found.

This is the busiest single building in the country, with over one and a half million visitors a year, so you should anticipate **queues** at most times of the day except in the depths of winter; in summer the best way to beat the crowds is to visit for the last couple of hours or pre-book a time to visit (see box on p.62). Finally, be prepared to find some of the rooms closed for one reason or another – at the height of the summer it's not unusual to discover nearly half the gallery locked up.

All state-run museums in Florence, including the Uffizi, give free admission to visitors from EU countries aged under 18 or over 65, and half-price admission to people under 26. Most accept only a passport or identity card as proof of age.

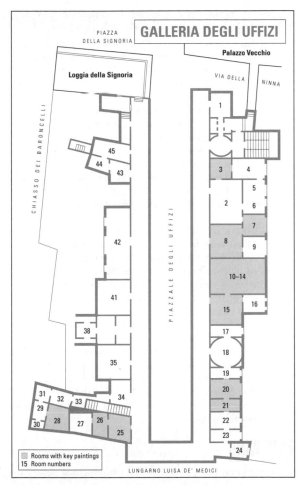

GALLERIA DEGLI UFFIZI

PIAZZA DELLA SIGNORIA

Loggia della Signoria

Palazzo Vecchio

VIA DELLA NINNA

CHIASSO DEI BARONCELLI

PIAZZALE DEGLI UFFIZI

Rooms with key paintings

15 Room numbers

LUNGARNO LUISA DE' MEDICI

UFFIZI OPENING AND RESERVATIONS

The **Uffizi** is open Tues–Sun 8.15am–6.50pm; in high summer and at festive periods the gallery sometimes stays open until 10pm. The ticket office closes at 6pm. The Uffizi forms one of the group of thirteen state museums and galleries, **Firenze Musei**, which allow you to book a time for entry into the museum in advance: call ☎055.294.883 and an English-speaking operator will give you a reservation number and time for the day you wish to visit. Tickets can be picked up at the allocated time (not earlier) at the meeting point for advanced reservations, to the left of the main gallery entrance. The full entry ticket costs €7.80 but, as with all state galleries in Italy, EU citizens aged 18–25 pay half price and entry is free to under-18s and over-65s. A booking fee of €1.20 is charged for advance reservations.

The gallery is housed in what were once government offices (*uffizi*) built by **Vasari** for Cosimo I in 1560. After Vasari's death, work on the elongated U-shaped building was continued by Buontalenti, who was asked by Francesco I to glaze the upper storey so that it could house his art collection. Each of the succeeding Medici added to the family's trove of art treasures. The accumulated collection was preserved for public inspection by the last member of the family, Anna Maria Lodovica, whose will specified that it should be left to the people of Florence and never be allowed to leave the city. Last century a large proportion of the statuary was transferred to the Bargello, while most of the antiquities went to the Museo Archeologico, leaving the Galleria degli Uffizi as essentially a gallery of paintings supplemented with some classical sculptures.

EAST WING

On the ground floor, in rooms that once formed part of the

eleventh-century church of San Pier Scheraggio, are shown **Andrea del Castagno**'s frescoes of celebrated Florentines; the imaginary portraits include Dante and Boccaccio, both of whom spoke in debates at the church. Close to a Botticelli *Annunciation*, a lift goes up to the galleries; if you take the staircase instead, you'll pass the entrance to the prints and drawings collection, the bulk of which is reserved for scholarly scrutiny, though samples are often on public show.

The Uffizi's main galleries are ranged along the two wings of the third floor, off a long, cool corridor lined with an array of portraits, busts and statues. The main rooms of the gallery lie to the left, proceeding in roughly chronological order from the thirteenth to the sixteenth centuries. The rooms beyond the Tribune (18), about two thirds of the way down, house a miscellany of non-Florentine pieces, mainly from the Venetian and Flemish Renaissance.

Works of special note are highlighted in green in the text

Cimabue to Uccello

Room 1, housing an assembly of antique sculptures, many of which were used as a kind of source book by Renaissance artists, is often shut. The beginnings of the stylistic evolution of that period can be traced in the three altarpieces of the *Maestà* (Madonna Enthroned) that dominate **Room 2**: the Madonna Rucellai, Maestà di Santa Trìnita and Madonna d'Ognissanti, by **Duccio**, **Cimabue** and **Giotto** respectively. These great works, which dwarf everything around them, show the softening of the hieratic Byzantine style into a more tactile form of representation. Painters from fourteenth-century Siena fill **Room 3**, with several pieces by Ambrogio and Pietro Lorenzetti and

EAST WING

Simone Martini's glorious **Annunciation**, the Virgin cowering from the angel amid a field of pure gold.

Other trecento artists follow in **Rooms 5 and 6**, among them Florence's first-rank Gothic painters, **Orcagna** and **Lorenzo Monaco**, whose majestic **Coronation of the Virgin** catches the eye first. The **Adoration of the Magi** by **Gentile da Fabriano** is the summit of the precious style known as International Gothic, spangled with gold that in places is so thick that the crowns of the kings, for instance, are like low-relief jewellery. It's crammed with so much detail that there's no real distinction between what's crucial and what's peripheral, with as much attention lavished on incidentals such as a snarling cheetah as on the supposed protagonists. The right-hand panel of the predella, below, was stolen by Napoleon and replaced with a copy that, unlike the rest of the painting, is not painted directly onto gold – hence the relative matt dullness of its surface. Nearby is Starnina's *Thebiad*, a baffling but beguiling little narrative that can perhaps best be described as a monastic fairy tale.

Gothic golds are left behind in **Room 7**, which reveals the sheer diversity of early Renaissance painting. **The Madonna and Child with SS Francis, John the Baptist, Zenobius and Lucy** is one of only twelve extant paintings by **Domenico Veneziano**, who spent much of his life in Venice but died destitute in Florence. Veneziano's greatest pupil, **Piero della Francesca**, is represented by the Flemish-influenced paired portraits of **Federico da Montefeltro and Battista Sforza**, the duke and duchess of Urbino. These panels were painted two years after Battista's death – in the background of her portrait is the town of Gubbio, where she died giving birth to her ninth child and first son, Guidobaldo.

Paolo Uccello's **The Battle of San Romano** once hung in Lorenzo the Magnificent's bedchamber, in company with its two companion pieces now in the Louvre and

London's National Gallery. Warfare is the ostensible subject, but this is really a semi-abstract compendium of perspectival effects – a toppling knight, a horse and rider keeled onto their sides, the foreshortened legs of a kicking horse, a thicket of lances – creating a fight scene with no real sense of violence.

Filippo Lippi to Leonardo

Most space in **Room 8** is given over to **Filippo Lippi**, whose *Madonna and Child with Two Angels* supplies one of the gallery's most popular faces, and one of its least other-worldly devotional images – the model was Lucrezia Buti, a convent novice who became the object of one of his more enduring sexual obsessions. That liaison produced a son, the aptly named **Filippino** "Little Philip" **Lippi**, whose lustrous *Madonna Degli Otto* shows the later influence of Leonardo. Lippi's pupil, Botticelli, steals some of the thunder in **Room 9**, where the artists centre-stage are **Piero** and **Antonio del Pollaiuolo**; their sinewy *SS Vincent, James and Eustace*, one of their best works, is chiefly the work of Antonio. This room also contains the *Portrait of Young Man in a Red Hat*, sometimes referred to as a self-portrait by Filippino, but now widely believed to be an eighteenth-century fraud.

It's in the merged Rooms **10–14** that the greatest of **Botticelli**'s productions are gathered. A century ago most people walked past his pictures without breaking stride; nowadays – despite their elusiveness – the *Primavera* and the *Birth of Venus* stop all visitors in their tracks. The identities of the characters in the **Primavera** are not contentious: on the right Zephyrus, god of the west wind, chases the nymph Cloris, who is then transfigured into Flora, the pregnant goddess of spring; Venus stands in the centre, to the side of the three Graces, who are targeted by Cupid; on the left Mercury wards off the clouds of winter. What this all means, however, has occupied scholars for decades. Some see it as an allegory of the four seasons, but the consensus now seems to be that it shows the triumph of Venus, with the Graces as the physical embodiment of her beauty and Flora the symbol of her fruitfulness – an interpretation supported by the fact that the picture was placed outside the wedding suite of Lorenzo di Pierfrancesco de' Medici.

Botticelli's most winsome painting, the **Birth of Venus**, probably takes as its source the grisly myth that the goddess emerged from the sea after having been impregnated by the castration of Uranus – an allegory for the creation of beauty through the mingling of the spirit (Uranus) and the physical world. The supporting players are the nymph, Cloris, and Zephyrus, god of the west wind. Zephyrus blows the risen Venus to the shore where the goddess is clothed by Hora, daughter and attendant of Aurora, goddess of dawn. A third allegory hangs close by – *Pallas and the Centaur*, perhaps symbolizing the ambivalent triumph of reason over instinct.

It's hardly obvious to a casual eye, but Botticelli's *Birth of Venus* marks a significant and often overlooked development in technique: it was one of the first large-scale works to be painted onto stretched canvas.

His devotional paintings are generally less perplexing. The *Adoration of the Magi* is traditionally thought to contain a gallery of Medici portraits: Cosimo il Vecchio as the first king, his sons Giovanni and Piero as the other two kings, Lorenzo the Magnificent on the far left, and his brother Giuliano as the black-haired young man in profile on the right. Only the identification of Cosimo is reasonably certain, along with that of Botticelli himself, on the right in the yellow robe. In later life, influenced by Savonarola's teaching, Botticelli confined himself to devotional pictures and moral fables, and his style became increasingly severe.

The transformation is clear when comparing the easy grace of the *Madonna of the Magnificat* and the *Madonna of the Pomegranate* with the more rigidly composed *Pala di Sant' Ambrogio* or the angular and agitated *Calumny.* Even the *Annunciation* (1489), painted just as Savonarola's preaching began to grip Florence, reveals a new intensity in the expression of the angel and in the twisting treatment of the body of the Virgin, who appears almost blown back by the force of the message.

Not quite every masterpiece in this room is by Botticelli. Set away from the walls is the **Adoration of the Shepherds** by his Flemish contemporary **Hugo van der Goes**. Brought to Florence in 1483 by Tomasso Portinari, the Medici agent in Bruges, it provided the city's artists with their first large-scale demonstration of the realism of

SANDRO BOTTICELLI

Possibly a pupil of Filippo Lippi, **Sandro Botticelli** (c.1445–1510) was certainly influenced by the Pollaiuolo brothers, whose paintings of the *Virtues* he completed. Among his earliest works are the frescoes in Ognissanti (see p.161). The mythological paintings for which he is celebrated – including the *Birth of Venus* and *Primavera* – are distinguished by their emphasis on line rather than mass, and by their complicated symbolic meaning, a reflection on his involvement with the neoplatonist philosophers whom the Medici gathered about them.

In the last decade of his life his lucid, slightly archaic style suffered from comparison with the more radical paintings of Michelangelo and Leonardo da Vinci, and his devotional pictures, as seen in the Uffizi at least, became almost clumsily didactic – a result, perhaps, of his involvement with Savonarola and his followers.

northern European oil painting, and had a great influence on the way the medium was exploited here.

One wall of **Room 15** traces the formative years of **Leonardo da Vinci**, whose distinctive touch appears first in the Baptism of Christ (14) by his master Verrocchio. Vasari claimed that only the wistful angel in profile was by the 18-year-old apprentice, and the misty landscape in the background, but recent X-rays have revealed that he also worked heavily on the figure of Christ. A similar terrain of soft-focus mountains and water occupies the far distance in Leonardo's slightly later Annunciation, in which a diffused light falls on a scene where everything is observed with a scientist's precision – the petals of the flowers on which the angel alights, the fall of the Virgin's drapery, the carving on the lectern at which she reads.

In restless contrast to the aristocratic poise of the *Annunciation*, the sketch of The Adoration of the Magi – abandoned when Leonardo left Florence for Milan in early 1482 – presents the infant Christ as the eye of a vortex of figures, all drawn into his presence by a force as irresistible as a whirlpool.

Most of the rest of the room is given over to Raphael's teacher, **Perugino**, who is represented by a typically contemplative *Madonna and Child with Saints* (1493), and a glassily meditative *Pietà* (1494–5). It also contains a bizarre *Incarnation* by **Piero di Cosimo**, the wild man of the Florentine Renaissance. Shunning civilized company, Piero did everything he could to bring his life close to a state of uncompromised Nature, living in a house that was never cleaned, in the midst of a garden he refused to tend, and eating nothing but hard-boiled eggs. Where his contemporaries might seek inspiration in commentaries on Plato, he would spend hours staring at the sky, at peeling walls, at the pavement – at anything where abstract patterns might conjure fabulous scenes in his imagination. His wildness is most obviously realized in the nightmarish *Perseus Freeing Andromeda*, where even the rocks and the sea seem to twist and boil monstrously; it was hanging in Room 19 at the time of writing, but should return to Room 15.

The Tribuna to the Arno

Room 18, the octagonal **Tribuna**, now houses the most important of the Medici's collection of Classical sculptures, chief among which is the *Medici Venus*, a first-century BC copy of the Praxitelean *Aphrodite of Cnidos*. She was kept in the Villa Medici in Rome until Cosimo III began to fret that she was having a detrimental effect on the morals of the city's art students, and ordered her removal to Florence. The move clearly didn't affect the statue's sexual charisma, however, as it became traditional for eighteenth-century visitors to Florence to caress her buttocks.

Around the walls are hung some fascinating portraits by **Bronzino** – Cosimo de' Medici, Eleanor of Toledo, Bartolomeo Panciatichi and his wife Lucrezia Panciatichi, all painted as figures of porcelain, placed in a bloodless, sunless world. More vital is Andrea del Sarto's flirtatious *Ritratto d'Ignotta (Portrait of a Young Woman)*, and there's a deceptive naturalism to Vasari's portrait of Lorenzo the Magnificent and Pontormo's of Cosimo il Vecchio, both painted long after the death of their subjects.

The last section of this wing throws together Renaissance paintings from outside Florence, with some notable Venetian and Flemish works. **Signorelli** and **Perugino** – with some photo-sharp portraits – are the principal artists in **Room 19**, and after them comes a room largely devoted to **Cranach** and **Dürer**. Each has an *Adam and Eve* here, Dürer taking the opportunity to show off his proficiency as a painter of wildlife. Dürer's power as a portraitist is displayed in the *Portrait of the Artist's Father*, his earliest authen-

EAST WING

ticated painting, and Cranach has a couple of acute pictures of Luther on display, one of them a double with his wife.

A taste of the Uffizi's remarkable collection of Venetian painting follows, with an impenetrable *Sacred Allegory* by **Giovanni Bellini**, and three of the few works by **Giorgione** to be found anywhere, including a mesmerizing (attributed) portrait of a young soldier traditionally known as the *Gattemelata*. A brace of northern European paintings is chiefly notable for **Holbein**'s *Portrait of Sir Richard Southwell*, while a crystalline triptych by **Mantegna** in Room 21 is not in fact a real triptych, but rather a trio of small paintings shackled together after the event. To the side are a couple of other pictures by Mantegna – a swarthy portrait of Carlo de' Medici and the tiny *Madonna of the Stonecutters*, set against a mountain that looks like a gigantic fir cone.

WEST WING

If you're determined to carry straight on through to the opposite wing of the gallery, the short corridor linking the two sections is a good point to refresh tired eyes; the views extend south, along the Arno, and north past the Palazzo della Signoria to Brunelleschi's looming dome.

Michelangelo to Titian

Beyond the stockpile of classical pieces in the short corridor overlooking the Arno, the main attraction in **Room 25** is **Michelangelo**'s Doni Tondo, the only easel painting he came close to completing. (Regarding sculpture as the noblest of the visual arts, Michelangelo dismissed all non-fresco painting as a demeaning chore.) Nobody has yet explained the precise significance of every aspect of this picture, but plausible explanations for parts of it have been put forward. The five naked figures behind the Holy Family seem to be standing in a half-moon-shaped cistern or font, which would relate to the infant Baptist to the right, who – in the words of St Paul – prefigures the coming of Christ just as the new moon is "a shadow of things to come". In the same epistle, Paul goes on to commend the virtues of mercy, benignity, humility, modesty and patience, which are perhaps what the five youths represent.

Room 26 contains **Andrea del Sarto**'s sultry *Madonna of the Harpies* and a number of compositions by **Raphael**, including the lovely *Madonna of the Goldfinch* and the late *Pope Leo X with Cardinals Giulio de' Medici and Luigi de' Rossi* – as shifty a group of ecclesiastics as was ever gathered in one frame. The Michelangelo tondo's contorted gestures, hermetic meaning and virulent colours were greatly influential on the Mannerist painters of the sixteenth century, as can be gauged from *Moses Defending the Daughters of Jethro* by **Rosso Fiorentino**, one of the seminal figures of the movement, whose works hang in **Room 27**, along with two major religious works by Bronzino and his adoptive father, Pontormo – one of the very few painters not seen at his best in the Uffizi.

Room 28 is entirely given over to another of the titanic figures of sixteenth-century art, **Titian**, with nine paintings on show. His *Flora* and *A Knight of Malta* are stunning, but most eyes tend to swivel towards the Venus of Urbino, the most fleshy and provocative of all Renaissance nudes.

Mark Twain once described Titian's sensual *Venus of Urbino* as "the foulest, the vilest, the obscenest picture the world possesses".

Parmigianino to Chardin

A brief diversion through the painters of the sixteenth-century Emilian school follows, centred on **Parmigianino**, whose *Madonna of the Long Neck* is one of the pivotal Mannerist creations. Parmigianino was a febrile and introverted character who abandoned painting for alchemy towards the end of his short life, and many of his works are marked by a sort of morbid refinement – none more so than this one. The Madonna's tunic clings to every contour, an angel advances a perfectly turned leg, the infant Christ drapes himself languorously on his mother's lap – prefiguring the dead Christ of the Pietà – while in the background an emaciated figure unrolls a scroll of parchment by a colonnade so severely foreshortened that it looks like a single column.

Rooms 31 to 34 feature artists from Venice and the Veneto, with outstanding paintings such as **Moroni**'s *Portrait of Count Pietro Secco Suardi*, **Paolo Veronese**'s *Annunciation* and *Holy Family with St Barbara*, and **Tintoretto**'s *Leda*. In any other company, Sebastiano del Piombo's *Death of Adonis* would draw all the attention. In May 1993, the painting was nearly lost altogether when a huge terrorist bomb tore through much of this westernmost part of the gallery. Given that del Piombo's masterpiece was reduced to little more than postage-stamp tatters, the recently completed restoration is nothing short of miraculous.

Room 41, entered off the main corridor, is dominated by **Rubens** and **Van Dyck**. The former's *Portrait of Isabella Brandt* makes its point more quietly than most of the stuff around it. Rubens lets rip in *Henry IV at the Battle of Ivry* and *The Triumphal Entry of Henry IV into Paris* – Henry's marriage to Marie de' Medici is the connection with Florence. Rubens's equally histrionic contemporary, **Caravaggio**, has a cluster of pieces in **Room 43**, including a screaming severed head of *Medusa*, a smug little bore of a *Bacchus*, and a *Sacrifice of Isaac* – religious art as tabloid journalism.

The next room, **44**, is in effect a showcase for the portraiture of **Rembrandt**. His sorrow-laden *Self-Portrait as an Old Man*, painted five years or so before his death, makes a poignant contrast with the self-confident self-portrait of thirty years earlier. Although there are some good pieces from **Tiepolo**, portraits again command the attention in the following room of eighteenth-century works, especially the two of Maria Theresa painted by **Goya**, and **Chardin**'s demure children at play. On the way out, in the hall at the top of the exit stairs, squats one of the city's talismans, the *Wild Boar*, a Roman copy of a third-century BC Hellenistic sculpture; it was the model for the *Porcellino* fountain in the Mercato Nuovo.

The Corridoio Vasariano

A door on the west corridor, between rooms 25 and 34, opens onto the **Corridoio Vasariano**, a passageway built by Vasari in 1565 to link the Palazzo Vecchio to the Palazzo Pitti through the Uffizi. Winding its way down to the river, over the Ponte Vecchio, through the church of Santa Felìcita and into the Giardino di Boboli, it gives a fascinating series of clandestine views of the city. As if that weren't pleasure enough, the corridor is completely lined with paintings, the larger portion of which comprises a **gallery of self-portraits**. Once past the portrait of Vasari, the series proceeds chronologically, littered with illustrious names: Raphael, Andrea del Sarto, Bronzino, Bernini, Rubens, Rembrandt, Velázquez, David, Delacroix and Ingres.

Visits have to be arranged by telephone (☎055.265.4321) or at the gallery's ticket office; **tours** are conducted in the morning, usually on Wednesday and Friday only, the precise time varying with the availability of staff. The numbers are limited to thirty people on each tour – apparently because Vasari failed to include a fire escape – so the tours tend to get booked up months in advance.

For more on the Ponte Vecchio, the Palazzo Pitti, and the course of the Corridoio beyond the river, see Chapter 11.

WEST WING •

The Bargello and around

T he dense network of streets to the north and east of the Piazza della Signoria is dominated by the forbidding bulk of the **Bargello**. Once the city's prison, this dour, battlemented fortress is now home to one of the most exhilarating collections of sculpture to be seen anywhere. The giants – Michelangelo, Donatello and the rest – are all represented here, as well as an alluring and little-advertised collection devoted to the decorative arts. If you want to get a full idea of the achievement of the Florentine Renaissance, this ranks alongside the Uffizi as one of the two essential museums in the city.

Immediately opposite the Bargello stands the **Badia Fiorentina**, an art-filled abbey church and the most important of several buildings in the area with strong associations with Florence's foremost poet, **Dante Alighieri** (see p.84). The changing face of the city itself, meanwhile, is chronicled in the charming and little-known **Museo di Firenze com'era**.

Exiled from the city, Dante described his fellow Florentines
as gente avara, invidiosa e superba – a "mean, envious and
proud people".

MUSEO NAZIONALE DEL BARGELLO

Map 2, G5. Via del Proconsolo 4. Tues–Sat 8.15am–1.50pm, plus
same hours second & fourth Sun and first, third & fifth Mon of the
month; €4.10.

In Renaissance Florence, **sculpture** assumed an importance
unmatched in any other part of Italy, perhaps because this
most public of arts was especially appropriate to a city with
such a highly developed sense of itself as a special and cohe-
sive community. On a less abstract level, Florence is surrounded by quarries, and the art of stonecutting had always
been nurtured here. Whatever the reason for this pre-
eminence, the sculpture collection of the **Museo Nazionale
del Bargello** from this period is the richest in Italy.

Sculpture apart, the museum also devotes a vast amount
of space to the **decorative arts**: superb carpets, enamels,
ivories, glassware, tapestries, silverware and other *objets d'art*.
Although they receive scant attention from the tour guides,
it would be as easy to spend as much time on the dozen or
more rooms filled with these treasures as the four rooms
devoted to sculpture.

The Bargello's home, the daunting Palazzo del Bargello,
was built in 1255 immediately after the overthrow of the
aristocratic regime. The first of the city's public palaces, it
soon became the seat of the *Podestà*, the city's chief magistrate, and the site of the main law court. Numerous male-
factors were tortured, tried, sentenced and executed here,
the elegant courtyard having been the site of the city's gal-
lows and block. The building acquired its present name

after 1574, when the Medici abolished the post of *Podestà*, the building becoming home to the chief of police – the *Bargello*. Torture and execution were banned in 1786, though the building remained a prison until 1859.

Ground floor

You've no time to catch your breath in the Bargello: the first room to the right of the ticket office is crammed with treasures, chief of which are the work of **Michelangelo**, in whose shadow every Florentine sculptor laboured from the sixteenth century onwards. The tipsy, soft-bellied figure of *Bacchus* (1496–97) was his first major sculpture, carved at the age of 22, a year or so before his great *Pietà* in Rome. Michelangelo's style later evolved into something less immediately striking, as is shown by the delicate *Tondo Pitti* of the *Madonna and Child* (1503–5). The square-jawed *Bust of Brutus* (1539–40) is the artist's sole work of this kind; a powerful portrait sketch in stone, it's a coded celebration of anti-Medicean republicanism, made soon after the murder of the nightmarish Duke Alessandro de' Medici (see p.336).

Works by Michelangelo's followers and contemporaries are ranged in the immediate vicinity; some of them would command prolonged attention in less exalted company. **Benvenuto Cellini**'s huge *Bust of Cosimo I* (1545–47), his first work in bronze, was a sort of technical trial for the casting of the *Perseus*, his most famous work. Alongside the two preparatory models for the *Perseus* in wax and bronze are displayed the original relief panel and four statuettes from the statue's pedestal; the reproductions that took their place in the Loggia della Signoria (see p.43) look rather better, seen from the intended distance.

Close by, **Giambologna**'s voluptuous *Florence Defeating Pisa* (1575) – a disingenuous pretext for a glamour display if ever there were one – takes up a lot of space, but is eclipsed by his best-known creation, the wonderful and much imitated *Mercury* (1564). Comic relief is provided by the reliably awful Bandinelli, whose coiffured *Adam and Eve* look like a grandee and his wife taking an *au naturel* stroll through their estate. Most persuasive, and considerably more erotic, is **Ammannati**'s winsome *Leda and the Swan* (1440–50), inspired by a painting of the subject by Michelangelo that was later destroyed.

Part two of the ground floor's collection lies across the Gothic **courtyard**, which is plastered with the coats of arms of the *Podestà*. Against the far wall stand six allegorical figures by Ammannati from the fountain of the Palazzo Pitti courtyard. The left of the two rooms across the yard features largely fourteenth-century works, notably pieces by Arnolfo di Cambio and Tino da Camaino. Temporary exhibitions are often held in the room to the right.

First floor

At the top of Giuliano da Sangallo's courtyard **staircase** (1502), the first-floor loggia has been turned into a menagerie for Giambologna's quaint bronze animals and birds, imported from the Medici villa at Castello, just outside Florence. The nearer doorway to the right opens into the tall, Gothic **Salone del Consiglio Generale**, the museum's second key room. Here again the number of masterpieces is breathtaking, though this time the presiding genius is **Donatello**, the fountainhead of Renaissance sculpture.

Vestiges of the sinuous Gothic manner are evident in the drapery of his marble *David* (1408), but there's nothing antiquated in the **St George** (1416), carved for the tabernacle of the armourers' guild at Orsanmichele and installed in a replica of its original niche at the far end of the room. If any one sculpture could be said to embody the shift of sensibility that occurred in quattrocento Florence, this is it – whereas Saint George had previously been little more than a symbol of valour, this alert, tensed figure represents not the act of heroism but the volition behind it. The slaying of the dragon is depicted in the small, badly eroded marble panel underneath, a piece as revolutionary as the figure of the saint, with its seamless interweaving of foreground and background.

Also here is the famous and sexually ambivalent bronze **David**, the first freestanding nude figure since Classical times (1430–40). A decade later the sculptor produced the strange prancing figure known as *Amor-Atys*, afterwards mistaken for a genuine statue from Classical antiquity. This was the highest compliment the artist could have wished for – as is attested by the story of Michelangelo's heaping soil over one of his first works, a sleeping cupid, in order to give it the appearance of an unearthed Classical piece. Donatello was just as comfortable with portraiture as with Christian or pagan imagery, as his breathtakingly vivid terracotta *Bust of Niccolò da Uzzano* demonstrates; it may be the earliest Renaissance portrait bust. When the occasion demanded, Donatello could produce a straightforwardly monumental piece like the nearby *Marzocco* (1418–20), Florence's heraldic lion.

In *The Stones of Florence*, Mary McCarthy memorably described Donatello's bronze David as "a transvestite's and fetishist's dream of alluring ambiguity".

Donatello's master, **Ghiberti**, is represented by his relief of *Abraham's Sacrifice*, his entry in the competition to design the Baptistery doors in 1401, easily missed on the right-hand wall; the treatment of the theme submitted by Brunelleschi, effectively the runner-up, is hung alongside. Set around the walls of the room, **Luca della Robbia**'s simple sweet-natured humanism is embodied in a sequence of glazed terracotta Madonnas.

The rest of this floor is occupied by a superb collection of European and Islamic applied art, with dazzling specimens of ivory-carving from Byzantium and medieval France – combs, boxes, chess pieces, and devotional panels featuring scores of figures crammed into a space the size of a paperback. Pay special attention to Room 9, the **Cappella di Santa Maria Maddalena**. The chapel's frescoes (1340), discovered in 1841 when the room was converted from a prison cell, were long attributed to Giotto – they're now thought to be by followers. The scenes from *Paradiso* on the altar (end) wall feature a portrait of Dante holding *The Divine Comedy* – he's the figure in maroon in the right-hand group, fifth from the left. The chapel's beautiful pulpit, lectern and stalls (1483–88) all came from San Miniato al Monte (see p.203), while the impressive altar triptych is a mid-fifteenth-century work by Giovanni di Francesco.

Second floor

Sculpture resumes upstairs, with a room of works from the della Robbia family, a prelude to the **Sala dei Bronzetti**, Italy's best assembly of small Renaissance bronzes. Giambologna's spiralling designs predominate, a testament to his popularity in late sixteenth-century Florence. His better-known pieces – such as the *Mercury*, which is also displayed on the ground floor – will be more familiar on a larger scale, but look out for the Hercules series (Ercole, in Italian) showing the hero variously wrestling and clubbing his opponents into submission. Despite the subject matter, Giambologna shows off a mannered, almost static poise that contrasts well with **Antonio del Pollaiuolo**'s earlier and much more violent *Ercole ed Antaeo* (c.1478), which stands on a pillar nearby. Like Leonardo, Pollaiuolo unravelled the complexities of human musculature by dissecting corpses.

Lastly, there's a room devoted mainly to **Renaissance portrait busts**, including Mino da Fiesole's busts of Giovanni de' Medici and Piero il Gottoso (the sons of Cosimo de' Medici). Antonio del Pollaiuolo's *Young Cavalier* is probably another thinly disguised Medici portrait, while the bust labelled *Ritratto d'Ignoto (Portrait of an Unknown Man)*, beside Verocchio's *Madonna Col Bambino*, may in fact depict the face of Macchiavelli. The weight of patronage also secured Benedetto da Maiano's powerful portrait of Florentine merchant Pietro Mellini (1474) in old age.

Also look out Francesco Laurana's *Battista Sforza*, an interesting comparison with the Piero della Francesca portrait in the Uffizi, and the *Woman Holding Flowers* by Verrocchio. The centre of the room is shared by Verrocchio's *David*, clearly influenced by the Donatello figure downstairs, and a wooden crucifix (c 1471) attributed to the same artist.

BADIA FIORENTINA

Map 2, G5. Via Dante Alighieri-Via del Proconsolo. Mon 3–6pm only; free.

Step outside the Bargello and directly opposite lies the **Badia Fiorentina**, approaching the end of many years of restoration. Visits are only allowed on Monday afternoons, but the church remains open for prayer at other times, following the monastic rules of the Fraternity of Jerusalem, whose church this is; the ten monks live ordinary lives in urban communities, but reserve time for prayer and silence.

The dark interior and fresco-covered cloister are well worth a few minutes. The Badia (Abbey) is also a place of reverence for admirers of Dante, for this was the parish church of **Beatrice Portinari**, for whom he conceived a lifelong love as he watched her at Mass here (see p.84). Furthermore, it was here that Boccaccio delivered his celebrated lectures on Dante's theological epic.

Founded in 978 by Willa, widow of the Margrave of Tuscany, in honour of her husband, the Badia was one of the focal buildings in medieval Florence: the city's sick were treated in a hospital founded here in 1031, while the main bell marked the divisions of the working day. The hospital also owed much to Willa's son, Ugo, who further endowed his mother's foundation after a vision of the hellish torments which awaited him by "reason of his worldly life, unless he should repent".

The 1280s saw the church overhauled along Cistercian Gothic lines, probably under the direction of Arnolfo di Cambio, architect of the Duomo and Palazzo Vecchio. Only a few years later, in 1307, part of the new structure was demolished as punishment to the resident monks for refusal to pay a tax. Later Baroque additions smothered much of the old church in 1627, though the narrow **campanile** – Romanesque at its base, Gothic towards its apex – escaped unharmed. Completed between 1310 and 1330, its hexagonal outline remains a prominent feature of the Florentine skyline.

Works of special note are highlighted in green in the text.

The interior

The church's interior highlight, on the left as you enter, is Filippino Lippi's superb **Apparition of the Virgin to St Bernard**, painted in 1485 for the Benedictine monastery at Campora and commissioned by Piero del Pugliese: Lippi has included a portrait of the donor at the bottom of the painting, which is still gloriously enclosed by its original

BADIA FIORENTINA

frame. The work was brought here for safekeeping in 1529 as the threat of a siege of the city grew. Bernard is shown in the act of writing a homily aimed at those caught between the "rocks" of tribulation and the "chains" of sin. This is an allusion to the active and contemplative life, and to the latter in particular, hence the presence of the four monks – exemplars of the contemplative life – shown in the background to the right.

Close by is the church's second highlight, a **tomb monument** to Ugo, sculpted by Mino da Fiesole between 1469 and 1481. Mino was also responsible for the nearby **tomb of Bernardo Giugni** and an altar frontal of the **Madonna and Child with SS Leonard and Lawrence**. Giugni was a lawyer and diplomat, hence the figures of Justice and Faith accompanying his effigy.

A staircase leads from the choir – take the door immediately right of the high altar – to the upper storey of the **Chiostro degli Aranci**, or Cloister of the Oranges (from the fruit trees that used to be grown here). Two of its flanks are graced with an anonymous but highly distinctive fresco cycle (1436–39) on the life of St Benedict. A later panel – showing the saint throwing himself into bushes to resist temptation – is by the young Bronzino (1526–28). The cloister itself (1432–38) is the work of Bernardo Rossellino, one of the leading lights of early Renaissance architecture.

THE DANTE TRAIL

After visiting the Badia Fiorentina, dedicated literary pilgrims might want to explore the small knot of buildings with Dantesque associations – some of them admittedly spurious – that cluster together in the grid of minor streets between Piazza del Duomo and Piazza della Signoria. Start your peregrinations at the Baptistery (see p.25), Dante's "bel San Giovanni", and one of only three Florentine churches mentioned by the poet. Nearby, south of the Duomo, search out the so-called **Sasso di Dante** (Dante's Stone), set between Via dello Studio and Via del Proconsolo. Dante is supposed to have sat here and watched the construction of the cathedral. Walk down Via dello Studio, and at its junction with Via del Corso lies the **Palazzo Salviati** (**Map 2, F3**), site of Beatrice's former home. The courtyard still contains the so-called Nicchia di Dante (Dante's Niche), from which the young Dante is said to have watched his *inamorata*.

Casa di Dante

Map 2, F4. Via Santa Margherita 1. Mon & Wed–Sat: summer 10am–6pm, winter 10am–4pm; Sun 10am–2pm; €2.60.

Cross Via del Corso from the Palazzo Salviati, head down Via Santa Margherita and you come to a small piazza fronting the somewhat fraudulent **Casa di Dante**. Marketed as Dante's house, the present building is actually a medieval pastiche dating from 1910. The modest museum upstairs is a homage to the poet rather than a shrine: it contains nothing directly related to his life, and in all likelihood Dante was born not on the house's site but somewhere in the street that bears his name. Numerous editions of the *Divina Commedia* are on show – including a poster printed with the whole text in minuscule type – along with copies of Botticelli's illustrations to the poem.

Churches

As contentious as the Casa di Dante's claims is the story that Dante married Gemma Donati in **Santa Margherita de' Cerchi** (**Map 2, F4**; Mon–Thurs & Sat 10am–noon &

THE DANTE TRAIL

DANTE

Dante signed himself "Dante Alighieri, a Florentine by birth but not by character", a bitter allusion to the city he served as a politician but which later cast him into exile and was to inspire some of the most vitriolic passages in his great epic poem, *La Divina Commedia* (The Divine Comedy).

The poet was born in 1265, into a minor and impoverished noble family. He was educated at Bologna and later at Padua, where he studied philosophy and astronomy. The defining moment in his life came in 1274 when he met the 8-year-old **Beatrice Portinari**, a young girl whom Boccaccio described as possessed of "habits and language more serious and modest than her age warranted". Her features were "so delicate and so beautifully formed," he went on, "and full, besides mere beauty, of so much candid loveliness that many thought her almost an angel."

Dante – just 9 at the time of the meeting – later described his own feeling following the encounter: "Love ruled my soul," he wrote, "and began to hold such sway over me… that it was necessary for me to do completely all his pleasure. He commanded me often that I should endeavour to see this so youthful angel, and I saw in her such noble and praiseworthy deportment that truly of her might be said these words of the poet Homer – *She appeared to be born not of mortal man but of God.*"

Unhappily, Beatrice's family had decided their daughter was to marry someone else – Simone de' Bardi – the ceremony

3–5pm, Fri 10am–noon), the ancient little church up the street from the Casa di Dante on the right. Documented as early as 1032, the building does, however, contain several tombs belonging to the Portinari, Beatrice's family name; the porch also features the Donati family crest, as this was also their local parish church. These are probably the limits

taking place when she was 17. Seven years later she was dead. Dante, for his part, had been promised – aged 12 – to Gemma Donati. The wedding took place in 1295, when the poet was 30.

Romantic hopes dashed, Dante settled down to a military and political career. In 1289 he fought for Florence against Arezzo and helped in a campaign against Pisa. Later he joined the Apothecaries' Guild, serving on a variety of minor civic committees. In 1300 he was dispatched to San Gimignano, where he was entrusted with the job of coaxing the town into an alliance against Pope Boniface VIII, who had designs on Tuscany. In June of the same year he sought to settle the widening breach between the Black (anti-imperial) and White (more conciliatory) factions of Florence's ruling Guelph party.

The dispute had its roots in money: the Whites contained leading bankers to the imperial powers (the Cerchi, Mozzi, Davanzati and Frescobaldi), while the Blacks counted the Pazzi, Bardi and Donati amongst their number, all prominent papal bankers. Boniface, not surprisingly, sided with the Blacks, who eventually emerged triumphant.

Dante's White sympathies sealed his fate. In 1302, following trumped-up charges of corruption, he was sentenced with other Whites to two years' exile. While many of the deportees subsequently returned, Dante rejected his city of "self-made men and fast-got gain". He wandered instead between Forlì, Verona, Padua, Luni and Venice, writing much of *The Divine Comedy* as he went, finally settling in Ravenna, where he died in 1321.

of the Dantesque associations, though the church is worth a look anyway, chiefly for a nice altarpiece of the *Madonna and Four Saints* by Neri di Bicci.

Over Via Dante Alighieri from the poet's house, on Piazza San Martino, lies the tiny **San Martino del Vescovo** (**Map 2, F4**; Mon–Sat 10am–noon & 3–5pm),

DANTE

●

built on the site of a small oratory founded in 986 that served as the Alighieri's parish church. Rebuilt in 1479, it later became the headquarters of a charitable body, the Compagnia di Buonomini, who commissioned the church's ten celebrated lunette frescoes showing various altruistic acts and scenes from the life of St Martin. Painted by the workshop of Ghirlandaio, the pictures present as absorbing a record of daily life in Renaissance Florence as the artist's better-known works in Santa Maria Novella (see p.153). The chapel also contains a couple of fine Madonnas, one Byzantine, the other probably by Niccolò Soggia, a pupil of Perugino.

MUSEO DI FIRENZE COM'ERA

Map 3, I7. Via dell'Oriuolo 24. Mon–Thurs, Sat & Sun 9am–1.30pm; L5000/€2.58.

The top of Via del Proconsolo, just a few yards from the Museo dell'Opera del Duomo, forms a major junction with Via dell'Oriuolo, home to the **Museo di Firenze com'era**. This so-called "Museum of Florence as it used to be" is one of Florence's unsung little museums, but none the worse for that: both its contents and setting – in a pleasant garden-fronted palazzo – are delightful.

The city's story begins in the new room on the left, a rather dry collection of models, plans and photographs of the mammoth excavation of the Piazza della Signoria that took place in the 1980s. As one would expect, a number of discoveries were made, but for want of any better ideas the piazza was simply paved over once the dig was complete. A large, somewhat speculative model of the **Roman city** stands at the far end of the room, with coloured sections showing the buildings whose locations the archeologists are sure of.

The long, vaulted main gallery stands on the other side of the entrance corridor. Maps, prints, photos and topographical paintings chart the growth of Florence from the fifteenth century to the present, and while none of the exhibits are masterpieces, most of them are at least informative. Perhaps the most impressive item comes right at the start: a meticulous 1887 reproduction of a colossal 1470 aerial view of Florence called the *Pianta della Catena* (Chain Map), the original of which is in Berlin.

Almost as appealing are the twelve lunette pictures (1555) of the **Medici villas**, reproductions of which you'll see on postcards and posters across the city. They're the work of Flemish painter Justus Utens and were painted for the Medici's Villa dell'Artimino. A poignant wooden model portrays the labyrinthine jumble of the **Mercato Vecchio**, the city's ancient heart, which was demolished to make space for the Piazza della Repubblica at the end of the nineteenth century. Justification for the clearance was given as the need to control outbreaks of cholera, not to mention crime and prostitution, but it had as much to do with the resurgent middle-class pride that followed Florence's role as transitional capital of Italy (1865–71). Elsewhere, a graphic picture portrays Savonarola's execution (see p.132), and eighteenth-century Florence is celebrated in the elegiac engravings of Giuseppe Zocchi.

MUSEO DI FIRENZE COM'ERA

Santa Croce

The grand, fresco-filled Franciscan church of **Santa Croce** is one of the most compelling in Florence, and forms the centrepiece of a fascinating area with a lively, raffish charm of its own. Prior to the 1966 flood, this was one of Florence's more densely populated districts. When the Arno burst its banks, this low-lying quarter, packed with tenements and small workshops, was virtually wrecked, and many of its residents moved out permanently in the following years.

These days the district is enjoying a renaissance. The more traditional shops, bars and restaurants that survived the flood have been joined by a growing number of new – and for the most part – extremely good bars and *osterie*. This makes it one of the city's more appealing areas to explore – the **Sant'Ambrogio** market district in particular is worth an hour so.

Next door to the church is the gate to the small **Museo dell'Opera di Santa Croce**, with Brunelleschi's serene **Cappella dei Pazzi**, one of Florence's architectural masterpieces, standing in the cloister garden within. A little to the south is the **Museo Horne**, a modest but pleasing museum devoted to the art treasures of a nineteenth-century private collector. A little to the north is a much smarter but in many ways less satisfying museum dedicated to Michelangelo, the **Casa Buonarroti**.

No trip to the Santa Croce district is complete without a visit to Vivoli, regarded by many as purveyors of Tuscany's best ice cream (see p.240).

PIAZZA SANTA CROCE

Map 4, J3.

Piazza Santa Croce, the area fronting the church of Santa Croce, is one of Florence's larger squares, and traditionally one of the city's main arenas for ceremonials and festivities. Thus when Lorenzo the Magnificent was married to the Roman heiress Clarice Orsini, the event was celebrated on this square, with a tournament that was more a fashion event than a contest of skill – Lorenzo's knightly outfit, for instance, was adorned with pearls, diamonds and rubies. It's still used as the pitch for the *Gioco di Calcio Storico*, a football tournament between the city's four *quartieri*; the game, held three times in St John's week (the last week of June), is characterized by incomprehensible rules and a level of violence which the sixteenth-century costumes do little to inhibit.

While in the piazza it's worth studying Santa Croce's **facade**, a neo-Gothic sham which dates from as recently as 1863. The church had languished for centuries without a suitable frontage, a situation remedied when someone claimed to have discovered long-lost plans for the "original" facade. In truth the scheme was no more than a giant-sized pastiche of Orcagna's tabernacle in Orsanmichele (see p.168); construction of the new structure, oddly enough, was paid for by an Englishman, Sir Francis Sloane.

THE CHURCH OF SANTA CROCE

Map 4, J3. Piazza Santa Croce. Mon–Sat: Easter–Oct 8am–5.45pm,
Nov–Easter 9.30am–12.30pm & 3–5.45pm; Sun 3–5.45pm.

Santa Croce has long acted as the city's pantheon: the
walls and nave floor are lined with the **tombs** of over 270

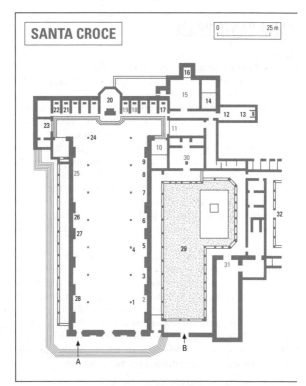

illustrious Florentines, including grandees such as Michelangelo, Galileo, Machiavelli and Dante – though the last is actually buried in Ravenna, where he died in exile. Evidence of the church's grand status can be seen in the extraordinary **fresco cycles** lavished on the chapels over the years, particularly during the fourteenth century, when

1 Madonna del Latte (1478), Antonio Rossellino
2 Tomb of Michelangelo (1570), Giorgio Vasari
3 Cenotaph to Dante (1829), Stefano Ricci
4 Pulpit (1472–6), Benedetto da Maiano
5 Monument to Vittorio Alfieri (1810), Antonio Canova
6 Tomb of Niccolò Machiavelli (1787), Innocenzo Spinazzi
7 Annunciation (1435), Donatello
8 Tomb of Leonardo Bruni (1446–7), Bernardo Rossellino
9 Tomb of Giacchino Rossini (1900), Giuseppe Cassioli
10 Cappella Castellani: frescoes (1385), Agnolo Gaddi
11 Cappella Baroncelli: frescoes (1332–8), Taddeo Gaddi
12 Cappella Medici (1434), designed by Michelozzo
13 Madonna and Child altarpiece (1480), Andrea della Robbia
14 Church shop and leather workshop
15 Sacristy
16 Cappella Rinuccini: frescoes (1365), Giovanni da Milano
17 Cappella Velluti: altarpiece, Giovanni di Biondo
18 Cappella Peruzzi: Life of St John and St John the Baptist (1326–30), Giotto
19 Cappella Bardi: Life of St Francis (1315–20), Giotto
20 Chancel: Frescoes and stained glass (1380), Agnolo Gaddi
21 Cappella Pulci-Beradi: Martyrdom of SS Lorenzo and Stefano (1330) frescoes, Bernardo Daddi
22 Cappella Bardi di Vernio: Scenes from the Life of San Silvestro (1340) frescoes, Maso di Banco
23 Cappella Bardi: wooden crucifix (1412), Donatello
24 Monument to Leon Battista Alberti (d. 1472), Lorenzo Bartolini (early nineteenth-century)
25 Tomb of Carlo Marsuppini (1453), Desiderio da Settignano
26 Pietà (1560), Agnolo Bronzino
27 Tomb of Lorenzo Ghiberti and his son Vittorio (pavement slab)
28 Tomb of Galileo (1737), Giulio Foggini
29 First Cloister
30 Cappella dei Pazzi
31 Refectory and museum
32 Second Cloister
A Entrance to Santa Croce
B Entrance to Museo dell'Opera di Santa Croce

●

artists of the stature of Giotto and the Gaddi family worked here. (You'll need a pocketful of L200 coins – or the euro equivalent – and the patience of a saint to study the frescoes properly, however, as the lights are on a hasty timer.) Over and above the works of art, the graceful Gothic structure itself is a delight: broader and less soaring than the slender cathedrals of northern Europe, but no less beautiful for that.

Santa Croce is the Franciscans' principal church in Florence – a rival to the Dominicans' Santa Maria Novella – and is said to have been founded by St Francis himself. In truth it was probably begun seventy or so years after Francis's death, in 1294, possibly by the architect of the Duomo, **Arnolfo di Cambio**. It replaced a smaller church on the site, a building that had become too small for the vast congregations gathering to hear the Franciscans' homilies on poverty, chastity and obedience in what was then one of the city's poorest areas.

Francis – who never became a priest – had intended his monks to live as itinerants, begging for alms when necessary, and preaching without the use of churches, never mind churches the size of Santa Croce. After his death, this radical stance was quickly abandoned by many of his followers, with the backing of a papacy anxious to institutionalize a potentially dangerous mass movement. Ironically, it was the city's richest families who funded the construction of the church, to atone for the sin of usury on which their fortunes were based. Several of the lavish and beautifully decorated chapels – the Bardi, Peruzzi, Baroncelli and so on – are named after their sponsors.

The interior

Stepping into Santa Croce's vast and lovely **interior** is a far more satisfying experience than crossing the threshold of the Duomo or Santa Maria Novella. The view down the airy naves would once have been interrupted by a large partition, built to separate the area set aside for the monks from that reserved for the congregation (a similar partition existed at Santa Maria Novella). Both the partition and choir were torn down in 1566 on the orders of Cosimo I, acting on Counter-Reformation dictates which proscribed such arrangements. Unfortunately the changes gave Vasari a chance to meddle, opening up the side altars and damaging frescoes by Orcagna, tantalizing traces of which still adorn parts of the walls.

Many an historic event has been acted out in this great interior. It was here that the full sessions of the **Council of Florence** took place in 1439, in an attempt to reconcile the differences between the Roman and Eastern churches. Attended by the pope, the Byzantine emperor and the Patriarch of Constantinople, the council arrived at a compromise that lasted only until the Byzantine delegation returned home. Its more enduring effect was that it brought scores of Classical scholars to the city, some of whom stayed on to give an important impetus to the Florentine Renaissance.

Works of special note are highlighted in green in the text and on the plan on pp.90–91.

The south aisle

Hurry towards the high altar and the Giotto-painted chapels to its right if all you want to see are the church's most famous works of art. Otherwise, take a more measured walk down the right-hand, or **south aisle**, where almost every object is of funerary, historic or artistic interest. Against the first pillar is the tomb of Francesco Nori, one of the victims of the Pazzi Conspiracy (see p.28), surmounted by Antonio Rossellino's lovely relief of the

Madonna del Latte (1). Nearby is Vasari's tomb of Michelangelo (2), whose body was brought back from Rome to Florence in July 1574, ten years after his death and 34 years after he left the city for good.

Michelangelo's tomb is said to have been positioned close to the church's entrance at his own request, so that when the graves fly open on the Day of Judgement, the first thing to catch his eye will be Brunelleschi's cathedral dome.

The Neoclassical **cenotaph to Dante (3)** is a monument rather than a tomb, as the exiled poet is buried in Ravenna, where he died in 1321 (see p.84). Three centuries before the poet finally received this bland nineteenth-century tribute, Michelangelo had offered to carve the poet's tomb – a tantalizing thought. Against the third pillar there's a marvellous **pulpit (4)** by Benedetto da Maiano, adorned with niche statuettes of the virtues and scenes from the life of St Francis.

Canova's **monument to Alfieri (5)** commemorates an eighteenth-century Italian poet and dramatist as famous for his amatory liaisons as his literary endeavours. The tomb was paid for by his mistress, the so-called Countess of Albany, erstwhile wife of Charles Edward Stuart – Bonnie Prince Charlie. Albany herself modelled for the tomb's main figure, an allegory of Italy bereaved by Alfieri's death. The nearby **tomb of Machiavelli (6)**, carved 260 years after his death, is unexceptional save for its famous inscription – *Tanto nomini nullum par elogium* – "No praise can be high enough for so great a name." The side door at the end of the aisle is flanked by Donatello's gilded stone relief of the Annunciation (7).

Nearby is Bernardo Rossellino's much-imitated **tomb of Leonardo Bruni (8)**, chancellor of the Republic, humanist scholar and author of the first history of the city – his effigy is holding a copy. Bruni, who died in 1444, was the first man of any great eminence to be buried in the church, his presence surprising given his predominantly humanist rather than Christian beliefs. The tomb, one of the most influential of the Renaissance, makes the point: for the first time the human figure dominates, with the Madonna and Child banished to a peripheral position high in the lunette. The inscription, penned by Carlo Marsuppini, his successor as chancellor, reads: "After Leonardo departed life, history is in mourning and eloquence is dumb..." Marsuppini himself is buried in the opposite aisle (see p.98).

The apse and sacristy

The chapels in the **apse** and the east end of Santa Croce are a compendium of Florentine fourteenth-century painting, showing the art of Giotto and some of his most accomplished contemporaries and followers at its most eloquent.

First up is the **Cappella Castellani (10)**, strikingly, if patchily, covered in frescoes by Agnolo Gaddi and his pupils. To the right are depicted the stories of St John the Baptist and St Nicholas of Bari: the latter, the patron saint of children – he's the "St Nicholas" of Santa Claus fame – is shown saving three girls from prostitution and reviving three murdered boys. The left wall features episodes from the lives of St John and St Antony Abbot – the latter gave away his wealth, making him a favourite of the poverty-inspired Franciscans. Also note the chapel's fine tabernacle, the work of Mino da Fiesole, and its funerary monuments, including that of the Countess of Albany (see opposite).

The adjoining **Cappella Baroncelli (11)** was decorated by Agnolo's father, Taddeo, a long-time assistant to Giotto. Taddeo's cycle, largely devoted to the life of the Virgin, features one of the first night scenes in Western painting, *The Annunciation to the Shepherds*. The main altar painting, the *Coronation of the Virgin*, may also be by Taddeo, though an increasing number of critics now attribute it to his master, Giotto.

The corridor to the right ends at the **Cappella Medici (12)**, usually open only for those taking Mass. It's notable for the large terracotta altarpiece by Andrea della Robbia and a nineteenth-century forged Donatello; the chapel, like the corridor, was designed by Michelozzo, the Medici's pet architect. Finely carved wooden doors lead off the corridor into the beautifully panelled **Sacristy (15)**, where the highlight is a marvellous *Crucifixion* by Taddeo on the left. The tiny **Cappella Rinuccini (16)**, separated from the sacristy by a grille, is impressively covered with frescoes on the life of the Virgin (on the left) and St Mary Magdalene (on the right): the Lombard artist responsible, Giovanni da Milano, was one of Giotto's most accomplished followers.

Giotto's frescoes and the chancel

Both the **Cappella Peruzzi (18)** and the **Cappella Bardi (19)** – the two chapels on the right of the chancel – are entirely covered with frescoes by Giotto, with some assistance in the latter. Their deterioration was partly caused by Giotto's having painted some of the pictures onto dry plaster, rather than the wet plaster employed in true fresco technique, but the vandalism of later generations was far more destructive. In the eighteenth century they were covered in whitewash, then they were heavily retouched in the nineteenth; restoration in the 1950s returned them to as close to their original state as was possible.

Scenes from the lives of St John the Evangelist and St John the Baptist cover the Peruzzi chapel, while a better-preserved cycle of the life of St Francis fills the Bardi. Despite the areas of paint destroyed when a tomb was attached to the wall, the *Funeral of St Francis* is still a composition of extraordinary impact, the grief-stricken mourners suggesting an affinity with the lamentation over the body of Christ – one of them even touches the wound in Francis's side, echoing the gesture of Doubting Thomas. The *Ordeal by Fire*, showing Francis about to demonstrate his faith to the sultan by walking through fire, shows Giotto's mastery of understated drama, with the sultan's entourage skulking off to the left in anticipation of the monk's triumph. On the wall above the chapel's entrance arch is the most powerful scene of all, *St Francis Receiving the Stigmata*, in which the power of Christ's apparition seems to force the chosen one to his knees.

Agnolo Gaddi was responsible for the design of the **stained glass** in the lancet windows round the high altar, and for all the chancel **frescoes (20)**, which depict the legend of the True Cross – a complicated tale tracing the wood of the Cross from its origins as the Tree of Paradise. The vast polyptych on the high altar is a composite of panels by several artists.

The **Cappella Bardi di Vernio (22)** was painted by Maso di Banco, perhaps the most inventive of Giotto's followers. Tradition dictated that the frescoes – *Scenes from the Life of San Silvestro* – portray the saint baptizing Emperor Constantine, notwithstanding the fact that Sylvester died some time before the emperor's actual baptism. The second **Cappella Bardi (23)** houses a wooden crucifix by Donatello, supposedly criticized by Brunelleschi as resembling a "peasant on the Cross". According to Vasari, Brunelleschi went off and created his own crucifix for Santa Maria Novella to show Donatello how it should be done (see p.155).

The north aisle

As you walk back towards the church entrance along the north aisle, the first pillar features a nineteenth-century **monument to Leon Battista Alberti (24)**, a Renaissance architect and artistic theorist whose writings did much to influence Rossellino in his carving of the Bruni tomb across the nave. The Bruni tomb in turn influenced the outstanding **tomb of Carlo Marsuppini (25)** by Desiderio da Settignano. Marsuppini's lack of Christian qualifications for so prominent a church burial, however, is even more striking than Bruni's – he's said to have died without taking confession or communion. The tomb inscription opens with the words: "Stay and see the marbles which enshrine a great sage, one for whose mind there was not world enough…"

A **Pietà (26)** by the young Bronzino, a future Mannerist star, briefly disturbs the parade of tombs which follows. A surprisingly modest pavement slab marks the **tomb of Lorenzo Ghiberti (27)** – the artist responsible for the Baptistery's marvellous doors – and his son Vittorio. The **tomb of Galileo (28)** is more ostentatious, though it was some ninety years after his death in 1642 that the "heretic" scientist was deemed worthy of a Christian burial in Florence's Pantheon.

Cappella dei Pazzi

Daily except Wed: March–Oct 10am–7pm; Nov–Feb 10am–6pm; L8000/€4.13.

A door to the right of the main facade of Santa Croce leads through into the church's first cloister (29), at the far end of which is Brunelleschi's famous **Cappella dei Pazzi (30)**. It typifies the learned, harmonious spirit of early Renaissance architecture. Begun in 1429 as a chapter-house for Santa Croce, it was commissioned by Andrea de' Pazzi, a member of a banking dynasty that played a prominent role in the Pazzi Conspiracy (see p.28). Its exterior remained unfinished at the time of the plot, however, and it seems none of the family was ever buried here.

Brunelleschi worked on the chapel between 1442 and his

death in 1446, though financing problems meant work was only completed in the 1470s. Although a trifle austere to modern eyes, the building is geometrically perfect without seeming pedantic, and is exemplary in the way its decorative detail harmonizes with the design. The polychrome lining of the portico's shallow cupola is by Luca della Robbia, as is the garland of fruit which surrounds the Pazzi family crest. The frieze of angels' heads is by Desiderio da Settignano, though Luca was responsible for the tondo of *St Andrew* (1461) over the door. The portico itself may be the work of Giuliano da Maiano, while the majestic wooden doors (1472) are the product of a collaboration between the brothers Maiano, Giuliano and Benedetto.

In the **interior**, Luca also produced the twelve blue and white tondi of the *Apostles*. The four vividly coloured tondi of the *Evangelists* in the upper roundels were produced in the della Robbia workshop, possibly to designs by Donatello and Brunelleschi.

Museo dell'Opera di Santa Croce

Same hours and ticket as Capella dei Pazzi.

The **Museo dell'Opera di Santa Croce** (31), which flanks the main cloister on the right, houses a miscellany of works of art, the best of which are gathered in the Refettorio (refectory). Foremost of these is Cimabue's famous *Crucifixion*, very badly damaged in 1966 and now the emblem of the havoc caused by the flood. Other highlights include a detached fresco of the *Last Supper* (1333), considered the finest work by Taddeo Gaddi (end wall), and the earliest surviving example of the many Last Suppers (*Cenacoli*) dotted around the city. This theme was of obvious relevance given its position, which – as here – was invariably the refectory where monks gathered to eat. Equally compelling is Donatello's enormous gilded *St Louis*

FLORENCE'S FLOODS

Florence's infamous **1966 flood** had plenty of precedents. Early chroniclers traced the city's foundation to Noah, great areas of the city were destroyed by a flood in 1178, and in 1269 the Carraia and Trìnita bridges were carried away on a torrent so heavy that "a great part of the city of Florence became a lake". In 1333 another huge flood was preceded by a four-day storm so violent that all the city's bells were tolled to drive away the evil spirits and, as the chronicler Giovanni Villani recorded, "in the houses they beat kettles and brass basins, raising loud cries to God of 'misericordia, misericordia' (have mercy on us)."

In 1557 Cosimo I instituted an urban beautification scheme after a deluge left the city under six metres of muddy water. On that occasion the Trìnita bridge was hit so suddenly that everyone on it was drowned, all except for two children who were left stranded on a pillar in midstream – they were fed for two days by means of a rope slung over from the Palazzo Strozzi. And in 1884, Trollope wrote with apparent glee of a flood which produced a "truly terrible and magnificent sight, " the river "one turbid, yellow mass... bringing down with it fragments of timber and carcasses of animals". No wonder Dante described the Arno as *la maladetta e sventurata fossa* – a cursed and luckless ditch.

Rarely was the river as fickle as in 1966. By November 4 of that year – doomsday – it had been raining almost continuously for forty days. Nearly half a metre of rain had fallen in the preceding two days. When the water pressure in an upstream reservoir threatened to break the dam, it was decided to open the sluices. The only people to be warned were the jewellers of the Ponte Vecchio, whose private nightwatchman phoned them in the small hours of the morning with news that the bridge was starting to shake. Police watching the shopkeepers clearing their displays were asked why they weren't spreading the alarm. Their reply – "We have received no orders."

When the banks of the **Arno** finally broke, a flash flood unleashed some 500,000 tonnes of water and mud on the streets, moving with such speed that early-rising commuters were drowned in the underpass of Santa Maria Novella train station. In all, 35 Florentines were killed and hundreds made homeless. Women and children were winched from rooftops – most men had to take their chances until the water subsided. Over 15,000 cars were wrecked. Electricity and water were off for days, plunging the city into nighttime darkness. Bread and milk had to be distributed from the Palazzo Vecchio.

Thousands of works of art were damaged, many ruined by heating oil, just delivered for the winter, that flushed out of basements. Slurry lapped around the Uffizi's cellars, crammed with 8000 stored paintings, while five of Ghiberti's panels from the Baptistery doors were torn off and found two kilometres away. Over a million volumes in the Biblioteca Nazionale were damaged beyond repair.

Within hours an impromptu army of **rescue workers** – many of them students – had been formed to haul pictures out of slime-filled churches and gather fragments of paint in plastic bags. Donations came in from all over the world, but the task was so immense that the restoration of many pieces is still unaccomplished. In total around two-thirds of the 3000 paintings damaged in the flood are now on view again, and two massive laboratories – one for paintings and one for stonework – are operating full-time in Florence, developing restoration techniques that are taken up by galleries all over the world.

FLORENCE'S FLOODS

of Toulouse (1424), made for Orsanmichele. Other fine works saved from Vasari's meddling in the main church include six fresco fragments by Orcagna (on the side walls) and Domenico Veneziano's *SS John and Francis*.

A series of rooms sparsely filled with various damaged fragments leads through towards a spacious **inner cloister (32)**, another late project by Brunelleschi. Completed in 1453, after the architect's death, it is the most peaceful spot in the centre of Florence, an atmosphere achieved by the slow rhythm of the narrow, widely spaced columns.

CASA BUONARROTI

Map 4, J2. Via Ghibellina 70. Daily except Tues 9.30am–1.30pm; L12,000/€6.20.

The **Casa Buonarroti** sounds enticing, but the name is misleading. Michelangelo Buonarroti certainly owned three houses here in 1508, and probably lived on the site intermittently between 1516 and 1525. Thereafter the properties' associations with the sculptor become increasingly tenuous. On Michelangelo's death, for example, they passed to his nephew, Leonardo, whose son converted them into a single palazzo, leaving little trace of the earlier houses (though he built a gallery dedicated to his great-uncle). Michelangelo's last descendant, Cosimo, left the building to the city on his death in 1858.

Today the house contains a smart but low-key museum. Many of the rooms are pleasing enough, all nicely decorated in period style and adorned with beautiful furniture, *objets d'art*, frescoed ceilings and the like. But among the jumble of works collected here, only a handful are by Michelangelo – most were created simply in homage to the great man.

Etruscan and Roman fragments have been wrested back from the Archeological Museum to languish on the ground floor once more, but the two main treasures are to be found in the room on the left at the top of the stairs. The **Madonna della Scala** (c. 1490–92) is Michelangelo's earliest known work, a delicate shallow relief carved when he was no older than 16. The similarly unfinished **Battle of the Centaurs** was carved shortly afterwards, when the boy was living in the Medici household. In the adjacent room you'll find the artist's wooden model (1517) for the facade of San Lorenzo. Close by is the largest of all the sculptural models on display, the torso of a **River God** (1524), a work in wood and wax probably intended for the Medici chapel in San Lorenzo. Other rooms contain small and fragmentary pieces, possibly by the master, possibly copies of works by him.

SANT'AMBROGIO

Sant'Ambrogio is a busy residential area with a big, bustling food market and a plethora of new bars, clubs and restaurants. During the day, it's an agreeable place to potter around and visit the market before pausing for refreshment at the *Caffé Cibreo*, one of the city's most beautiful bars (see p.243). At night, make a booking for the *Cibreo* restaurant, or the *Pizzaiuolo* opposite (see p.234 and p.239). Alternatively, duck into some of the happening bars in the streets nearby – the best evening option is *Rex* (see p.256).

Two of Florence's markets lie close by. To the north, the Piazza dei Ciompi is the venue for the flea market, or **Mercato delle Pulci** (**Map 3, K8**; Mon–Sat 8am–1pm & 3.30–7pm, plus last Sun of month 9am–7pm). Much of the junk maintains the city's reputation for inflated prices, though you can find a few interesting items at modest cost – old postcards, posters and so on. The market explodes in size on the last Sunday of every month. Vasari's **Loggia del Pesce** (1567) gives the square a touch of style; built for the fishmongers of the Mercato Vecchio in what is now Piazza della Repubblica, it was dismantled when that square was laid out and rebuilt here in 1951.

A short distance to the east, out of the orbit of ninety percent of tourists, is the **Mercato di Sant'Ambrogio**, (**Map 3, L2**; Mon–Sat 7am–2pm), a smaller, tattier and even more enjoyable version of the San Lorenzo food hall. The *tavola calda* (snacks and meals stall) here is one of Florence's lunchtime bargains, and – as at San Lorenzo – the stalls bring their prices down in the last hour of trading. An alternative is to stop at one of the barrows serving **lampredotto**, the deeply traditional speciality of hot tripe, usually served in a bun with a spicy sauce and a small cup of wine. The vendor can tell you that *lampredotto* is in fact made from two particular cuts of tripe – *la gala*, famed for its delicate, pink-crested ridges and exquisite taste, and the fattier, heavier *spannocchia* – but it's probably best not to enquire closely, if at all. The taste is indeed unparalleled, but the slippery texture certainly isn't for all stomachs.

Nearby **Sant'Ambrogio** (**Map 3, L8**) is one of Florence's older churches, having been documented in 988, though rebuilding over the centuries means that it is now somewhat bland in appearance. Painting-wise it's worth a visit for *The Madonna Enthroned with SS John the Baptist and Bartholomew* (second altar on the right), attributed to Orcagna (or the school of Orcagna), and for the recently restored triptych at the end of the wall (chapel right of the main altar) attributed to Lorenzo di Bicci or Bicci di Lorenzo.

More compelling than either painting, though, is the **Cappella del Miracolo**, the chapel to the left of the high altar, and its **tabernacle** (1481–83) by Mino da Fiesole, an accomplished sculptor whose name crops up time and again across Tuscany. This was one of Mino's last works – he died in 1484 – making it fitting that he should be buried close to

SANT'AMBROGIO

the work, his tomb marked by a pavement slab at the chapel entrance. Another artist, the multi-talented Verrocchio (d. 1488) – a painter, teacher and sculptor – is buried in the fourth chapel.

The narrative **fresco** (1486) alongside Mino's tabernacle alludes to the miracle which gave the Cappella del Miracolo its name. The work of Cosimo Rosselli, best known for his frescoes in Santissima Annunziata (see p.144), it describes the finding and display of a chalice full of blood in 1230. The Florentines believed the chalice saved them from, among other things, the effects of a virulent plague outbreak of 1340. The painting is full of portraits of Rosselli's contemporaries, making it another of Florence's vivid pieces of Renaissance social reportage: Rosselli himself is the figure in the black beret at the extreme left of the picture.

MUSEO HORNE

Map 4, I4. Via dei Benci 6. Daily except Sun 9am–1pm; L10,000/€5.16.

On the south side of Santa Croce, down by the river, stands one of Florence's more recondite museums, the **Museo della Fondazione Horne**. Its collection was left to the state by the English art historian Herbert Percy Horne (1864–1916), instrumental in his day in rescuing Botticelli from neglect with a pioneering biography. The half-a-dozen or so rooms of paintings, sculptures, pottery, furniture and other domestic objects contain no real masterpieces, but are diverting enough if you've already done the major collections. With winning eccentricity, the exhibits are labelled with numbers only and you have to carry round a key in the form of a long list – available from the ticket office.

The Museo Horne is easily seen in conjunction with the
Museo Bardini across the river (see p.199), similarly devoted
to one man's private collection.

The museum building, the **Palazzo Corsi-Alberti**
(1489), is worth a special glance even if you're not going
into the museum. Commissioned by the Corsi family, it's a
typical merchant's house of the period, with huge cellars in
which wool would have been dyed, and an open gallery
above the courtyard for drying the finished cloth.

The pride of Horne's collection was its drawings, which
are now salted away in the Uffizi, though a small, usually
captivating display is maintained in the room on the right of
the ground floor. Of what's left, the pick in the left-hand
downstairs room is a bas-relief of the Madonna and Child
attributed to Jacopo Sansovino. In the three rooms on the
first floor, the highlights of Room 1 are a worn crucifix
by Filippino Lippi; part of a predella with a tiny age-bowed
panel of *St Julian* by Masaccio; a dark *Deposition* by Gozzoli,
his last documented work; and a group of saints by Pietro
Lorenzetti. The next room contains the collection's big
draw, Giotto's *St Stephen* (a fragment from a polyptych), followed in Room 3 by Beccafumi's *Holy Family*, shown in its
original frame. The wooden figure of *St Jerome* nearby is by
Verrocchio.

One of the main exhibits on the **second floor** is a piece
of little artistic merit but great historical interest – a copy of
part of Leonardo's *Battle of Anghiari*, once frescoed on a wall
of the Palazzo Vecchio (see p.48). Here, too, are further
works by such big names as Filippo and Filippino Lippi,
Simone Martini and Beccafumi, as well as some lovely
pieces of furniture.

MUSEO HORNE

San Lorenzo

Walk a couple of blocks from the train station or Duomo and you'll see both the tawdriest and the liveliest aspects of central Florence. Hard up against the bustling Via Nazionale and Via Faenza, with their rabbit-hutch hotels and nocturnal hustle, lies the San Lorenzo district, the city's main market area, with scores of stalls encircling a vast and wonderful food hall that rarely sees a foreign face. The racks of T-shirts, leather jackets and belts almost engulf the church of **San Lorenzo** – a building of major importance that's often overlooked in the rush to the Duomo and the Uffizi.

Annexed to the church is another of the city's major draws, the **Cappelle Medicee** (Medici Chapels). While various of the Medici's most important members are buried in San Lorenzo, dozens of lesser lights are interred in these often gaudy chapels: two of the most venal family members – ironically – are celebrated by some of **Michelangelo**'s finest funerary sculpture. The Medici also account for the area's third major site, the **Palazzo Medici-Riccardi**, one of the clan's erstwhile palaces, though it's less the palace than an exquisite fresco-covered chapel within it that draws the crowds.

SAN LORENZO

Map 3, F6. Piazza San Lorenzo. Mon–Sat 10am–4.30pm, Sun mass only; L5000/€2.58.

San Lorenzo was founded in 393, lending credence to its claim to be the oldest church in Florence. For some three hundred years it was the city's cathedral, in time renouncing its title to Santa Reparata, itself eventually replaced by the present-day Duomo. By 1060 a sizeable Romanesque church had been built on the site, a building which in time became the Medici's parish church, benefiting greatly over the years from the family's munificence.

The family was in a particularly generous mood in 1419, when a committee of eight parishioners headed by Giovanni di Bicci de' Medici, founding father of the Medici fortune, offered to finance a new church. Brunelleschi was commissioned to begin the project, starting work on the **Sagrestia Vecchia** (Old Sacristy) before being given the go-ahead two years later to build the entire church. Construction lapsed over the next twenty years, hampered by financial problems, political upheavals and Brunelleschi's simultaneous work on the cathedral dome. Giovanni's son, Cosimo de' Medici, eventually gave the work fresh impetus with a grant of 40,000 *fiorini* (florins) – at a time when 150 florins would support a Florentine family for a year. Cosimo's largesse saved the day, but was still not sufficient to provide the church with a facade. No less a figure than Michelangelo laboured to remedy the omission, one of many to devote time to a scheme to provide a suitable frontage: none of the efforts was to any avail – to this day the exterior's bare brick has never been clad.

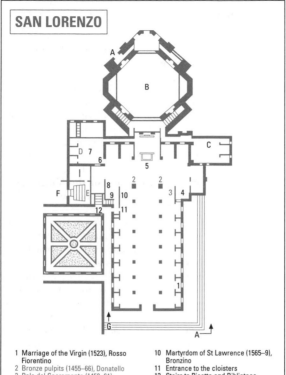

SAN LORENZO

1 Marriage of the Virgin (1523), Rosso Fiorentino
2 Bronze pulpits (1455–66), Donatello
3 Pala del Sacramento (1458–61), Desiderio da Settignano
4 Sarcophagus, fresco and crucifix (1470), Antonio da Pollaiuolo
5 Tomb of Cosimo de' Medici (Cosimo il Vecchio)
6 Tomb of Giovanni and Piero de' Medici (Cosimo's sons)
7 Tomb of Giovanni and Piccarda de' Medici (Cosimo's parents)
8 Funerary memorial to Donatello
9 Annunciation (1440), Filippo Lippi
10 Martyrdom of St Lawrence (1565–9), Bronzino
11 Entrance to the cloisters
12 Stairs to Ricetto and Biblioteca

A Entrance to the Cappelle Medicee (see p.114)
B Cappella dei Principi (see p.115)
C Sagrestia Nuova (see p.116)
D Sagrestia Vecchia
E Ricetto (vestibule), Michelangelo
F Biblioteca Medicea-Laurenziana
G Entrance to the Biblioteca Medicea-Laurenziana

The interior

Works of special note are highlighted in green in the text and on the plan on p.109.

Stepping in from outside – past the ticket barrier – the contrast with the bustle of the market area could hardly be greater. San Lorenzo was the earlier of Brunelleschi's great Florentine churches (the other is Santo Spirito) but already displays his mastery of Classical decorative motifs and mathematically planned proportions: the effect is cool and measured. Close to the entrance, in the second chapel on the right, is Rosso Fiorentino's **Marriage of the Virgin (1)**, a painting with a uniquely golden-haired and youthful Joseph.

More eye-catching are the two bronze pulpits (2) by **Donatello**, near the centre of the church, clad with reliefs depicting scenes preceding and following the Crucifixion. These are the artist's last works (c. 1460), completed by his pupils as increasing paralysis limited their master's ability to model in wax. Jagged and discomforting, charged with more energy than the space can contain, these panels are more like brutal sketches in bronze than conventional reliefs. The overpopulated *Deposition* has demented mourners sobbing beneath crosses which disappear into the void beyond the frame, while in the background a group of horsemen gather on a hill whose contours are left unmarked. Donatello is buried in the church, and commemorated by a **memorial (8)** on the right wall of a chapel in the north transept.

Just right of Donatello's pulpits there's a fine tabernacle, the Pala del Sacramento (3) by Desiderio da Settignano. Round the corner to the right lies a **chapel (4)** containing a Roman sarcophagus, a fresco fragment of the Virgin, a wooden crucifix by Antonio del Pollaiuolo and two modern works in *pietra dura*, a peculiarly Florentine kind of technicolour marquetry using semi-precious stones. In the centre of the church, the modesty of the **tomb of Cosimo de' Medici (5)**, known as Cosimo il Vecchio, is belied by the inscription "Pater Patriae" (Father of the Fatherland) – a title once borne by Roman emperors.

At the top of the north aisle, take in Filippo Lippi's 1440 altarpiece of the *Annunciation* (9) in the chapel just outside the Old Sacristy. Then move left and pass Bronzino's enormous fresco of *The Martyrdom of St Lawrence* (10) – the saint was martyred by being roasted on a grill.

Sagrestia Vecchia

Four more leading Medici members lie buried in the neighbouring **Sagrestia Vecchia (D)** or Old Sacristy, a minor architectural masterpiece that is far more than simply a Medici mausoleum. One of Brunelleschi's earliest projects (1421–26) – and the only one completed in his lifetime – the design, a cube and hemispherical dome, could hardly be more simple and yet more perfect. Brunelleschi's biographer, Manetti, wrote that "it astounded all men both of the city and foreigners ... for its new and beautiful manner. And so many people came continuously that they greatly bothered those who worked there." Nowadays most visitors are drawn to the architect's later Pazzi chapel (see p.98), so there's a chance of enjoying the sacristy in relative peace.

The space was commissioned by Giovanni Bicci de' Medici, the principal founder of the Medici fortune, as a private chapel. The dedication is to St John the Evangelist, patron saint of Giovanni (John), but note that it is the Medici *palle* motif (see p.120) that dominates. On his death, Giovanni, along with his wife Piccarda, was buried beneath the massive marble slab at the centre of the **chapel (7)**. Another **tomb (6)**, easily missed, lies immediately on the

SAN LORENZO

left as you enter, the last resting place of Giovanni's grandsons, Giovanni and Piero de' Medici – it was commissioned from Verrocchio in 1472 by Lorenzo de' Medici. To the modern eye the tomb looks relatively plain, but a Florentine of the day would have been abundantly aware that it was made from the three most precious materials of antiquity – marble, porphyry and bronze.

More arresting than either of the tombs, however, is the chapel's ornamentation. Here Brunelleschi's genius was complemented by the decorative acumen of Donatello, who worked in the sacristy between 1434 and 1443, some twenty years before sculpting the pulpits in the main body of the church. He was responsible for both the cherub-filled frieze and the eight extraordinary tondos above it, four of the latter a striking orangey-pink, the rest crafted in a more muted white against grey. The tondos' subjects are the four Evangelists and a quartet of scenes from the life of St John the Evangelist. The terracotta bust of St Lawrence (Lorenzo) is attributed to either Donatello or Desiderio da Settignano.

Two large **reliefs**, also probably by Donatello, adorn the space above the two doors on the end wall: one shows SS Lawrence and Stephen, twin protectors of Florence, the other SS Cosmas and Damian. These last two, twins and early Christian martyrs, were the patron saints of doctors (*medici*) and thus of the Medici, who were probably descended from doctors or apothecaries. By happy coincidence, Cosimo de' Medici, the church's chief patron, was born on the saints' feast day (27 September), so the two are often seen in paintings or buildings commissioned or connected with him.

Donatello was also responsible for the two bronze doors below with their combative martyrs to the left, and the Apostles and Fathers of the Church to the right. The chapel beyond the left door has a sublime little marble *lavabo*, probably by Verrocchio: many of its fantastic creatures have Medici connections – the falcon and lamb, for example, are the heraldic symbols of Piero de' Medici, who commissioned the work.

Lastly, the **stellar fresco** on the dome above the recessed altar inevitably draws your eye: opinion differs as to whether the position of the painted stars is synonymous with the state of the heavens on July 16, 1416, the birthday of Piero de' Medici, or on July 6, 1439, the date on which the union of the Eastern and Western churches was celebrated at the Council of Florence.

Biblioteca Medicea-Laurenziana

Map 3, F6. Piazza San Lorenzo. Mon–Sat 9am–1pm; free; longer hours and ticket during occasional exhibitions.

A gateway in the left corner of the piazza leads through a pleasant gardened cloister and up to the first floor entrance to the **Biblioteca Medicea-Laurenziana (F)**. Wishing to create a suitably grandiose home for the precious manuscripts assembled by Cosimo and Lorenzo de' Medici, Pope Clement VII (Lorenzo's nephew) asked Michelangelo to design a new Medici library in 1524. The **Ricetto (E)**, or vestibule (1559–71), of the building he eventually came up with is a revolutionary showpiece of Mannerist architecture, delighting in paradoxical display-brackets that support nothing, columns that sink into the walls rather than stand out from them, and a flight of steps so large that it almost fills the room, spilling down like a solidified lava flow.

From this eccentric space, the visitor passes into the tranquil **reading room**; here, too, almost everything is the work of Michelangelo, even the inlaid desks. Exhibitions in the connecting rooms draw on the 15,000-piece Medici collection, which includes manuscripts as diverse as a fifth-century copy of Virgil – the collection's oldest item – and a treatise on architecture by Leonardo. Note how the coffered ceiling and terracotta floor mirror each other's designs.

Cappelle Medicee

Map 3, F6. Piazza Madonna degli Aldobrandini. Tues–Sun 8.15am–5pm (plus same hours first, third & fifth Sun and second & fourth Mon of month); L11,000/€5.68.

Michelangelo's most celebrated contribution to the San Lorenzo complex forms part of the **Cappelle Medicee**, entered from Piazza Madonna degli Aldobrandini, at the back of the church. These chapels divide into three sections: the crypt, burial place of many minor Medici; the **Cappella dei Principi**, housing the tombs of six of the more major Medici; and the **Sagrestia Nuova**, home to three major groups of Michelangelo sculpture.

The crypt

Hardly any of the Medici, however humble, suffered the indignity of a modest grave. Some might have expected more, though, than the low-vaulted **crypt** of the Cappelle Medicee, home to the brass-railed tombs of many of the family's lesser lights. Most were placed here in 1791 by Ferdinand III with what appears to have been scant regard for his ancestors: one contemporary recorded how the duke had the corpses thrown "together pell-mell... caring scarcely to distinguish one from the other".

This haphazard arrangement prevailed until 1857, when it was decided – after much controversy – to exhume 49 of the bodies and provide them with a more dignified interment. William Wetmore Story, an American sculptor present at the exhumation, described the event with obvious relish: "Dark and parchment-dried faces were seen, with thin golden hair, rich as ever, and twisted with gems and pearls and golden nets... Anna Luisa, almost a skeleton, lay robed in rich violet velvet, with the electoral crown sur-mounting a black, ghastly face… Francesco, her uncle, lay beside her, a mass of putrid robes and rags."

Cappella dei Principi

After filing through the crypt, you climb steps at its rear into the larger of the chapels, the **Cappella dei Principi** (Chapel of the Princes), a morbid and dowdy marble-plated hall built as a mausoleum for Cosimo I and the grand dukes who succeeded him. The octagonal chapel took as its inspiration the floorplan of no less a building than the Baptistery, and the extent of Medici conceit was underlined by the chapel's intended centrepiece – the Holy Sepulchre of Christ, a prize that had to be forfeited when the pasha refused to sell it and an expedition sent to Jerusalem to steal it returned empty-handed.

The poet Byron called the Medici's gloomy Cappella dei Principi a "fine frippery in great slabs of various expensive stones, to commemorate rotten and forgotten carcasses".

This was the most expensive building project ever financed by the Medici, and the family were still paying for it in 1743 when the last of the line, Anna Maria Ludovica, joined her forebears in the basement. It could have looked even worse – the massive statues in the niches were intended to be made from semiprecious stones, like those used in the heraldic devices set into the walls (the crests are those of Tuscan and other towns within the Medici domain). Captured Turkish slaves formed the bulk of the workforce set to haul and hack the stone into manageable pieces. Only two of the massive statues were ever completed.

Scaffolding, suitably rich in gold and black, has adorned the walls since a section of cornice fell off in January 2000, revealing major structural faults.

Sagrestia Nuova

The vulgarity of the Cappella dei Principi makes it easy to forget that earlier members of the Medici family had been responsible for commissioning some of the most beautiful works of art in Europe. The **Sagrestia Nuova**, entered via a corridor off the Cappella, is a case in point, designed by Michelangelo as a tribute to, and subversion of, Brunelleschi's Sagrestia Vecchia in the main body of San Lorenzo (see p.111).

Architectural connoisseurs go into raptures over the sophistication of the architecture, notably the complex empty niches above the doors, which make imaginative use of classical motifs – one of the reasons why the chapel is considered to be perhaps the first example of Mannerism. The lay person, however, will be drawn to the three fabulous **Medici tombs** (1520–34), two wholly and one partly by Michelangelo. The sculptor was awarded the commission by Pope Leo X – a Medici – and the pope's cousin, Cardinal Giulio de' Medici.

With your back to the entrance door, the tomb on the left belongs to **Lorenzo, duke of Urbino**, the grandson of Lorenzo the Magnificent. Michelangelo depicts him as a man of thought, and his sarcophagus bears figures of *Dawn* and *Dusk*, the times of day whose ambiguities appeal to the contemplative mind. Opposite stands the tomb of Lorenzo de' Medici's youngest son, **Giuliano, duke of Nemours**; as a man of action, his character is symbolized by the clear antithesis of *Day* and *Night*. As a contemporary writer recorded, the sculptor gave his subjects "a greatness, a proportion, a dignity... which seemed to him would have brought them more praise, saying that a thousand years hence no one would be able to know that they were otherwise".

The protagonists were very much otherwise: Giuliano was in fact an easy-going but feckless individual, while

MICHELANGELO

One of the titanic figures of the Italian Renaissance, **Michelangelo Buonarotti** (1475–1564) was born in Caprese in eastern Tuscany. His family soon moved to Florence, where he became a pupil of Ghirlandaio, making his first stone reliefs for Lorenzo de' Medici. After the Medici were expelled from the city the young Michelangelo went to Rome in 1496. There, he secured a reputation as the most skilled sculptor of his day with the *Bacchus* (now in the Bargello – see p.76) and the *Pietà* for St Peter's.

After his return to Florence in 1501, Michelangelo carved the **David** and the *St Matthew* (both in the Accademia). He was also employed to paint a fresco of the *Battle of Cascina* in the Palazzo Vecchio. Only the cartoon was finished, but this became the single most influential work of art in the city, its twisting nudes a recurrent motif in later Mannerist art. Work was suspended in 1505 when Michelangelo was called to Rome by Pope Julius II to create his tomb; the *Slaves* in the Accademia were intended for this grandiose project which, like many of Michelangelo's schemes, was never finished.

In 1508 Michelangelo began his other superhuman project, the decoration of the **Sistine Chapel** ceiling in Rome. Back in Florence, he started work on the San Lorenzo complex in 1516, staying on in the city to supervise its defences when it was besieged by the Medici and Charles V in 1530. Four years later he left for ever, and spent his last thirty years in Rome, the period that produced the *Last Judgement* in the Sistine Chapel. Florence has one work from this final, tortured phase of Michelangelo's long career, the **Pietà** (now in the Museo dell'Opera del Duomo – see p.36) that he intended for his own tomb.

Lorenzo combined ineffectuality with arrogance. Both died young and unlamented of tuberculosis, combined in Lorenzo's case with syphilis. Michelangelo was not unaware of the ironies; critics have suggested that Lorenzo's absurd hat may well have been a gentle hint as to the subject's feeble-mindedness.

The two principal effigies were intended to face the equally grand tombs of Lorenzo de' Medici and his brother Giuliano, two Medici who at least had genuine claims to fame and honour (the latter was murdered in the Pazzi Conspiracy: see p.28). The only part of the project completed by Michelangelo is the **Madonna and Child**, the last image of the Madonna he ever sculpted. The figures to either side are Cosmas and Damian, patron saints of doctors (*medici*) and the Medici. Although completed by others, they follow Michelangelo's original design.

Wax and clay models exist in the Casa Buonarroti (see p.103) and British Museum of other figures Michelangelo planned for the tomb. Among these were allegorical figures of Heaven and Earth and statues of river gods representing the Tiber and Arno, the last two intended to symbolize the provinces of Tuscany and Lazio, both briefly ruled by Giuliano. Neither these nor the chapel were ever completed: in 1534, four years after the Medici had returned to Florence in the unfathomably wretched form of Alessandro, Michelangelo decamped to Rome, where he stayed for the rest of his life. There are more Michelangelo drawings behind the altar which can be seen on supervised (free) trips every thirty minutes.

PALAZZO MEDICI-RICCARDI

Map 3, G6. Via Cavour 1. Mon, Tues & Thurs–Sat 9am–7pm, Sun 9am–1pm; L8000/€4.13.

Close to the Duomo and San Lorenzo stands the **Palazzo**

Medici-Riccardi, built for Cosimo de' Medici by Michelozzo between 1444 and 1462, possibly to a plan by Brunelleschi. Another story has it that Cosimo did indeed ask Brunelleschi to design the new palace, but the result was so grand that Cosimo rejected it on political grounds, saying "envy is a plant one should never water". Brunelleschi, who was renowned for his temper, is said to have smashed the splendid model in rage.

The palace remained the family home and Medici business headquarters until Cosimo I moved to the Palazzo Vecchio in 1540. In Cosimo de Medici's prime, around fifty members of the Medici clan lived in the palace, though after the deaths of his son Giovanni and grandson Cosimino, the embittered, gouty old man was said to repeatedly complain that the palace had become "too large a house for so small a family". In its day, Donatello's statue of Judith and Holofernes (now in the Palazzo Vecchio – see p.54) adorned the walled garden, a rarity in Florence; the same artist's David, now in the Bargello, stood in the entrance courtyard.

With its heavily rusticated exterior, the monolithic palace was the prototype for several major Florentine buildings, most notably the Palazzo Pitti and Palazzo Strozzi. According to Michelozzo, rustication – the practice of facing buildings with vast, rough-hewn blocks of stone – was desirable as it united "an appearance of solidity and strength with the light and shade so essential to beauty under the glare of an Italian sun". After 1659 the palace was greatly altered by its new owners, the Riccardi, and it now houses the offices of the provincial government, burdened with a pall of bureaucratic gloom that no sun, Italian or otherwise, can penetrate. Ironically, given its history as the seat of Medici power, it was to this palace that Florence's police withdrew in the tense days of 1922, allowing Mussolini's fascists to take over the city's government unimpeded.

PALAZZO MEDICI-RICCARDI

THE MEDICI BALLS

You come across the **Medici emblem** – a cluster of red balls (palle) on a gold background – all over Florence, yet its origins are shrouded in mystery. Legend claims the family was descended from a Carolingian knight named Averardo, who fought and killed a giant in the Mugello, north of Florence. During the encounter his shield received six massive blows from the giant's mace, so Charlemagne, as a reward for his bravery, allowed Averardo to represent the dents as red balls on his coat of arms.

Rival families claimed that the balls had less exalted origins, that they were medicinal pills or cupping glasses, recalling the family's origins as apothecaries or doctors (*medici*). Others claim they are *bezants*, Byzantine coins, inspired by the arms of the *Arte del Cambio*, the money-changers' guild to which the Medici belonged. In a similar vein, some say the balls are coins, the traditional symbols of pawnbrokers.

Whatever the origin, the number of *palle* was never constant. In the thirteenth century, for example, there were twelve. By Cosimo de' Medici's time the number had dropped to seven, though San Lorenzo's Old Sacristy, a Cosimo commission, strangely has eight, while Verrocchio's roundel in the same church's chancel has six and Grand Duke Cosimo I's tomb, in the Cappella dei Principi, has five. Cosimo Il Vecchio was said to be so fond of displaying the *palle* on the buildings he had funded that a rival alleged that even the monk's privies in San Marco were adorned with Medici balls.

The frescoes

Today all that survives of the original palace is Michelozzo's deep, colonnaded courtyard, which closely follows the new architectural style established by Brunelleschi in the foundling hospital (see p.139), and a tiny **chapel**, reached by stairs leading directly from the court. It is the latter which draws the crowds, its interior covered by some of the city's most charming frescoes: Benozzo Gozzoli's three-panel sequence depicting *The Journey of the Magi*, painted around 1460 and recently restored to magnificent effect. The landscape scenes to either side of the altar are by the same artist.

A maximum of fifteen people may view the Medici-Riccardi chapel at any one time. To avoid the queues, book tickets and times in advance at the ticket office, located off the garden through the palace courtyard (or call ☎055.276.0340). The stairs to the chapel itself are immediately on the right upon entering the palace.

Despite the frescoes' ostensible subject, the cycle probably portrays the pageant of the Compagnia dei Magi, the most patrician of the city's religious confraternities, whose annual procession took place at Epiphany. Several of the Medici, inevitably, were prominent members, including Piero de' Medici, who may have commissioned the frescoes. It's known that several of the Medici household are featured in the procession, but putting names to these prettified faces is a problem.

Portraits of the most powerful Medici lurk amongst the gaudy, red-hatted crowd on the far left of the fresco facing you as you enter: the central figure in a black tunic probably portrays old Cosimo himself, with his son Piero on his left, leading the cavalcade. They are led by Caspar, dressed in gold, who is thought to represent either the young Lorenzo the Magnificent (others argue that this is one of the boys in red tunics in the second row) or the House of Medici itself. The artist himself looks out enigmatically from between the two prodigiously bearded men, who may well portray the Byzantine emperor John III Paleologus, who had attended the Council of Florence twenty years before the fresco was painted. Gozzoli's red beret, of a style much favoured by scholars of the time, is signed "OPUS BENOTII" in gold.

The first floor

Another set of stairs leads from the passageway beside the courtyard up to the **first floor**, where a display case in the lobby of the main gallery contains a *Madonna and Child* by **Filippo Lippi**, one of Cosimo de' Medici's more troublesome protégés. Even as a novice in the convent of Santa Maria del Carmine, Filippo managed to earn himself a reputation as a drunken womanizer: in the words of Vasari, he was "so lustful that he would give anything to enjoy a woman he wanted... and if he couldn't buy what he wanted, then he would cool his passion by painting her portrait". Cosimo set up a workshop for him in the Medici palace, from which he often absented himself to go chasing women. On one occasion Cosimo actually locked the artist in the studio, but Filippo escaped down a rope of bed sheets; having cajoled him into returning, Cosimo declared that he would in future manage the painter with "affection and kindness", a policy that seems to have worked more successfully.

The ceiling of the grandiloquent and much mirrored **gallery** (under restoration at the time of writing) glows with Luca Giordano's enthusiastic fresco of *The Apotheosis of the Medici*, from which one can only deduce that Giordano had no sense of shame. Perhaps he had no time to consider the commission – he was known as Luca "Fa-presto" (Luca Does-it-on-the-quick). Accompanying his father on the flight into the ether is the last male Medici, Gian Gastone (d. 1737), in reality a man so inert that he could rarely summon the energy to get out of bed in the morning.

Even more sumptuous interior decoration can be seen in the **Biblioteca Riccardiana-Moreniana**, on the opposite side of the palace (entered from Via Ginori; Mon–Sat 9am–1pm; free), one of the Riccardi's more successful remodellings. It is still a working library, but brief, silent visits can be made to see the array of gilded eighteenth-century shelves, overlooked by Luca Giordano's allegory of *Intellect Liberated from the Bonds of Ignorance* (1685).

MERCATO CENTRALE

Map 3, F5. Mon–Sat 7am–2pm; winter also Sat 4–8pm.

The **Mercato Centrale** is Europe's largest covered food hall, built in stone, iron and glass by Giuseppe Mengoni, architect of Milan's famous Galleria. Opened in 1874, it received a major overhaul a century later, reopening in 1980 with a new first floor. Butchers, *alimentari*, tripe-sellers, greengrocers, pasta stalls – they're all gathered under the one roof, and all charging prices lower than you'll readily find elsewhere in the city. Get there close to the end of the working day and you'll get some good reductions.

For a taste of simple Florentine food, call in at *Nerbone* (open until about 1.30pm), a small *tavola calda* at the far southwestern corner of the Mercato Centrale on the Via dell'Ariento side.

Each day from 8am to 7pm the streets around the Mercato Centrale are thronged with **stalls** selling bags, belts, shoes, trousers – some of it of variable quality. This is the busiest of Florence's daily street markets, and a half-hour's immersion in the haggling mass of customers provides as good a break as any from a pursuit of the city's art.

MERCATO CENTRALE

San Marco

Via Cavour may be the grandest of the long boulevards stretching north from the Duomo towards the busy traffic hub of Piazza della Libertà, but the street otherwise has little to recommend it. Halfway along, however, lies Piazza San Marco, the core of the tightknit **San Marco** district. On the square itself stands one of the city's top attractions, the **Museo di San Marco**, once a monastery and now a museum devoted largely to the paintings of Fra' Angelico. A couple of minutes away lies the museum that comes second only to the Uffizi in the popularity stakes, the **Accademia**, famous chiefly as the home of Michelangelo's *David*.

A similar distance away is the graceful **Piazza Santissima Annunziata**, frequently lauded as Florence's most beautiful square, and well worth the detour for Brunelleschi's revolutionary **Spedale degli Innocenti**, a building created as an orphanage in the fifteenth century, and the fresco cycle in the entrance atrium of **Santissima Annunziata**, the church which dominates the square's northern flank.

GALLERIA DELL'ACCADEMIA

Map 3, H4. Via Ricasoli 60. Tues–Sun 8.15am–6.50pm; L12,000/€6.20.

Florence's first academy of drawing, the Accademia del Disegno, was founded in 1563 by Bronzino, Ammannati and Vasari. Initially based in Santissima Annunziata, it moved in 1764 to Via Ricasoli, and soon afterwards was transformed into a general arts academy, the Accademia di Belle Arti. Twenty years later the Grand Duke Pietro Leopoldo I founded the nearby **Galleria dell'Accademia**, filling its rooms with paintings for the edification of the students. Later augmented with pieces from suppressed religious foundations and other sources, the Accademia has an extensive collection of paintings, especially of Florentine work of the fourteenth and fifteenth centuries.

The **picture galleries** which flank the main sculpture hall are quite small and generally unexciting, with copious examples of the work of "Unknown Florentine" and "Follower of… ". The pieces likeliest to make an impact are Pontormo's *Venus and Cupid* (1532), painted to a cartoon by Michelangelo; a *Madonna of the Sea* (1470) attributed to Botticelli; and the painted fifteenth-century *Adimari Chest*, showing a Florentine wedding ceremony in the Piazza del Duomo. A cluster of rooms near the exit house gilded religious works from the thirteenth and fourteenth centuries, including an altarpiece of the Pentecost by Andrea Orcagna (c.1365).

You can avoid having to queue by booking tickets for the Accademia in advance on ☎055.294.883 (see p.62).

Michelangelo's David

Yet the pictures are not what draw the crowds: the real attraction is **Michelangelo**, half a dozen of whose major sculptures are here, among them the **David** – symbol of the city's republican pride and of the illimitable ambition of the Renaissance artist. Commissioned by the Opera del

GALLERIA DELL'ACCADEMIA

Duomo in 1501, its theme – David defeating the tyrant Goliath – was conceived to invoke parallels with Florence's freedom from outside domination (despite the superior force of its enemies) and its recent liberation from Savonarola and the Medici.

The work's an incomparable show of technical bravura, all the more impressive given the difficulties posed by the marble from which it was carved. The four-metre block of stone – thin, shallow and riddled with cracks – had been quarried from Carrara in western Tuscany forty years earlier. Several artists had already attempted to work with it, notably Agostino di Duccio, Andrea Sansovino and Leonardo da Vinci. Michelangelo succeeded where others had failed, completing the work in 1504 when he was still just 29.

Four days and a team of forty men were then required to move the statue from the Opera del Duomo to its site in the Piazza della Signoria; another three weeks were needed to raise it atop its plinth. During the move the statue required protection day and night to prevent it being stoned by Medici supporters all too aware of its intended symbolism. They did eventually smash the left arm in 1527, when the Medici were again expelled from the city; the pieces were gathered up and reassembled. Since 1991, when one of David's toes was smashed with a hammer, a glass barrier has prevented visitors and potential iconoclasts from getting too close.

The statue remained in its outdoor setting, exposed to the elements, until 1873, losing its gilded hair and a band across its chest in the process. Also missing these days is a skirt of copper leaves added to spare the blushes of Florence's more sensitive citizens. What remains is the fact that the *David* was intended as a piece of public sculpture, not a gallery exhibit, hence the deliberate deformities designed to emphasize its monumentality. Closely surveyed in the Accademia's chapel-like space, therefore, the *David* appears a monstrous adolescent, with massive head and hands and gangling arms – the ugliest masterpiece of Western sculpture.

The Slaves

Michelangelo once described the process of carving as being the liberation of the form from within the stone, a notion that seems to be embodied by the remarkable unfinished **Slaves** (or Prisoners) close to the *David*. His procedure, clearly demonstrated here, was to cut the figure as if it were a deep relief, and then to free the three-dimensional figure; often his assistants would perform the initial operation, so it's possible that Michelangelo's own chisel never actually touched these stones.

Probably carved in the late 1520s, the statues were originally destined for the tomb of Julius II, intended perhaps to symbolize the liberal arts left "enslaved" by Julius's demise. The tomb underwent innumerable permutations before its eventual abandonment, however, and in 1564 the artist's nephew gave the carvings to the Medici, who installed them in the grotto of the Boboli Garden. Four of the original six statues came to the Accademia in 1909. Two others found their way to the Louvre in Paris.

Close by is another unfinished work, *St Matthew* (1505–6), started soon after completion of the *David* as a commission from the Opera del Duomo; they actually requested a full series of the Apostles from Michelangelo, but this is the only one he ever began. It languished half-forgotten in the cathedral vaults until 1831.

MUSEO DI SAN MARCO

Map 3, I4. Piazza San Marco 1. Tues–Fri 8.15am–1.50pm, Sat 8.15am–6.50pm (plus first, third & fifth Mon of the month

8.15am–1.50pm; and second & fourth Sunday of month
8.15am–7pm); L8000/€4.13.

A whole side of Piazza San Marco is taken up by the Dominican convent and church of San Marco, the former building now home to the **Museo di San Marco**. The Domincans acquired the site in 1436, after being forced to move from their former home in Fiesole following the joint connivance of Cosimo de' Medici and Pope Eugenius IV.

The complex would become the recipient of Cosimo's most lavish patronage. In the 1430s he financed Michelozzo's enlargement of the conventual buildings (1437–52), and went on to establish a vast library here. Abashed by the wealth he was transferring to them, the friars of San Marco suggested to Cosimo that he need not continue to support them on such a scale, to which he replied, "Never shall I be able to give God enough to set him down as my debtor."

Ironically, the convent became the centre of resistance to the Medici later in the century – Girolamo Savonarola, leader of the government of Florence after the expulsion of the Medici in 1494, was the prior of San Marco. It was also here that he was besieged and captured before his trial and execution (see p.132). In 1537, Duke Cosimo expelled the Dominicans once more, reminding them pointedly that it was another Cosimo de Medici who had established the building's magnificence in the first placc.

Ground floor

Today San Marco's deconsecrated convent houses the Museo di San Marco, in essence a museum – opened in 1869 – dedicated to the art of Fra' Angelico. Its first port of call, immediately beyond the **entrance (1)**, is the **Chiostro di Sant'Antonino (2)**, designed by Michelozzo in the 1440s and now dominated by a vast cedar of

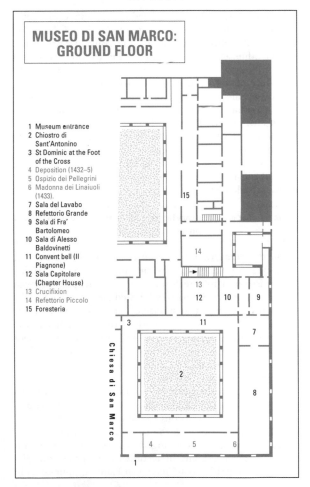

MUSEO DI SAN MARCO: GROUND FLOOR

1 Museum entrance
2 Chiostro di Sant'Antonino
3 St Dominic at the Foot of the Cross
4 Deposition (1432–5)
5 Ospizio dei Pellegrini
6 Madonna dei Linaiuoli (1433).
7 Sala del Lavabo
8 Refettorio Grande
9 Sala di Fra' Bartolomeo
10 Sala di Alesso Baldovinetti
11 Convent bell (Il Piagnone)
12 Sala Capitolare (Chapter House)
13 Crucifixion
14 Refettorio Piccolo
15 Foresteria

Chiesa di San Marco

MUSEO DI SAN MARCO

Lebanon. Most of the cloister's faded frescoes are sixteenth-century depictions of episodes from the life of Antonino Pierozzi, Angelico's mentor and the convent's first prior. Angelico himself painted the frescoes in its four corners, of which the most striking is the lunette depicting **St Dominic at the Foot of the Cross (3)**.

This weather-bleached work pales alongside the twenty or so paintings by the artist gathered in the **Ospizio dei Pellegrini (5)**, or Pilgrims' Hospice, which lies between the cloister and the piazza. Many of the works – including several of Angelico's most famous – were brought here from churches and galleries around Florence; all display the artist's brilliant colouring and spatial clarity, and an air of imperturbable piety.

Works of special note are highlighted in green in the text and on the plan on p.129.

On the right wall as you enter is a **Deposition (4)**, 1432–35, originally hung in the church of Santa Trìnita. Commissioned by the Strozzi family, the painting was begun by Lorenzo Monaco, who died after completing the upper trio of triangular pinnacles, and continued by Fra Angelico. At the opposite end of the room hangs the **Madonna dei Linaiuoli (6)** (1433), Angelico's first major public painting, commissioned by the *linaiuoli* or flax-workers' guild, for their headquarters. The grandiose marble frame is the work of Ghiberti.

Halfway down the room, on the inner wall, the so-called *Pala di San Marco* (1440), though badly damaged by the passage of time and a disastrous restoration, demonstrates Fra' Angelico's familiarity with the latest developments in artistic theory. Its figures are arranged in lines that taper towards a central vanishing point, in accordance with the principles laid out in Alberti's *Della Pittura* (On Painting), published in

Italian just two years before the picture was executed. The work was commissioned by the Medici as an altarpiece for the church of San Marco (see p.137), hence the presence of the family's patron saints Cosmas and Damian, who can be seen at work as doctors (*medici*), in the small panel immediately to the right.

Returning to the cloister, an entrance in its top right-hand corner opens into the **Sala del Lavabo (7)**, where the monks washed before eating (from *lavare* – to wash). Its entrance wall has a *Crucifixion with Saints* by Angelico and its right wall two panels with a pair of saints, also by Angelico. The left wall contains a damaged lunette fresco of the *Madonna and Child* by Paolo Uccello, plus part of a predella by the same artist. The impressive room to the right, the **Refettorio Grande (8)**, or Large Refectory, is dominated by a large fresco of the *Crucifixion* by the sixteenth-century painter Giovanni Sogliani. Of more artistic interest are the rooms off to the left, devoted to paintings by **Fra' Bartolomeo (9)** and **Alesso Baldovinetti (10)** respectively. Note in particular Fra' Bartolomeo's suitably intense portrait of Savonarola, and his unfinished *Palla della Signoria* (1512), originally destined for the Salone dei Cinquecento in the Palazzo Vecchio (see p.48).

Further round the cloister lies the **Sala Capitolare (12)**, or Chapter House, which now houses a large conventual bell, the **Piagnona (11)**, famously rung to summon help on Savonarola's arrest on the eve of April 8, 1498: it became a symbol of anti-Medici sentiment ever after. Here, too, is a powerful fresco of the Crucifixion (13), painted by Angelico and assistants in 1441. At the rear of this room, entered via a passage left of the Chapter House, lies the Refettorio Piccolo (14), or Small Refectory, with an unmissable, lustrous *Last Supper* (1480) by Ghirlandaio. This forms an anteroom to the **Foresteria (15)**, home to the convent's former guest rooms, which is cluttered with

131

SAVONAROLA

Girolamo Savonarola was born in 1452, the son of the physician to the Ferrara court. An abstemious and melancholic youth, he spent much of his time reading the Bible and writing dirges. At the age of 23 he absconded to a Dominican monastery in Bologna, informing his father that he was "unable to endure the evil conduct of the heedless people of Italy". The Dominicans dispatched him to preach all over northern Italy and, though hampered by his unprepossessing appearance, uningratiating voice and inelegant gestures, he eventually built up a committed following through the intensity of his preaching.

Savonarola settled in the monastery of **San Marco** in 1489, and by 1491 his sermons had become so popular that he was asked to deliver his Lent address in the Duomo. Proclaiming that God was speaking through him, he berated the city for its decadence, for its paintings that made the Virgin "look like a whore", and for the tyranny of its Medici-led government. When **Charles VIII of France** marched into Italy in September 1494 to press his claim to the throne of Naples, Savonarola presented him as the instrument of God's vengeance. With support for resistance ebbing, Piero de' Medici capitulated to Charles; within days the Medici had fled and their palace had been plundered.

Florence was declared a **republic**, but Savonarola was now in effect its ruler, issuing decrees from San Marco: profane carnivals were outlawed; fasting was to be observed more frequently; children were to inform the authorities whenever their parents transgressed the Eternal Law. Irreligious books and paintings, expensive clothes, cosmetics, mirrors, board games, trivialities and luxuries of all types were destroyed in colossal **"bonfires of the vanities"** on the city's major squares. Artists, possibly including Botticelli and

Fra Bartolomeo, are even said to have destroyed their own paintings, having come to see their subjects as wickedly lascivious.

Meanwhile, Charles VIII was installed in Naples. The **Holy League** – a formidable alliance of the papacy, Milan, Venice, Ferdinand of Aragon and the Emperor Maximilian – assembled to overthrow him, but in July 1495 its army was badly defeated by the French. Savonarola was summoned to the Vatican to explain why he had been unable to join the campaign. He declined to attend, claiming that it was not God's will, setting off a chain of exchanges that ended with his **excommunication** in June 1497.

When Savonarola celebrated Mass in the Duomo on Christmas Day, the pope threatened the entire city with excommunication unless the charismatic preacher was sent to the Vatican or imprisoned in Florence. The people began to desert him. The crops had failed, plague had broken out and the city was at war with Pisa. The Franciscans now issued a terrible **challenge**: one of their community and one of Savonarola's would walk through an avenue of fire in the Piazza della Signoria; whichever survived would be seen to be the true instrument of God. A thunderstorm, or perhaps the prevarication of the friars, prevented the trial from taking place, but the mood in the city had turned irrevocably. A mob besieged San Marco, burning down the doors to gain entry regardless of the efforts of the Dominicans, who hurled down masonry from above. On the following day, Palm Sunday 1498, Savonarola was arrested. Accused of heresy, he was tortured and then **burned at the stake** in front of the Palazzo Vecchio with two of his supporters. When the flames were finally extinguished, the ashes were thrown into the river to prevent anyone from gathering them as relics.

SAVONAROLA

architectural bits and pieces salvaged during nineteenth-century urban improvement schemes. The corridor provides good views into the (closed) Chiostro di San Domenico.

FRA' ANGELICO

As Michelozzo was altering and expanding San Marco, the convent's walls were being decorated by one of its friars and a future prior, **Fra' Angelico**, a Tuscan painter in whom a medieval simplicity of faith was uniquely allied to a Renaissance sophistication of manner. He was born in Vicchio di Mugello (30km northeast of Florence), son of a wealthy landowner, some time between the late 1380s and 1400. He entered the Dominican monastery of nearby Fiesole aged around 20, where he was known as Fra' Giovanni da Fiesole. Already recognized as an accomplished artist, his reputation flourished in earnest when he came to San Marco.

Here he was encouraged by the theologian Antonino Pierozzi – the future St Antonine or Antoninus – the convent's first prior and later archbishop of Florence. By the time Fra' Giovanni succeeded Pierozzi as prior, the pictures he had created for the monastery over the course of a decade and others for numerous churches in Florence and elsewhere – principally Orvieto cathedral and the Vatican – had earned him the title "the angelic painter", the name by which he's been known ever since. He was also made a beatific – a halfway house to sainthood – hence the other name by which he was long known, Beato Angelico. He achieved full sainthood in 1983.

First floor

Stairs off the cloister by the entrance to the Foresteria lead up to the first floor, where almost immediately you're confronted with one of the most sublime paintings in Italy. For

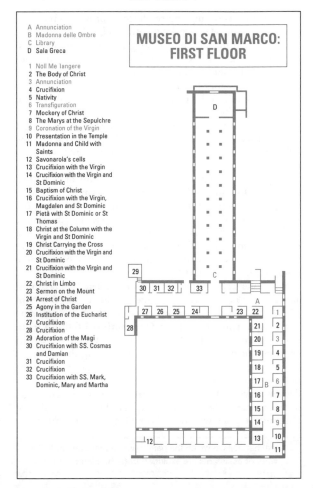

A Annunciation
B Madonna delle Ombre
C Library
D Sala Greca

1 Noli Me Tangere
2 The Body of Christ
3 Annunciation
4 Crucifixion
5 Nativity
6 Transfiguration
7 Mockery of Christ
8 The Marys at the Sepulchre
9 Coronation of the Virgin
10 Presentation in the Temple
11 Madonna and Child with
    Saints
12 Savonarola's cells
13 Crucifixion with the Virgin
14 Crucifixion with the Virgin and
    St Dominic
15 Baptism of Christ
16 Crucifixion with the Virgin,
    Magdalen and St Dominic
17 Pietà with St Dominic or St
    Thomas
18 Christ at the Column with the
    Virgin and St Dominic
19 Christ Carrying the Cross
20 Crucifixion with the Virgin and
    St Dominic
21 Crucifixion with the Virgin and
    St Dominic
22 Christ in Limbo
23 Sermon on the Mount
24 Arrest of Christ
25 Agony in the Garden
26 Institution of the Eucharist
27 Crucifixion
28 Crucifixion
29 Adoration of the Magi
30 Crucifixion with SS. Cosmas
    and Damian
31 Crucifixion
32 Crucifixion
33 Crucifixion with SS. Mark,
    Dominic, Mary and Martha

MUSEO DI SAN MARCO: FIRST FLOOR

MUSEO DI SAN MARCO

the drama of its setting and the lucidity of its composition, nothing in San Marco matches Angelico's **Annunciation** (A). The pallid, submissive Virgin is one of the most touching images in Renaissance art, and the courteous angel, with his scintillating unfurled wings, is as convincing a heavenly messenger as any ever painted. An inscription on this fresco reminds the passing monks to say a Hail Mary as they venerate the image.

Angelico and his assistants also painted the simple and piously restrained pictures in each of the 44 **dormitory cells** on this floor, into which the brothers would withdraw for solitary contemplation and sleep. Such privacy was a novelty, allowed only after a papal concession of 1419 that freed the Dominicans from sleeping in dormitories. Given the speed with which the monks began their construction, the cells must have been a welcome change, but they came with a price. The realism of the frescoes, in particular the copious amounts of blood present in some of the Crucifixion scenes, is said to have caused some of the more timorous monks to faint.

The outer cells of the corridor on the left (1–11) almost all have works by Angelico himself – don't miss the **Noli Me Tangere (1)**, the **Annunciation (3)**, the outstanding **Transfiguration (6)** and the **Coronation of the Virgin (9)**. The marvellous **Madonna delle Ombre (B)**, or Madonna of the Shadows, on the wall facing these cells, is probably also by Angelico. Several of the scenes include one or both of a pair of monastic onlookers, serving as intermediaries between the occupant of the cell and the personages in the pictures: the one with the star above his head is St Dominic; the one with the split skull is St Peter Martyr.

Note that cells in which the paintings are predominantly the work of assistants are excluded from the plan on p.135.

At the end of the far corridor is a knot of more elaborate rooms (12) once occupied by **Savonarola**. These now contain various relics – a belt, a cape, a torn vest – more or less questionably authenticated as worn by the man himself; most dubious of all is the piece of wood from his funeral pyre. At the end of the nearer corridor – turn right at the *Annunciation* – note the double-frescoed cells 29 and 30, which are larger than their neighbours: these more luxuriously appointed retreats were the personal domain of Cosimo de' Medici. The fresco of the Adoration of the Magi (29) may well be the work of Angelico's star pupil Benozzo Gozzoli. Its subject may have been suggested by Cosimo himself, who liked to think of himself as a latter-day wise man, or at least as a gift-giving king.

Just before the VIP cells lies the entrance to Michelozzo's Library (C), 1441–44, built to a design that exudes an atmosphere of calm study, though as the plaque tells, it was here that Savonarola was finally cornered and arrested in 1498. On the left-hand wall, halfway down, the original "meditative green" colour of the walls has been exposed. Cosimo's agents roamed as far as the Near East garnering precious manuscripts and books for him; in turn, Cosimo handed all the religious items over to the monastery, stipulating that they should be accessible to all, making it Europe's first public library. At the far end, a door leads through to the **Sala Greca** (**D**; usually open for guided visits on the hour), added to house a growing collection of Greek codices.

The church

Map 3, I4. Piazza San Marco. Mon–Sat 9.30am–noon & 4–5.30pm. Greatly altered since Michelozzo's intervention, the church of **San Marco** to the left of the museum complex is worth a quick call for two works on the second and third altars on the right: a *Madonna and Saints* painted in 1509 by Fra'

MUSEO DI SAN MARCO

137

Bartolomeo, and an eighth-century mosaic of *The Madonna in Prayer* (surrounded by later additions), brought here from the Constantine basilica in Rome. This had to be cut in half in transit, and you can still see the break across the Virgin's midriff.

CENACOLO DI SANT'APOLLONIA

Map 3, G4. Via XXVII Aprile 1. Tues–Sat 8.15am–1.50pm (plus same hours second & fourth Sun and first, third & fifth Mon of the month); free.

Running off the west side of Piazza San Marco, Via Arazzieri soon becomes Via XXVII Aprile, where the former Benedictine convent of **Sant'Apollonia** stands at no. 1. Most of the complex has now been turned into flats, but one entire wall of the former refectory houses Andrea del Castagno's *Last Supper* – perhaps the most disturbing version of the event painted in the Renaissance. Blood red is the dominant tone, and the most commanding figure is the diabolic black-bearded Judas, who sits on the near side of the table. The seething patterns in the marbled panels behind the Apostles seem to mimic the turmoil in the mind of each, as he hears Christ's announcement of the betrayal.

Painted around 1450, the fresco was plastered over by the nuns before being uncovered in the middle of the last century. Above the illusionistic recess in which the supper takes place are the faded remains of a *Resurrection, Crucifixion and Deposition* by Castagno, revealed when the frescoes were taken off the wall for restoration. The *sinopie* (preparatory drawings) of these and of a *Pietà* are displayed opposite.

PIAZZA SANTISSIMA ANNUNZIATA

Map 3, I5.

Nineteenth-century urban renewal schemes left many of

Florence's squares rather grim places, which makes **Piazza Santissima Annunziata**, with its distinctive arcades, all the more attractive a public space. It has a special importance for the city, too. Until the end of the eighteenth century the Florentine year used to begin on March 25, the Festival of the Annunciation – hence the Florentine predilection for paintings of the Annunciation, and the fashionableness of the Annunziata church (see p.140), which has long been the place for society weddings. The festival is still marked by a huge fair in the piazza and the streets leading off it; later in the year, on the first weekend in September, the square is used for Tuscany's largest crafts fair.

Brunelleschi began the piazza in the 1420s, with additions made later by Ammannati and Antonio da Sangallo. The **equestrian statue of Grand Duke Ferdinand I** (1608) at its centre was Giambologna's final work, and was cast by his pupil Pietro Tacca from cannons captured at the Battle of Lepanto. Tacca was also the creator of the bizarre **fountains** (1629), on each of which a pair of aquatic monkeys dribble water at two whiskered sea slugs.

Spedale degli Innocenti

Map 3, I5. Piazza Santissima Annunziata 12. Daily except Wed 8.30am–2pm; L5000/€2.58.

Piazza Santissima Annunziata's predominant tone is set by the **Spedale degli Innocenti** (or Ospedale). Opened in 1445 as the first foundlings' hospital in Europe, it is still an orphanage today. Commissioned in 1419 by the Arte della Seta, the silk-weavers' guild, it was largely designed by Brunelleschi, whose activity as a goldsmith, strangely, allowed him membership of the guild. The nine-arched loggia (1419–26) across the building, the first time a loggia had been extended in such a way, was one of Europe's earliest examples of the new Classically influenced style that became known as "Renaissance".

Andrea della Robbia's blue-backed ceramic tondi (1487) of well swaddled babies advertise the building's function, but their insouciance belies the misery associated with it. Slavery was part of the Florentine economy even as late as the fifteenth century, and many of the infants given over to the care of the Innocenti were born to domestic slaves. A far from untypical entry in the Innocenti archives records the abandonment of twins "from the house of Agostino Capponi, born of Polonia his slave… They arrived half dead: if they had been two dogs they would have been better cared for." From 1660 children could be abandoned anonymously in the *rota*, a small revolving door whose bricked up remains are still visible at the extreme left of the facade: it remained in use until 1875.

The building within centres on two beautiful cloisters, Brunelleschi's central **Choistro degli Uomini** (Men's Cloister) and the narrow, graceful **Choistro delle Donne** (Women's Cloister) to the right. Stairs from the left-hand corner of the former lead up to the **Museo dello Spedale degli Innocenti**, a miscellany of Florentine Renaissance art that includes one of Luca della Robbia's most charming Madonnas and an *Adoration of the Magi* (1488) by Domenico Ghirlandaio. The latter, commissioned as the altarpiece of the building's church, features a background depicting the *Massacre of the Innocents*. The parallel of the slaughter of Bethlehem's first-born with the orphanage's foundlings, or *innocenti*, was deliberately made.

SANTISSIMA ANNUNZIATA

Map 3, I5. Piazza Santissima Annunziata. Daily 7am–12.30pm & 4–6.30pm.

Santissima Annunziata is the mother church of the

Servites, or Servi di Maria (Servants of Mary), a religious order founded by Filippo Benizzi and six Florentine aristocrats in 1234. From humble beginnings, the order blossomed after 1252, when a painting of the Virgin begun by one of the monks – abandoned in despair because of his inability to create a truly beautiful image – was completed by an angel while he slept. So many people came to venerate the image that by 1444 a new church, financed by the Medici, was commissioned from Michelozzo (who happened to be the brother of the Servites' head prior). The project, completed by Leon Battista Alberti in 1481, involved laying out the present-day **Via dei Servi**, designed to link Santissima Annunziata and the cathedral, thus uniting the city's two most important churches dedicated to the Madonna.

Chiostrino dei Voti

As the number of pilgrims to the church increased, so it became a custom to leave wax votive offerings (*voti*) in honour of its miraculous Madonna. In the early days these were placed around the walls. Later they were hung from the nave ceiling. Eventually they became so numerous that in 1447 a special atrium, the **Chiostrino dei Voti**, was built onto the church. In time this came to house some 600 statues, many of them life-sized depictions of the donor, often with full-size wax horse in close attendance. The collection was one of the city's great tourist attractions until 1786, when the whole lot was melted down to make candles.

More lasting alterations to the cloister's appearance, in the shape of a major **fresco cycle**, were made in 1516 on the occasion of the canonization of Filippo Benizzi, the Servites' founding father. Three leading artists of the day, Andrea del Sarto, Jacopo Pontormo and Rosso Fiorentino,

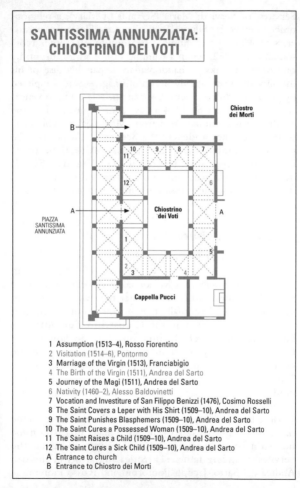

SANTISSIMA ANNUNZIATA: CHIOSTRINO DEI VOTI

1 Assumption (1513–4), Rosso Fiorentino
2 Visitation (1514–6), Pontormo
3 Marriage of the Virgin (1513), Franciabigio
4 The Birth of the Virgin (1511), Andrea del Sarto
5 Journey of the Magi (1511), Andrea del Sarto
6 Nativity (1460–2), Alesso Baldovinetti
7 Vocation and Investiture of San Filippo Benizzi (1476), Cosimo Rosselli
8 The Saint Covers a Leper with His Shirt (1509–10), Andrea del Sarto
9 The Saint Punishes Blasphemers (1509–10), Andrea del Sarto
10 The Saint Cures a Possessed Woman (1509–10), Andrea del Sarto
11 The Saint Raises a Child (1509–10), Andrea del Sarto
12 The Saint Cures a Sick Child (1509–10), Andrea del Sarto
A Entrance to church
B Entrance to Chiostro dei Morti

were involved, together with several lesser painters. Some of the panels are in a poor state – all were removed from the walls and restored after the 1966 flood – but their overall effect is superb.

The entrance wall, together with the right (south) and far (east) walls, depict scenes from the *Life of the Virgin* – an obvious theme given the church's Marian dedication – while the remaining two walls portray scenes from the *Life of St Filippo Benizzi*. Moving right around the cloister, the sequence works backwards from the Virgin's death, beginning with an **Assumption (1)** by Rosso Fiorentino, one of his first works, painted when he was aged around 19. The authorities immediately found fault with it, asking Andrea del Sarto to paint a new version. In the event it was never altered.

Works of special note are highlighted in green in the text and on the plan on opposite.

Alongside lies Pontormo's Visitation (2), said to have taken some 18 months to paint; del Sarto's **Journey of the Magi** (5), by contrast, across the atrium, took a little over three months (see below). In the next alcove note Franciabigio's **Marriage of the Virgin** (3), in which the painter is said to have taken a hammer to the Virgin's face: apparently he was angry at the monks for having secretly looked at the work before its completion; after the artist's tantrum no one had the courage to repair the damage.

Before the next lunette comes a fine marble bas-relief of the *Madonna and Child* attributed to Michelozzo, followed by the cloister's masterpiece, Andrea del Sarto's Birth of the Virgin (4). To the right of the large church door is the same artist's **Journey of the Magi (5)**, which includes a self-portrait in the right-hand corner. Left of the door lies

SANTISSIMA ANNUNZIATA

Alesso Baldovinetti's Nativity (6), its faded appearance the result of poor initial preparation on the part of the artist. The sequence devoted to Filippo Benizzi begins on the next wall with Cosimo Rosselli's **Vocation and Investiture of the Saint (7)**; the five remaining damaged panels **(8–12)** are all the work of Andrea del Sarto (see plan on p.142 for details).

The interior

Few Florentine interiors are as striking at first sight as Santissima Annunziata. Beyond the startling first impressions, though, the church contains few genuine treasures – much of the gilt and stucco fancy dress is a decorative gloss perpetrated in the seventeenth and eighteenth centuries. One notable exception is the ornate **tabernacle** (1448–61) immediately on your left as you enter, designed by Michelozzo and containing the original miraculous image of the Madonna. Michelozzo's patron, Piero di Cosimo de' Medici, made sure that nobody remained unaware of the money he sank into the shrine – an inscription reads "Costò fior. 4 mila el marmo solo" (The marble alone cost 4000 florins). The painting encased in the marble has been repainted into illegibility, and is usually kept covered anyway. It is further obscured by a vast array of lamps, candles and votive offerings – Florentine brides still traditionally visit the shrine to leave their bridal bouquets with the Madonna.

To the tabernacle's right lies a chapel (1453–63) originally created as an oratory for the Medici, adorned with five panels of inlaid stone depicting the Virgin's principal symbols (sun, moon, star, lily and rose) and a small picture of the *Redeemer* (1515) by Andrea del Sarto. Piero de' Medici loaned out the space to visiting dignitaries to allow them a privileged view of the Madonna.

The **Cappella Feroni** next door, the first chapel in the church's north aisle, features a restrained fresco by **Andrea del Castagno** of *Christ and St Julian* (1455–56). The next chapel to the right contains a more striking fresco by the same artist, the *Holy Trinity and St Jerome* (1454). Now restored, both frescoes were obliterated after Vasari publicized the rumour that Castagno had poisoned his erstwhile friend, Domenico Veneziano, motivated by envy of the other's skill with oil paint. Castagno was saddled with this crime until the last century, when an archivist discovered that the alleged murderer in fact predeceased his victim by four years.

Separated from the nave by a triumphal arch is the unusual **tribune**, begun by Michelozzo but completed to designs by Alberti; you get into it along a corridor from the north transept. The chapel at the farthest point was altered by Giambologna into a monument to himself, complete with bronze reliefs and a crucifix by the sculptor. The chapel to its left contains a sizeable *Resurrection* (1550) by Bronzino. Look out, too, for the magnificent **organ** at the head of the aisle; built in 1628, it's the city's oldest organ and the second oldest in Italy.

The warm, spacious **Chiostro dei Morti** is worth visiting for Andrea del Sarto's intimate *Madonna del Sacco* (1525), one of his most famous works (it's the only fresco under glass). The cloister is entered through a gate to the left of the church portico or from the left transept, but both are often locked, so a word with the sacristan might be in order.

Andrea del Sarto's *Madonna del Sacco* (Madonna of the Sack) takes its curious name from the sack on which St Joseph is leaning; it actually depicts the Rest during the *Flight into Egypt*.

SANTISSIMA ANNUNZIATA

MUSEO ARCHEOLOGICO

Map 3, J5. Via della Colonna 38. Mon 2–7pm, Tues & Thurs
8.30am–7pm, Wed & Fri–Sun 8.30am–2pm; summer usually also Sat
9pm–midnight (hours are subject to frequent changes); L8000/€4.13.

On the other side of Via della Colonna from the side wall
of Santissima Annunziata is the **Museo Archeologico**, the
most important collection of its kind in northern Italy. It
suffered terrible damage in the flood of 1966 and the task
of restoring the exhibits is still not quite finished, so the
arrangement of the rooms is subject to sudden changes.

Its special strength is its **Etruscan** finds, many of them part
of the Medici bequest. On the ground floor there's a comprehensive display of Etruscan funerary figures, but even
more arresting than these is the *François Vase*, an Attic krater
(bowl) from the sixth century BC, discovered in an Etruscan
tomb at Chiusi. Pride of place in the first-floor **Egyptian
collection**, where the rooms are handsomely decorated in
mock-Egyptian funerary style, goes to a Hittite chariot made
of bone and wood and dating from the fourteenth century
BC. The grisly exposed mummies may be popular with kids.

The rest of this floor and much of the floor above are
given over to the **Etruscan, Greek and Roman collections**, arranged with variable clarity. Of the Roman pieces
the outstanding item is the *Idolino*, probably a copy of a fifth-
century BC Greek original. Nearby is a massive Hellenistic
horse's head, which once adorned the garden of the Palazzo
Medici, where it was studied by Donatello and Verrocchio.
In the long gallery you'll find the best of the Etruscan pieces:
the *Arringatore* (Orator), the only known Etruscan large
bronze from the Hellenistic period; and the *Chimera*, a triple-
headed monster of the fifth century BC. A symbol of the
three-season pre-Christian Mediterranean year, the *Chimera*
was much admired by Cosimo I's retinue of Mannerist artists
and all subsequent connoisseurs of the offbeat.

Santa Maria Novella

The district centred on the great church of **Santa Maria Novella** is most people's first taste of Florence – the rear of the church is virtually the first thing you see on emerging from the main train station. Although you'll probably start your sightseeing elsewhere, you should return to visit a church that ranks with Santa Croce as the city's most important after the Duomo and Baptistery.

On the other side of the church lies **Piazza Santa Maria Novella**, a square with a lethargic backwater feel, much favoured for picnic lunches and after-dark loitering. Nearby **Ognissanti** is a less compelling church than Santa Maria, but worth a visit for a trio of paintings. Any serious shopping expedition will involve scouring the streets of this area, particularly **Via de' Tornabuoni**, though many of its shops are effectively out of bounds to those who don't travel first class: Versace, Ferragamo, Gucci and Armani are just some of the big names here.

For more information on shopping in Florence, see
pp.279–291.

SANTA MARIA NOVELLA

Map 3, D6. Piazza Santa Maria Novella. Mon–Thurs 9.30am–5pm,
Fri & Sun 1–5pm; L5000/€2.58.

From its gay, freshly scrubbed green, white and pink marble
facade, you'd never guess that the church of **Santa Maria
Novella** was the Florentine base of the austere Dominican
order, fearsome vigilantes of thirteenth-century
Catholicism. A more humble church, Santa Maria delle
Vigne, which had existed here since the eleventh century,
was handed to the Dominicans in 1221; they then set about
altering the place to their taste.

By 1360 the interior was finished, but only the
Romanesque lower part of the **facade** had been completed. This state of affairs lasted until 1456, when Giovanni
Rucellai paid for Alberti to design a classicized upper storey
(1456–70) that would blend with the older section while
improving the facade's proportions. The sponsor's name is
picked out across the facade in Roman capitals
(IOHANES·ORICELLARIVS…), while the Rucellai family
emblem, the billowing sail of Fortune, runs as a motif
through the central frieze. Note the cemetery to the right
of the church, a feature unique in Florence – an arcade of
avelli, the collective burial vaults of upper-class families.

The interior

Santa Maria Novella's Gothic **interior** was designed specifically with the idea of preaching sermons to as large a congregation as possible – hence its size. Acoustic effects may

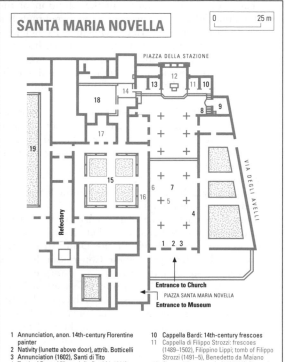

SANTA MARIA NOVELLA

0   25 m

PIAZZA DELLA STAZIONE

VIA DEGLI AVELLI

Refectory

Entrance to Church

PIAZZA SANTA MARIA NOVELLA

Entrance to Museum

1 Annunciation, anon. 14th-century Florentine painter
2 Nativity (lunette above door), attrib. Botticelli
3 Annunciation (1602), Santi di Tito
4 Tomb of Beata Villana delle Botti (d. 1361), a Dominican nun, by Bernardo Rossellini (1451) and Desiderio da Settignano
5 Pulpit (1443), Brunelleschi
6 Trinity (1427), Masaccio
7 Crucifix, Giotto (c. 1288–90)
8 Tomb of the Patriarch of Constantinople (d.1440)
9 Cappella Rucellai (1303–52): Madonna and Child (1348), Mino da Fiesole; tombplate of Leonardo Dati (1425–6), Ghiberti

10 Cappella Bardi: 14th-century frescoes
11 Cappella di Filippo Strozzi: frescoes (1489–1502), Filippino Lippi; tomb of Filippo Strozzi (1491–5), Benedetto da Maiano
12 Chancel: fresco cycle (1485–90), Domenico Ghirlandaio
13 Cappella Gondi: crucifix (1410–14), attrib. Brunelleschi
14 Cappella Strozzi: frescoes (1350–7), Narno di Cione; altarpiece (1357), Orcagna
15 Chiostro Verde
16 The Flood (1425–30), Paolo Uccello
17 Cappellone degli Spagnoli
18 Chiostrino dei Morti
19 Chiostro Grande

even have been a consideration in the adoption of the French Gothic fashion for stone vaults – timbered roofs had hitherto been the norm in Tuscan churches. Its architects were not content with sheer physical size alone, however, and created a further illusion of space with an ingenious trompe l'oeil – the distance between the columns diminishes with proximity to the altar, a perspectival illusion to make the nave seem longer.

Treasures aplenty fill the interior, not least a ground-breaking painting by Masaccio, a crucifix by Giotto and no fewer than three major **fresco cycles**. They'd be even more had it not been for the antics of Vasari and his minions in the 1560s, who ran amok here in a frenzy of "improvement", ripping out the rood screen and the choir, and bleaching over the frescoes; restorers in the last century managed to reverse much of his handiwork.

Entwined around the second nave pillar on the left is a **pulpit (5)**, designed by Brunelleschi but chiefly famous as the vantage point from which the Dominicans first denounced Galileo for espousing the Copernican theory of the heavens. The actual carving was completed by Buggiano, Brunelleschi's adopted son, who may well have advised Masaccio on the Renaissance architectural details present in the background of his extraordinary 1427 fresco of the Trinity (6), which is painted on the wall nearby. This was one of the earliest works in which the rules of perspective and classical proportion were rigorously employed, and Florentines queued to view the illusion on its unveiling, stunned by a painting which appeared to create three-dimensional space on a solid wall. Amazingly, the picture was concealed behind an altar in 1570 and only rediscovered in 1861.

The painting's theme was suggested by the fact that the Dominicans' calendar began with the Feast of the Trinity. Surmounting a stark image of the state to which all flesh is reduced, the main scene is a dramatized diagram of the mechanics of Christian redemption. The lines of the painting lead from the picture's donors, the judge Lorenzo Lenzi and his wife (the figures flanking the pair of painted pillars), through the Virgin and the Baptist (humanity's mystical link with the Holy Trinity), to the crucified Christ and the stern figure of God the Father at the pinnacle. The skeleton beneath the picture bears a motto with the none too cheery rhyming couplet: "I was that which you are, you will be that which I am."

Newly restored for the millennium, the refreshed colours of Masaccio's masterpiece had Florentines queuing up all over again in Easter 2001. They were also eager to see **Giotto's Crucifix (7)**, a radically naturalistic, probably juvenile work (c. 1288–90) that now hangs in what is thought to be its intended position, poised dramatically over the centre of the nave. Hitherto, it had been hidden away in the sacristy, veiled by a layer of dirt so thick that many scholars refused to recognize it as the work of the great master; the attribution is still disputed, a common complaint being that Christ's body is depicted in an unusually heavy way. But as seen from below, suspended in an eerily life-like manner, the weight of flesh seems only to contribute to its painful realism.

Works of special note are highlighted in green in the text and on the plan on p.149.

Nothing else in the main part of the church has quite the same resonance as these three works, but the wealth of decoration is astounding. In the right transept lies the tomb of the **Patriarch of Constantinople (8)**, who died in the adjoining convent in 1440 after unsuccessful negotiations to unite the Roman and Byzantine churches at the 1439 Council of Florence. Raised above the pavement of the transept, the **Cappella Rucellai (9)**, often closed, contains a marble *Madonna and Child* on the main altar signed by Nino Pisano, and – in the centre of the floor – Ghiberti's bronze tomb of the Dominican general Francesco Leonardo Dati.

Cappella di Filippo Strozzi

In 1486 the chapel (11) to the right of the chancel was bought by Filippo Strozzi, a wealthy banker, who then commissioned Filippino Lippi to paint a much-interrupted fresco cycle (1489–1502) on the life of his namesake, St Philip the Apostle – a saint rarely portrayed in Italian art. The paintings, a departure from anything seen in Florence at the time, were completed well after Strozzi's death in 1491. Lippi, it's interesting to note, received a payment of 300 florins for the work – ten times the cost of Strozzi's funeral.

Before starting the project Filippino spent some time in Rome, and the work he carried out on his return displays an archeologist's obsession with ancient Roman culture. In its deliberately awkward style, it also looks ahead to the unsettling work of the Mannerists. The right wall depicts Philip's *Crucifixion* and his *Miracle before the Temple of Mars*. In the latter, the Apostle uses the cross to banish a dragon which had been an object of pagan worship in a Temple of Mars. The enraged temple priests then capture and crucify the saint. The figures swooning from the dragon's stench are almost overwhelmed by an architectural fantasy derived from Rome's recently excavated Golden House of Nero. Look carefully in the top right-hand corner and you'll see a minuscule figure of Christ, about the same size as one of the vases behind the figure of Mars.

The left wall depicts *The Raising of Drusiana* and the *Attempted Martyrdom of St John*: the latter scene alludes to the persecutions of the emperor Domitian, during which John was dipped in boiling oil in an attempt to kill him –

apparently he emerged miraculously unscathed and rejuvenated by the experience. The vaults portray Adam, Noah, Jacob and Abraham and, like the chapel's stained glass and impressive trompe l'oeil decoration, were also the work of Lippi. Behind the altar of this chapel is **Strozzi's tomb** (1491–95), beautifully carved by Benedetto da Maiano.

Capella Tornabuoni

As a chronicle of fifteenth-century life in Florence, no series of frescoes is more fascinating than **Domenico Ghirlandaio**'s pictures around the chancel (12) and high altar. The artist's masterpiece, the pictures ostensibly depict scenes from the life of the Virgin (left wall) and episodes from the life of St John the Baptist, and were designed to replace works on similar themes by Orcagna destroyed a century earlier, reputedly by a bolt of lightning. To get close to the frescoes you'll need to arrive between 10am and 4pm, when the chancel is opened for brief, accompanied visits on the hour every hour. Or for a more considered viewing bring some binoculars – and bear in mind that the lowest row is mostly obscured by a monstrous reredos.

However, the fact that the paintings were commissioned by **Giovanni Tornabuoni**, a banker and uncle of Lorenzo de' Medici (Lorenzo the Magnificent), means they are liberally sprinkled with contemporary portraits and narrative details – which explains why certain illustrious ladies of the Tornabuoni family are present at the births of both John the Baptist and the Virgin. Such self-glorification made the frescoes the object of special ire after they were completed, drawing the vitriol of Savonarola during his hellfire and brimstone sermons (see p.132). Stuffier art critics have also labelled them too "superficial" for serious comment: John Ruskin, their most notable detractor, observed that "if you are a nice person, they are not nice enough," and "if you are a vulgar person, not vulgar enough".

SANTA MARIA NOVELLA

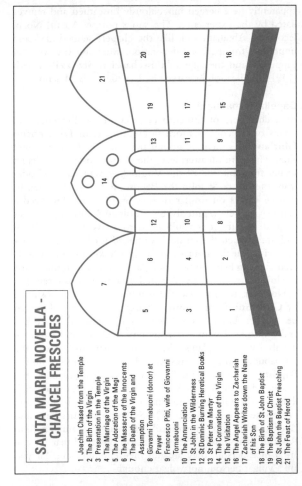

SANTA MARIA NOVELLA – CHANCEL FRESCOES

1. Joachim Chased from the Temple
2. The Birth of the Virgin
3. Presentation in the Temple
4. The Marriage of the Virgin
5. The Adoration of the Magi
6. The Massacre of the Innocents
7. The Death of the Virgin and Assumption
8. Giovanni Tornabuoni (donor) at Prayer
9. Francesco Pitti, wife of Giovanni Tornabuoni
10. The Annunciation
11. St John in the Wilderness
12. St Dominic Burning Heretical Books
13. St Peter the Martyr
14. The Coronation of the Virgin
15. The Visitation
16. The Angel Appears to Zachariah
17. Zachariah Writes down the Name of his Son
18. The Birth of St John Baptist
19. The Baptism of Christ
20. St John the Baptist Preaching
21. The Feast of Herod

In truth, there are few frescoes in the city with such immediate charm, and none which are so self-conscious a celebration of Florence at its zenith – it's no accident that one of the frescoes **(17)** includes a prominent Latin inscription (on an arch to the right) which reads: "The year 1490, when the most beautiful city renowned for abundance, victories, arts and noble buildings profoundly enjoyed salubrity and peace."

Having found the inscription, you might then want to identify some of the portraits scattered around the paintings. Ghirlandaio features as a self-portrait in **(1)**, in which Joachim, the Virgin's father, is chased from the temple because he has been unable to have children – the painter is the figure in the right-hand group with hand on hip. In the next fresco **(2)**, the young woman in the white and gold dress leading the group of women is Ludovica, Tornabuoni's only daughter, who died in childbirth aged 15: it's doubtless no accident that the scene painted in the fresco depicts the birth of the Virgin. Across the chancel, on the right wall, the **Visitation (15)** features Giovanna degli Albizi, Tornabuoni's daughter-in-law, who also died in childbirth – she's the first of the trio of women to the right of the Virgin. The **Birth of St John Baptist (18)** features Tornabuoni's sister, Lucrezia, better known as the mother of Lorenzo de' Medici (the Magnificent): she's the woman in front of the servant carrying the fruit on her head.

Cappella Strozzi

The next chapel beyond the chancel is the Cappella Gondi (12), which houses Brunelleschi's crucifix, supposedly carved as a riposte to the uncouthness of Donatello's cross in Santa Croce. It is the artist's only surviving sculpture in wood. Legend claims that Donatello was so struck on seeing his rival's work that he dropped a basket of eggs. Such minor treasures are eclipsed, however, by the great fresco cycle in the next chapel but one, the Cappella Strozzi (13).

The cappella lies above the level of the rest of the church at the end of the north (left) transept. Its frescoes (1350–57) were commissioned as an expiation of the sin of usury by Tommaso Strozzi, an ancestor of Filippo Strozzi, patron of the chapel across the church (see p.152). The pictures are the masterpiece of Nardo di Cione, brother of the better-known Orcagna (Andrea di Cione), with whom Nardo worked in conjunction to design the chapel's stained glass.

Orcagna alone painted the chapel's magnificent high altarpiece – *Christ Presenting the Keys to St Peter and the Book of Wisdom to Thomas Aquinas* (1357). A propaganda exercise on behalf of the Dominicans, the picture shows Christ bestowing favour on both St Peter and St Thomas Aquinas, the latter a figure second only to St Dominic in the order's hierarchy. The stern and implacable figures are perfect advertisements for the Dominicans' unbending authority.

Behind the altar, the central fresco depicts the *Last Judgement*, with Dante featured as one of the saved (in white, third from the left, second row from the top). So, too, are Tommaso Strozzi and his wife, shown being led by St Michael into paradise, with an angel helping the righteous up through a trapdoor; on the right of the altar, a devil forks the damned down into hell. The theme of judgement is continued in the bleached fresco of Dante's *Inferno* on the right wall, faced by a thronged *Paradiso* on the left. The entrance arch features a frieze of saints, while the vaults depict the Dominicans' own St Thomas Aquinas and the Virtues.

Museo di Santa Maria Novella

Map 2, A1. Piazza Santa Maria Novella. Daily except Fri 9am–2pm; L5000/€2.58.

More remarkable paintings are to be found in the spacious Romanesque conventual buildings to the left of Santa Maria Novella, home to the **Museo di Santa Maria Novella**. The first set of cloisters beyond the entrance, the **Chiostro Verde (16)** (1332–50), features frescoes of *Stories from Genesis* (1425–30) executed by Paolo Uccello and his workshop. The cloister takes its name from the green base *terra verde* pigment they used, and which now gives the paintings a spectral undertone.

The windswept image of The Flood (17), the best-preserved of the cloister's frescoes, is rendered almost unintelligible by the telescoping perspective and the double appearance of the ark (before and after the flood), whose flanks form a receding corridor in the centre of the picture: on the left, the ark is rising on the deluge, on the right it has come to rest as the waters subside. In the foreground, two men fight each other in their desperation to stay alive; the chequered lifebelt that one of these men is wearing around his neck is a favourite Uccello device for demonstrating a mastery of perspective – it's a *mazzocchio*, a 72-faceted wicker ring round which a turbanned headdress was wrapped. Another man grabs the ankles of the visionary figure in the foreground – presumably Noah, though he is a much younger and more beardless Noah than the hirsute patriarch leaning out of the ark on the right to receive the dove's olive branch. In the right foreground there's a preview of the universal devastation, with tiny corpses laid out on the deck, and a crow gobbling an eyeball from one of the drowned.

PAOLO UCCELLO

Some of the most curious and haunting images to come out of the Florentine Renaissance are the products of **Paolo Uccello**'s obsession with the problems of perspective and foreshortening. Born in 1396, he trained in Ghiberti's workshop before moving to Venice, where he was employed on mosaics for the Basilica di San Marco. He worked periodically in Florence, returning for an extended period in 1431. Five years later he was contracted to paint the commemorative portrait of Sir John Hawkwood in the Duomo (see p.18) – the trompe l'oeil painting which gives the first evidence of his interest in foreshortening.

After an interlude in Padua, Uccello completed the frescoes for the cloister of Santa Maria Novella, in which his systematic but non-naturalistic use of perspective is seen at its most extreme. In the following decade he painted the three-scene sequence of the **Battle of San Romano** (Louvre, London National Gallery and Uffizi) for the Medici – his most ambitious non-fresco paintings, and similarly notable for their unsettling multiple perspectives and strange use of foreshortening.

Uccello was driven halfway round the bend by the study of **perspective**, locking himself away for weeks at a time when he'd got his teeth into a particularly thorny problem. Chronically incapable of looking after his more mundane concerns, he was destitute by the time of his death in 1475: "I am old and without means of livelihood. My wife is sick and I am unable to work any more." Yet he left behind some of the most arresting paintings of the Renaissance, in which his preoccupation with mathematical precision coexists uneasily with a fundamentally Gothic sense of pageantry to produce images of fascinating obscurity.

Cappellone degli Spagnoli

Off the cloister opens what was once the chapter-house of the immensely rich convent of Santa Maria, the Cappellone degli Spagnoli (18), or Spanish Chapel. For a time it was also the headquarters of the Inquisition. It received its present name after Eleonora di Toledo, wife of Cosimo I, reserved it for the use of her Spanish entourage. Presumably she derived much inspiration from its majestic fresco cycle (1367–69) by Andrea di Firenze, an extended depiction of the triumph of the Catholic Church that was described by Ruskin as "the most noble piece of pictorial philosophy in Italy".

Virtually every patch of the walls is covered with frescoes, whose theme is the role of the Dominicans in the battle against heresy and in the salvation of Christian souls. The **left wall** as you stand with your back to the entrance depicts *The Triumph of Divine Wisdom*, a triumph exemplified by Thomas Aquinas, who is portrayed enthroned below the Virgin and Apostles amidst the winged Virtues and the "wise men" of the Old and New Testaments (the so-called Doctors of the Church). Below these are 14 figures who symbolize the Arts and Sciences, branches of learning brought to fruition by the Holy Spirit (symbolized by the dove above the Virgin) working through the Catholic faith.

The more spectacular **right wall** depicts *The Triumph of the Church*, or more specifically, the "Mission, Work and Triumph of the Dominican Order". Everything here conforms to a strict and logical hierarchy, beginning at the crown of the painting with the boat of St Peter, a symbol of the Church. At the bottom is a building supposed to be Florence's cathedral, a pinky-purple creation imagined eighty years before its actual completion – and longer still before the dome was even begun. Before it stand the pope and Holy Roman emperor, society's ultimate spiritual and temporal rulers. Before them stand ranks of figures representing religious orders, among which the Dominicans are naturally pre-eminent. In particular note St Dominic, the order's founder, unleashing the "hounds of the lord", or *Domini Canes*, a pun on the Dominicans' name: heretics, the dogs' victims, are shown as wolves being torn to pieces.

Among the group of pilgrims (in the centre, just below the Duomo) are several portraits, real or imagined: Cimabue (standing in a large brown cloak); Giotto (beside him in profile, wearing a green cloak); Boccaccio (further right, in purple, holding a closed book); Petrarch (above, with a cloak and white ermine hood); and Dante (alongside Petrarch in profile, with a white cap). Above and to the right, are scenes of young people dancing, hawking, playing music and engaging in other debauched pleasures of the sort that the Dominicans so heartily disapproved.

Those able to resist such abominations – the saved – are shown being marshalled by a nearby friar who hears their confession (which removes the taint of mortal sin) before dispatch towards St Peter and the Gate of Paradise. Once through the gate, the blessed are shown in adoration of God and the angels with the Virgin at their midst. Foremost among those confessing is the chapel's donor, one Buonamico Guidalotti (shown kneeling), who paid for the chapel in honour of his wife, who died during the 1348 plague.

The far wall contains scenes connected with the crucifixion, while the near (entrance) wall, which is excluded from the frescoes' unified theme, contains scenes from the life of St Peter the Martyr, one of the Dominicans' leading lights. The contemporaneous decoration of the **Chiostrino dei Morti (19)**, the oldest part of the complex, has not aged so robustly; it was closed for restoration at the time of writing. The Chiostro Grande, to the west, is also out of bounds, but for the more unusual reason that it is a practice parade ground for aspiring carabinieri (Italy's semi-military police force).

OGNISSANTI

Map 3, C7. Borgo Ognissanti. Daily 8am–noon & 5–7.30pm.

In medieval times one of the main areas of cloth production – the mainstay of the Florentine economy – was in the western part of the city. **Ognissanti**, or All Saints, the main church of this western quarter, was founded in 1256 by the Umiliati, a Benedictine order from Lombardy whose speciality was the weaving of woollen cloth – they it was who commissioned the great Giotto altarpiece of the *Maestà* in the Uffizi (see p.63). In 1561 the Franciscans took over the church, the new tenure being marked by a Baroque overhaul which spared only the medieval campanile.

The facade (1637) of the church is of historical interest as one of the earliest eruptions of the Baroque in Florence – it was abhorred by many Florentines at the time as an affront to the city's Renaissance traditions. The building within, however, is made appealing by earlier features – **frescoes** by Domenico Ghirlandaio and Sandro Botticelli. The young face squeezed between the Madonna and the dark-cloaked man in Ghirlandaio's *Madonna della Misericordia* (1473), the lower of two works over the second altar on the right, is said to be that of Amerigo Vespucci (1451–1512), an agent for the Medici in Seville, whose two voyages in 1499 and 1501 would lend his name to a continent.

The altar was paid for by the Vespucci, a family of silk merchants from the surrounding district, which is why other members of the clan appear beneath the Madonna's protective cloak. Among them is Simonetta Vespucci (at the Virgin's left hand), the mistress of Giuliano de' Medici and reputedly the most beautiful woman of her age – she is said to have been the model for Botticelli's *Venus*, now in the Uffizi.

The idea may not be so far-fetched, for Botticelli also lived locally, and the Vespucci and Filipepi families were on good terms. Botticelli is buried in the church, beneath a round tomb slab in the south transept, and his painting of *St Augustine's Vision of St Jerome* (1480) lies on the same wall as the Madonna, between the third and fourth altars. Facing it is Ghirlandaio's more earthbound *St Jerome*, also painted in 1480.

In the same year Ghirlandaio painted the well preserved *Last Supper* that covers one wall of the **refectory**, reached through the cloister entered to the left of the church (Mon, Tues & Sat 9am–noon; free). It's a characteristically placid scene, the most animated characters being the birds in flight over the fruit-laden lemon trees above the heads of the disciples.

Orsanmichele and around

Despite the urban improvement schemes of the last century and the bombings of the last war, several streets in central Florence retain their medieval character, especially in the district to the west of Piazza della Signoria. The church of **Orsanmichele**, easily seen just off Via dei Calzaiuoli, sets the prevailing tone, its exterior the stage for some outstanding sculpture, its atmospheric interior a calm retreat from the hubbub of the city centre.

Forming a border post to this quarter is the modest Mercato Nuovo (see p.290). From here, an amble through streets such as Via Porta Rossa, Via delle Terme and Borgo Santi Apostoli will give you some idea of the feel of Florence in the Middle Ages, when every important house was an urban fortress. Best of these medieval redoubts is the **Palazzo Davanzati**, whose interior, which looked little different from the way it did six hundred years ago, was one of the most charming things to visit in the city before the building was closed for a lengthy structural rescue job. Rounding off the district, the fine church of **Santa Trìnita** is home to an outstanding but relatively unsung fresco cycle by Domenico Ghirlandaio.

ORSANMICHELE

Map 2, C5. Via dell'Arte della Lana. Daily 9am–noon, 4–6pm (closed first & last Mon of the month); free.

Standing like a truncated military tower towards the southern end of Via dei Calzaiuoli, **Orsanmichele** is the oddest-looking church in Florence. Not only is the building itself a major monument, but its exterior was once the most impressive outdoor sculpture gallery in the city. Several of the pieces have been or are being restored, however, after which they will be displayed in the Bargello and elsewhere, while their places at Orsanmichele are taken by replicas. Copies or not, the church is unmissable.

The first building here was a small oratory secreted in the orchard or vegetable garden (*orto*) of a now-vanished Benedictine monastery. A larger church stood on the site from the ninth century – San Michele ad Hortum, later San Michele in Orte – hence the compacted form of Orsanmichele. Even after the church was replaced by a grain market in the thirteenth century, the place retained its religious associations. In 1300, the chronicler Giovanni Villani claimed "the lame walked and the possessed were liberated" after visiting a miraculous image of the Virgin painted on one of the market pillars.

After a 1304 fire, the building was eventually replaced by a loggia designed by Francesco Talenti to serve as a trade hall for the *Arti Maggiori*, the Great Guilds which governed the city. Between 1367 and 1380 the loggia was walled in, after which the site was again dedicated almost exclusively to religious functions (while leaving two upper storeys for use as emergency grain stores).

As far back as 1339, plans had been made to adorn each

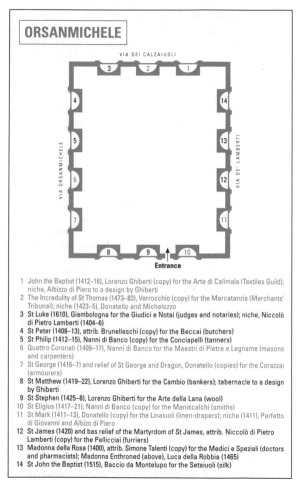

ORSANMICHELE

1 John the Baptist (1412–16), Lorenzo Ghiberti (copy) for the Arte di Calimala (Textiles Guild); niche, Albizzo di Piero to a design by Ghiberti

2 The Incredulity of St Thomas (1473–83), Verrocchio (copy) for the Mercatanzia (Merchants' Tribunal); niche (1423–5), Donatello and Michelozzo

3 St Luke (1610), Giambologna for the Giudici e Notai (judges and notaries); niche, Niccolò di Pietro Lamberti (1404–6)

4 St Peter (1408–13), attrib. Brunelleschi (copy) for the Beccai (butchers)

5 St Philip (1412–15), Nanni di Banco (copy) for the Conciapelli (tanners)

6 Quattro Coronati (1409–17), Nanni di Banco for the Maestri di Pietre e Legname (masons and carpenters)

7 St George (1416–7) and relief of St George and Dragon, Donatello (copies) for the Corazzai (armourers)

8 St Matthew (1419–22), Lorenzo Ghiberti for the Cambio (bankers); tabernacle to a design by Ghiberti

9 St Stephen (1425–8), Lorenzo Ghiberti for the Arte della Lana (wool)

10 St Eligius (1417–21), Nanni di Banco (copy) for the Maniscalchi (smiths)

11 St Mark (1411–13), Donatello (copy) for the Linaiuoli (linen-drapers); niche (1411), Perfetto di Giovanni and Albizo di Piero

12 St James (1420) and bas relief of the Martyrdom of St James, attrib. Niccolò di Pietro Lamberti (copy) for the Pellicciai (furriers)

13 Madonna della Rosa (1400), attrib. Simone Talenti (copy) for the Medici e Speziali (doctors and pharmacists); Madonna Enthroned (above), Luca della Robbia (1465)

14 St John the Baptist (1515), Baccio da Montelupo for the Setaiuoli (silk)

pillar of the building with a patron statue, each assigned to a different guild. In the event, only one statue was produced in sixty years – a St Stephen commissioned by the *Arte della Lana*. In 1408, weary of the delay, the city elders set a ten-year deadline, warning that the niches would be allocated to rival guilds if commissions remained unfulfilled. The delay was to posterity's benefit, for the statues eventually produced spanned the emergent years of the Renaissance: sixty years earlier far lesser talents than Donatello, Ghiberti, Verrocchio and Luca della Robbia might have been expected to work on the project.

The exterior

Beginning on the far left of Orsanmichele's Via dei Calzaiuoli flank, the first tabernacle is occupied by a replica of Ghiberti's **John the Baptist (1)**, the earliest life-size bronze statue of the Renaissance. It was made for the *Calimala*, the guild of wholesale cloth importers. Doubtful whether Ghiberti could cast the figure in one piece, his cautious patrons made him liable for the cost of the metal should he fail. In the event it came out intact, except for one toe, which had to be welded on later. The adjacent niche is occupied by a replica of **The Incredulity of St Thomas (2)** by Verrocchio, which replaced an earlier gilded statue by Donatello, *St Louis of Toulouse*, now in the Museo dell'Opera del Duomo; Giambologna's **St Luke (3)** similarly replaced an earlier statue by Lamberti now in the Bargello.

Round the corner, Brunelleschi's **St Peter (4)** is followed by two works from Nanni di Banco: **St Philip (5)** and the so-called **Quattro Coronati (6)**. These four Christian stonemasons executed by Diocletian for refusing to carve a pagan idol were patron saints of the masons' guild, sponsors of this niche. Their name comes from the manner of their execution – they were killed by having an iron crown (*corona*) driven onto their heads. The bas-reliefs of architects and sculptors at work are also by Nanni: the medallion above is by Luca della Robbia. A copy of Donatello's **St George (7)** occupies the next niche – the original is in the Bargello, as is the original accompanying bas-relief of *St George and the Dragon*.

Works of special note are highlighted in green in the text and on the plan on p.165.

On the church's west side stand **St Matthew (8)** and **St Stephen (9)**, both by Ghiberti, and **St Eligius (10)** by Nanni di Banco; the *St Matthew*, posed and clad like a Roman orator, makes a telling comparison with the same artist's *St John*, cast just ten years before but still semi-Gothic in its sharp-edged drapery and arching lines. Earlier than either is Donatello's **St Mark (11)**, made in 1411 when the artist was 25; the work is often considered one of the first statues of the Renaissance, a title based on the naturalism of St Mark's stance and the brooding intensity of his gaze. A replica of Pietro Lamberti's **St James (12)** precedes a benign **Madonna della Rosa (13)**, probably by Simone Talenti. The latter was damaged in 1493 when one Signor Marrona went berserk and set about axing lumps out of every statue of the Madonna he could find. A lynch mob of Savonarola's monks caught up with him just after he'd gouged out one of the eyes of the infant Christ. The weakest of the sculptures, Baccio da Montelupo's **John the Evangelist (14)**, brings up the rear.

Nanni di Banco – the story goes – misjudged the space available for his Quattro Coronati; when only three figures would fit in the niche, he consulted his friend Donatello, who simply had his assistants file away at the saints until they squeezed in.

The interior

Orsanmichele's interior centrepiece is an unmissable pavilion-sized glass and marble **tabernacle** by Orcagna, the only significant sculptural work by the artist. Decorated with lapis lazuli and gold, it cost 86,000 florins in 1355. The iconography is obscure, but concerns salvation through the Virgin. It frames a *Madonna delle Grazie* painted in 1347 by Bernardo Daddi as a replacement for the miraculous image of the Virgin destroyed by the 1304 fire (see p.164). The brotherhood that administered Orsanmichele paid for the tabernacle from thanksgiving donations in the aftermath of the Black Death; so many people attributed their survival to the Madonna's intervention that the money received in 1348 alone was greater than the annual tax income of the city coffers. Other paintings can be seen on the pillars: devotional images of the guilds' patron saints, they were commissioned as low-cost ancestors of the Orsanmichele statues.

The original lines of the bricked-up loggia (see p.164) are still clear, while the vaulted halls of the upper granary – one of the city's most imposing medieval interiors – also survive. The halls now house the **Museo di Orsanmichele**, entered via the footbridge from the Palazzo dell'Arte della Lana, the building opposite the entrance to the church. The museum is open for tours daily (9am, 10am & 11am) except for the first and last Mondays of the month, though in practice opening times can be affected by the use of the space for temporary exhibitions. If you get the chance be sure to visit, not only for the fine interior, but also for the chance to see several of the most important original **exterior statues**. As restoration work is completed, it is planned that all the statues will eventually be exhibited here, though no one expects to wrest the most famous of all, Donatello's St George, from the clutches of the Bargello.

PALAZZO DAVANZATI

Map 4, E2. Via Porta Rossa 13. ☏055.238.8610. Currently closed.

For a re-creation of medieval Florence – indeed, one of the few places where you get any real feel for the city's medieval rather than Renaissance past – you should visit the wonderful **Palazzo Davanzati**. Built in 1330, the palazzo was divided up into flats during the nineteenth century, but at the beginning of the twentieth was restored to something close to its appearance in the 1500s. This was slightly different to its original guise, a loggia having replaced the roof's earlier battlements, and the Davanzati – who bought the house in 1578 – having stuck their coat of arms on the front. Apart from those emendations, the place now looks much as it did when first inhabited.

Today the palazzo is maintained as the **Museo della Casa Fiorentina Antica**. Most of its interior rooms are beautifully painted and graced with exquisite wooden ceilings. Where the original furniture and fittings are missing, appropriate items have been introduced from the Bargello and elsewhere.

The building was closed in late 1995 for major structural restoration. In view of the length of time that this is likely to take, a worthless photographic exhibition of the holdings of the museum is on display in the entrance hall (Tues–Sat 8.15am–1.45pm; plus fourth Mon of month; closed second and fourth Sun of month). The description that follows gives you an idea of the interior of the museum before closure.

- -

Before entering the palazzo, take in the immense amount of metalwork on the exterior, used variously for tying up animals, draping wool and washing out to dry, suspending bird cages or fixing banners, carpets and other hangings on the occasion of festivities and processions.

- -

PALAZZO DAVANZATI

The house

The palace's original owners, the Davizzi, a family of wealthy wool merchants, were obviously well prepared for the adversities of urban living: the **courtyard** has siege-resistant doors, its own water supply, and huge storerooms: fully provisioned, they provided supplies for a year. Note the rear right-hand pillar, incidentally, carved with figures said to be portraits of the Davizzi family.

The courtyard's **well** was something of a luxury at a time when much of Florence was still dependent on public fountains: a complex series of ropes and pulleys allowed it to serve the entire house. So, too, were the palace's **toilets**, state-of-the art affairs by the standards of 1330. Such arrangements were far from common: Boccaccio describes the more basic facilities of most Florentines in the *Decameron* – two planks of wood suspended over a small pit.

An ancient staircase – the only one of its kind to survive in the city – leads to the **first floor** and the Sala Grande or **Sala Madornale**. This room, used for family gatherings, underlines the dual nature of the house: furnished in the best style of the day, it also has four wood-covered hatches in the floor to allow the bombarding of a besieging enemy. Merchants' houses in the fourteenth century would typically have had elaborately painted walls in the main rooms. The Palazzo Davanzati preserves some fine examples, especially in the dining room or **Sala dei Pappagalli**, where the imitation wall hangings of the lower walls are patterned with a parrot (*pappagallo*) motif, while the upper walls depict a garden terrace.

Tapestries, ceramics, sculpture and lacework alleviate the austerity of many of the rooms, and there's a fine collection of *cassoni*, the painted chests in which the wife's dowry would be stored. Plushest of the rooms is the first-floor **bedroom**, or Sala dei Pavoni – complete with en-suite bathroom. It takes its name from the beautiful frescoed frieze of trees, peacocks (*pavoni*) and other exotic birds: the coats of arms woven into the decoration are the crests of families related to the Davizzi. The rare Sicilian linen bed cover is decorated with scenes from the story of Tristan.

The upper floors

The arrangements of the rooms on the upper two floors, together with their beautiful array of furniture and decoration, mirror that of the first floor. For all the splendour of the lower rooms, the spot where the palace's occupants would have been likeliest to linger is the third-floor **kitchen**. Located on the uppermost floor to minimize damage if a fire broke out, it would have been the warmest room in the house. A fascinating array of utensils are on show here: the *girapolenta*, the polenta-stirrer, is extraordinary. Set into one wall is a service shaft connecting the kitchen to all floors of the building. The leaded glass – like the toilets – was considered a marvel at a time when many windows were covered with turpentine-soaked rags stretched across frames to repel rainwater.

SANTA TRÌNITA

Map 4, E2. Piazza Santa Trìnita. Mon–Sat 8am–noon & 4–6pm; Sun 4–6pm; free.

The antiquity of **Santa Trìnita** is manifest in the Latinate pronunciation of its name – modern Italian stresses the last, not the first syllable. Founded in 1092, the church was rebuilt between about 1300 and 1330, work being interrupted by the plague of 1348. Further rebuilding took place between 1365 and 1405, while the facade – by Buontalenti – was added in 1594. Piecemeal additions over the years have lent the church a pleasantly hybrid air: the largely Gothic interior contrasts with the Mannerist facade, itself at odds with its Romanesque interior wall.

SANTA TRÌNITA

1 Cappella Cialli-Sernigi: Mystic Marriage of St Catherine (1390–95), Spinello Aretino
2 Cappella Bartolini-Salimbeni: Scenes from the Life of the Virgin (1420–25), Lorenzo Monaco
3 Cappella Ardinghelli: Pietà (1424), Giovanni Toscani; altar tabernacle (1505–13), Benedetto da Rovezzano
4 Passage with remnants of avelli (graves) that once lined church's flanks
5 Sacristy: tomb of Onofrio Strozzi (1425), attrib. Michelozzo
6 Cappella Sassetti: Scenes from the Life of St Francis (1483–6); Adoration of the Shepherds altarpiece (1485), Domenico Ghirlandaio
7 Cappella Doni: "Miraculous" crucifix removed from the church of San Miniato al Monte
8 Chancel
9 Cappella Scali: tomb of Benozzo Federighi (1454–7), Luca della Robbia (left wall)
10 Cappella Spini: wooden statue of Mary Magdalen (1455), Desiderio da Settignano and Benedetto da Maiano
11 Cappella Compagni: entrance arch – San Giovanni Gualberto Pardons his Brother's Murderer (1440), Lorenzo di Bicci; right wall – Annunciation; altar wall – San Giovanni Gualberto and Members of the Vallambrosan Order (1455), Neri di Bicci
12 Cappella Davanzati: altarpiece – Coronation of the Virgin and Twelve Saints (1430), Bicci di Lorenzo; left wall – Tomb of Giuliano Davanzati (d.1444), attrib. Bernardo Rossellino (includes third-century Roman sarcophagus)

GIOVANNI GUALBERTO

The church of Santa Trìnita was originally founded by a Florentine nobleman called **Giovanni Gualberto**; scenes from his life are illustrated in the frescoes in the fourth chapel of the left aisle. One Good Friday, so the story goes, Gualberto set off intent on avenging the murder of his brother. On finding the murderer he decided to spare his life – it was Good Friday – and proceeded to San Miniato (see p.203), where a crucifix is said to have bowed its head to honour his act of mercy. Giovanni went on to become a Benedictine monk and found the reforming Vallombrosan order and – notwithstanding the mayhem created on Florence's streets by his militant support-ers – was eventually canonized.

The interior

Santa Trìnita's architecture is softened by a number of works of art, the best – Domenico Ghirlandaio's **Cappella Sassetti frescoes** – as good as any in the city. Resist the temptation to head straight for these, however, and work round the church (you'll need coins to light some altars, others need only a push on the red button on the wall), beginning at the **Cappella Cialli–Sernigi (1)**. This con-tains a damaged fresco and detached *sinopia* depicting the *Mystical Marriage of St Catherine* (1389) by Spinello Aretino, recently discovered below the frescoes in the adjoining chapel.

Works of special note are highlighted in green in the text and on the plan opposite.

The next chapel, the **Cappella Bartolini–Salimbeni (2)**, is one of only a handful in the city whose decorative scheme has remained uncorrupted by subsequent additions and changes. The arresting frescoes (1420–25) of episodes from the **Life of the Virgin (2)** are by Lorenzo Monaco, who also painted its *Annunciation* altarpiece. The lunette and right wall of the next chapel, the **Cappella Ardinghelli (3)**, features Giovanni Toscani's contemporaneous frescoes of the *Pietà* (1424–25) and an unfinished altar tabernacle by Benedetto da Rovezzano (1505–13): the latter, intended for the tomb of Giovanni Gualberto, was damaged during the 1530 siege of the city.

A small **passage (4)** lined with graves, or *avelli*, is usually closed, but the adjacent sacristy, or **Cappella di Onofrio Strozzi (5)**, designed by Ghiberti between 1418 and 1423, is often open; if not, the sacristan will show you around. The main altar once held Gentile da Fabriano's majestic *Adoration of the Magi*, now in the Uffizi. To the altar's left is the tomb of Onofrio Strozzi, scion of a major banking dynasty: long thought to be the work of Donatello, the tomb is now cautiously attributed to Michelozzo. Next comes the church's highlight, the Cappella Sassetti (6) (see box opposite), while displayed in the neighbouring **Cappella Doni (7)** is the miraculous crucifix, formerly in San Miniato, said to have bowed its head to Gualberto (see p.173). The **chancel (8)** features further early fresco fragments – similar tantalizing fragments are dotted around the church. Its high altar once held another major painting now in the Uffizi – Cimabue's pioneering *Maestà*.

The third of the church's major works, a powerful composition by Luca della Robbia – the tomb of Benozzo Federighi, bishop of Fiesole (9) – occupies the left wall of the Cappella Scali; moulded and carved for the church of San Pancrazio, it was transported here in 1896. The fine wooden **statue of Mary Magdalene (10)**, which owes much to Donatello's Magdalene in the Museo dell'Opera (see p.37), was begun by Desiderio da Settignano and completed, according to Vasari, by Benedetto da Maiano.

Before leaving, various of the fifteenth-century paintings in the remaining **side chapels (11–12)** are well worth a look.

THE CAPPELLA SASSETTI

The **Cappella Sassetti** (6) is rightly famous for its cycle of frescoes of scenes from the *Life of St Francis* (1483–86) by **Domenico Ghirlandaio**. Commissioned by Francesco Sassetti, a friend of Lorenzo the Magnificent, they were intended, in part, to compete with the frescoes of Sassetti's rival, Giovanni Tornabuoni, in Santa Maria Novella, also by Ghirlandaio (see p.153). Sassetti and his wife, the chapel's donors, are buried in Giuliano da Sangallo's black tombs under the side arches.

Ghirlandaio's frescoes are concerned as much with a portrayal of fifteenth-century Florence as with the narrative of their religious themes. St Francis is shown healing a sick child in Piazza Santa Trìnita: the church of Santa Trìnita is in the background, painted as it then appeared, still with its pre-Buontalenti Gothic facade. *St Francis Receiving the Rule* (in the lunette above the altar) sets the action in Piazza della Signoria – note the Loggia della Signoria – and features (right foreground) a portrait of Sassetti between his son, Federigo, and Lorenzo the Magnificent (Sassetti was general manager of the Medici bank). On the steps below them are the humanist Poliziano and three of his pupils, Lorenzo's sons. Ghirlandaio (hand on hip) is present as a self-portrait.

Ghirlandaio also painted the chapel's altarpiece, the *Adoration of the Shepherds* (1485), a persuasive Renaissance fusion of Classical and Christian iconography. Mary and the shepherds are painted amid Classical columns, a Roman sarcophagus (used as the manger) and a triumphal arch transplanted from the Roman forum. The figures of the donors – Sassetti and his wife, Nera Corsi – kneel to either side.

Central Oltrarno

Visitors to Florence might perceive the River Arno as a simple interruption in the urban fabric, but Florentines still tend to talk as though a ravine runs through their city. North of the river is known as *Arno di quà* (over here), while the other side, hemmed in by a ridge of hills that rises a short distance from the river, is *Arno di là* (over there). More formally, it's known as the **Oltrarno** – literally "beyond the Arno" – a terminology which has its roots in medieval times, when the district was not as accessible as the numerous bridges now make it.

Traditionally an artisans' quarter, the Oltrarno has nonetheless always contained more prosperous enclaves – many of Florence's ruling families chose to settle in this area, and nowadays some of the city's plushest shops line the streets parallel to the river's southern bank. Further in, the area around Santo Spirito and Piazza del Carmine is a good place to come in the evening, as it's here you'll find some of Florence's best and trendiest **bars and restaurants**. Window-shopping, eating and drinking are not the area's sole pleasures, however, as the district also contains several of the city's key sights.

The first of these, the famous **Ponte Vecchio**, links the northern bank to the Oltrarno's central area, home to the **Palazzo Pitti**, a rambling palace complex whose cluster of museums includes the city's second-ranking picture gallery. Close by lies the **Giardino di Boboli**, Italy's most visited garden, a leafy retreat from the sightseeing. Lesser attractions include the ancient church of **Santa Felìcita**, known for one of the city's stranger paintings, and the wonderfully bizarre medical waxworks of **La Specola**.

PONTE VECCHIO

Map 4, F3

The direct route from the city centre to the heart of the Oltrarno crosses the Arno via the **Ponte Vecchio**, the last in a line of bridges at the river's narrowest point that stretches back to Etruscan and Roman times. Some believe that this was the bridging point for the Via Cassia, the principal consular road between Rome and the north, while others maintain that the Roman crossing was a touch further upstream. Until 1218 the crossing here was the city's only bridge, though the version you see today dates from 1345, built to replace a wooden bridge swept away by floods twelve years earlier. The name, which means the "Old Bridge", was coined to distinguish it from the Ponte alla Carraia, built in 1218. Over its arcades stalks Vasari's concealed passageway (see p.73), commissioned by the Medicis in 1565 to allow them to pass unobserved from the Palazzo Vecchio to the Palazzo Pitti.

Much later in its history the Ponte Vecchio was the only bridge not mined by the Nazis in 1944 as they retreated before the advancing American 5th Army – Field Marshal Kesselring is said to have spared it on Hitler's express orders. Much of the rest of the city, including medieval quarters at either end of the bridge, was not so lucky, chiefly because the Nazis reneged on a promise to spare the city (as had happened in Rome), blowing up swathes of old buildings to hamper the Allied advance.

The bridge's present-day shops and hawkers can come as a shock, but the Ponte Vecchio has always been loaded with stores like those now propped over the water. Their earliest inhabitants were butchers and fishmongers, attracted to the site by the proximity of the river, which provided a convenient dumping ground for their waste. Next came the tanners, who used the river to soak their hides before tanning them with horses' urine. The current plethora of jewellers dates from 1593, when Ferdinando I evicted the butchers' stalls and other practitioners of what he called "vile arts". In their place he installed eight jewellers and 41 **goldsmiths**, also taking the opportunity to double the rents. Florence had long revered the art of the goldsmith, and several of its major artists were skilled in the craft: Ghiberti, Donatello and Cellini, for example. The third of the trio is celebrated by a bust (1900) in the centre of the bridge, the night-time meeting point for Florence's unreconstructed hippies and local lads on the make.

SANTA FELÌCITA

Map 2, D9. Piazza Santa Felìcita. Mon–Sat 9am–noon & 3–6pm; free.

Santa Felìcita is probably the oldest church in Florence, possibly founded in the second century by Greek or Syrian merchants, pioneers of Christianity in the city. It was built over an early Christian cemetery – commemorated by a column (1381) in Piazza della Felìcita – and close to the Roman Via Cassia. It's known for certain that a church existed on the site by the fifth century – a tombstone dated 405 has been found nearby – by which time it had been dedicated to St Felicity, an early Roman martyr. New churches were built on the site in the eleventh and fourteenth centuries, while in 1565 Vasari added an elaborate portico to accommodate the *corridoio* (see p.73) linking the Uffizi and Palazzo Pitti; a window from the corridor looks directly into the church. All but the facade was extensively remodelled between 1736 and 1739.

St Felicity is often shown in Renaissance paintings with her seven sons, each of whom was executed in front of her for refusing to renounce his faith. The saint herself was either beheaded or thrown into boiling oil.

The interior demands a visit for the **Cappella Capponi**, and the paintings of Pontormo in particular, which lie to the right of the main door surrounded by irritating railings. The chapel was designed in the 1420s by Brunelleschi, but subsequently much altered. Under the cupola are four tondi of the *Evangelists* (Bronzino probably supplied the *St Mark*), while on opposite sides of the window on the right wall are the Virgin and the angel of Pontormo's delightfully simple *Annunciation*, the arrangement alluding to the Incarnation as the means by which the Light came into the world.

The low level of actual light admitted by this window was one of the determining factors in the startling colour scheme of the weirdly erotic **Deposition** (1525–28) above the chapel's main altar, one of the masterworks of Florentine Mannerism. Electric lighting now floods the picture, but it will cost you a L1000 coin (or – eventually – the euro equivalent). Nothing here, in the words of one critic, is either "natural" or "ordinary". Thus there's no sign of the cross, the thieves, Roman soldiers or any of the other scene-setting devices usual in paintings of this subject. The sole background detail is a solitary ghostly cloud, while only the body of Christ is realistically coloured: the figures carrying his body, borne like a mournful trophy, are androgynous figures clad in billows of acidic sky-blue, puce

SANTA FELÌCITA

green and candy-floss pink drapery. The brown-cloaked figure on the extreme right is believed to be a self-portrait of the artist.

JACOPO PONTORMO

Born near Empoli, **Jacopo Pontormo** (1494–1556) studied under Andrea del Sarto in Florence in the early 1510s. His early independent works include the frescoes in the atrium of Santissima Annunziata in Florence, which have an edgy quality quite unlike that of his master. In the 1520s he was hired by the Medici to decorate part of their villa at Poggio a Caiano, after which he executed a *Passion* cycle for the Certosa, to the south of the city. His masterpiece in Florence is the *Deposition* in Santa Felicita (1525–28) – though the figures show a debt to Michelangelo's figures, the lurid colour scheme is unprecedented. The major project of his later years, a fresco cycle in San Lorenzo, has been totally destroyed, though some of his other paintings can be seen in the Uffizi.

Pontormo was a crucial figure in the evolution of the hyper-refined Mannerist style. The artist himself was every bit as strange as his bizarre *Deposition* suggests. A relentless hypochondriac – his diary is a tally of the state of his kidneys, bowel disorders and other assorted ailments – he seems to have found the company of others almost intolerable, spending much of his time in a top-floor room that could be reached only by a ladder, which he drew up behind him. So eccentric was his behaviour that he was virtually mythologized by his contemporaries. One writer attributed to him an all-consuming terror of death and called his room a "beast's lair", while another insisted that he kept corpses in a tub as models for a *Deluge* that he was painting – an antisocial research project that allegedly brought protests from the neighbours.

PALAZZO PITTI

Map 4, E5.

Beyond Santa Felìcita, the street opens out at Piazza Pitti, forecourt of the largest and most outrageously rusticated palace in Florence – the **Palazzo Pitti**. Banker and merchant Luca Pitti commissioned the palace to outdo his rivals, the Medici. Work started around 1457, possibly using a design by Brunelleschi which had been rejected by Cosimo de' Medici for being too grand. No sooner was the palace completed, however, than the Pitti's fortunes began to decline. By 1549 they were forced – ironically – to sell out to the Medici. The Pitti subsequently became the Medici's base in Florence, growing in bulk until the seventeenth century, when it achieved its present gargantuan proportions. Later, during Florence's brief tenure as the Italian capital between 1865 and 1871, it housed the Italian kings.

Today the Palazzo Pitti and the pavilions of the Giardino di Boboli (see p.186) contain eight museums, of which the foremost is the **Galleria Palatina**, an art collection second in importance only to the Uffizi. Separate tickets are required for the Galleria and **Museo degli Argenti**, the most compelling of the palace's collections, and for the **Galleria d'Arte Moderna** – these tickets, however, cover entry into other museums in the complex.

The Pitti is a building with notorious operational problems, so be prepared to find some parts closed when you visit.

The Galleria Palatina and Appartamenti Reali

Tues–Sat 8.15am–6.50pm, Sun 8.15am–1.50pm; ticket office shuts 45min before closing; L12,000/€6.20, including admission to the Appartamenti Reali.

Many of the paintings gathered by the Medici in the seventeenth century are now arranged in the **Galleria Palatina**, a suite of 29 rooms on the first floor of one wing of the palace. The ticket office and the grand staircase leading up to the gallery both lie off the main courtyard to the rear of the palace. Beyond the huge chandelier at the head of the stairs, the first two rooms – which have wonderful views – lead into two parallel suites of six rooms. If you want to head for the meat of the collection, walk straight to the end of the first section, then turn left and back down the parallel row of state rooms. It's here that you'll find the gallery's eleven paintings by **Raphael**, as well as the fourteen **Titians**.

The pictures are not arranged in the sort of didactic order observed by most galleries but hung as they would have been in the days of their acquisition, three deep in places, with the aim of making each room pleasurably varied. The best thing to do is wander at random until a picture takes your fancy. The big names just keep on coming, and the highlights are many, so you'll need the best part of a morning to see the collection properly.

The current itinerary takes you straight through into the suite containing mostly less famous works, though some individual paintings are well worth seeking out, including **Fra' Bartolomeo**'s *Deposition;* a tondo of the *Madonna and Child* (1452) by **Filippo Lippi**, in the Sala Prometeo; his son Filippino's *Death of Lucrezia,* in the next room; and, in the Sala dell' Educazione di Giove, a *Sleeping Cupid* (1608), by **Caravaggio**, and Cristofano Allori's sexy **Judith and Holofernes**. This last work was one of Italy's most universally admired seventeenth-century paintings, though few executions, actual or pictorial, can have been quite so bloodless, and few of the protagonists at such events so immaculately attired and coiffured. Allori himself, his mother and his mistress provided the models for the picture's principal characters. Two corridors lead off to the right of this section: the Corridoio del Volterrano houses mainly Florentine works of the seventeenth century, while the Corridoio dell Colonna has a Flemish theme.

In the second, more captivating part of the gallery, **Andrea del Sarto**, a contemporary of Raphael, is represented in strength, his seventeen works including a beautifully grave *Annunciation*. At the time of writing, many of **Raphael**'s paintings were hung in the Sala delle Nicchie, the last room of all, but following restoration work they should return to the Sala Saturno, the second of the major state rooms as you return towards the entrance staircase.

When Raphael settled in Florence in 1505, he was besieged with commissions from patrons delighted to find an artist for whom the creative process involved so little agonizing. In the next three years he painted scores of pictures for such people as Angelo Doni, the man who commissioned Michelangelo's *Doni Tondo*, now in the Uffizi. Raphael's portraits of Doni and his wife, Maddalena (1506–7), display an unhesitating facility and perfect poise; if the Maddalena's pose looks familiar, incidentally, it's because it's copied directly from Leonardo's *Mona Lisa*.

Similar poise illuminates Raphael's splendidly framed 1515 *Madonna della Seggiola*, or Madonna of the Chair, in which the figures are curved into the rounded shape of the picture with no sense of artificiality. The curve was deliberate, creating the effect of a distorting convex mirror, one of the first conscious uses of illusionism in Renaissance painting. The painting's round panel, or tondo, is said to have come from the bottom of a wine barrel. For centuries this was Italy's most popular image of the Virgin; nineteenth-century copyists had to join a five-year waiting list to study the picture.

La Gravida (1504–8), in the Sala dell'Iliade, shows Raphael in earthier vein; it's a rare work which tentatively portrays the pregnant bulge of an expectant mother. According to Vasari, the model for the famous *Donna Velata*, or Veiled Woman (1516), in the Sala di Giove, was a Roman baker's daughter and the painter's mistress.

If you're puzzled by the sudden appearance of Elizabeth I of England in the Sala dell'Iliade, it's because the Medici tried at one time to collect portraits of all the crowned heads of Europe.

Most of the paintings by the Venetian artist, **Titian**, are found in the Sala Venere, the penultimate room. These include a number of his most trenchant portraits. The lecherous and scurrilous Pietro Aretino – journalist, critic, poet and one of Titian's closest friends – was so thrilled by his 1545 portrait that he gave it to Cosimo I; Titian painted him on several other occasions, sometimes using him as the model for Pontius Pilate. Also here are likenesses of Philip II of Spain and the young Cardinal Ippolito de' Medici (1532) – who fought in the defence of Vienna against the Ottomans only to be poisoned at the age of 24 – and the so-called *Portrait of an Englishman* (1540), who scrutinizes the viewer with unflinching sea-grey eyes. To his left, by way of contrast, is the same artist's sensuous and much-copied *Mary Magdalene* (1531), the first of a series on this theme produced for the Duke of Urbino. In the same room, look out for Rosso Fiorentino's recently restored *Madonna Enthroned with Saints* (1522), and the gallery's outstanding sculpture, Canova's *Venus Italica*, commissioned by Napoleon as a replacement for the Venus de' Medici, which he had whisked off to Paris.

Much of the rest of the Pitti's first floor comprises the **Appartamenti Reali**, the Pitti's state rooms. They were renovated by the dukes of Lorraine in the eighteenth century, and then by Vittorio Emanuele when Florence became the country's capital, so the rooms display three distinct decorative phases. The gallery leads straight through into the apartments, and after Raphael and Titian it can be difficult to sustain a great deal of enthusiasm for such ducal elegance, for all the sumptuousness of the furnishings.

The other museums

Galleria d'Arte Moderna & Galleria dell Costume: Tues–Sat 8.15am–1.50pm (plus first, third & fifth Sun, and second & fourth Mon of each month); joint ticket L8000/€4.13. Museo degli Argenti: same hours; L4000/€2.07, or more during exhibitions. Ticket office shuts 45min before closing.

On the floor above the Palatina is the **Galleria d'Arte Moderna**, a chronological survey of primarily Tuscan art from the mid-eighteenth century to 1945. Most rewarding are the products of the *Macchiaioli*, the Italian division of the Impressionist movement; most startling, however, are the sculptures, featuring sublime kitsch such as Antonio Ciseri's *Pregnant Nun*.

The Pitti's **Museo degli Argenti**, entered from the main palace courtyard, is a museum not just of silverware – as its name implies – but of luxury artefacts in general. The lavishly frescoed reception rooms themselves fall into this category: the first hall, the Sala di Giovanni di San Giovanni, shows Lorenzo de' Medici giving refuge to the Muses; the other three ceremonial rooms have trompe l'oeil paintings by seventeenth-century Bolognese artists. As for the exhibits, the least ambivalent response is likely to be aroused by Lorenzo the Magnificent's trove of antique vases, all of them marked with their owner's name. The later the date of the pieces, though, the greater the discordance between the skill of the craftsman and the taste by which it was governed; by the time you reach the end of the jewellery show on the first floor, you'll have lost all capacity to be surprised or revolted by seashell figurines, cups made from ostrich eggs, portraits in stone inlay, and the like. Exhibitions are sometimes held here, which can affect the ticket price and opening hours.

Visitors without a specialist interest are unlikely to be riveted by the two remaining museums currently open. In the Palazzina della Meridiana, the eighteenth-century southern wing of the Pitti, the **Galleria del Costume** provides the opportunity to see the dress that Eleonora di Toledo was buried in, though you can admire it easily enough in Bronzino's portrait of her in the Palazzo Vecchio (see p.51). Also housed in the Meridiana is the **Collezione Contini Bonacossi** (free tours usually Thurs & Sat 9.45am – appointments have to be made a week before at the Uffizi, ☎055.23.885), on long-term loan to the Pitti. Its prize pieces are its Spanish paintings, in particular Velázquez's *Water Carrier of Seville*.

The well presented but dull **Museo delle Porcellane**, or Porcelain Museum, on the other side of the Boboli Garden, is currently closed for restoration (normally open Tues–Sun 9am–1.30pm; L4000/€2.07), while the **Museo delle Carrozze** (Carriage Museum) has been closed for years and, despite what the Pitti handouts tell you, will almost certainly remain so for years, to the chagrin of very few.

GIARDINO DI BOBOLI

Map 4, E5. Piazza Pitti. Daily: March–May 8.15am–5.30pm; June–Aug 8.15am–7.30pm; Sept & Oct 8.15am–6.30pm; Nov–Feb 8.15am–4.30pm; sometimes closes an hour early in bad weather; L4000/€2.07.

The delightful formal gardens at **Boboli** were once a quarry; the bedrock of the hillside here is one of the sources of the yellow, limey sandstone known as *pietra forte* (strong stone) that colours much of Florence. Much of the quarry's output didn't have to travel far: carefully shaped into a rough, boulder-like texture, the stones from Boboli were used to "rusticate" Palazzo Pitti's great facade. When the Medici acquired the house in 1549 they set to work transforming their back yard into an enormous 111-acre garden, its every statue, view and grotto designed to elevate "Nature" by the judicious application of "Art" – in the proper Renaissance manner.

The garden takes its name from the Boboli or Bobolini family, erstwhile owners of some of the surrounding land. Work continued into the early seventeenth century, by which stage this steep hillside had been turned into a maze of statue-strewn avenues and well trimmed vegetation. Opened to the public in 1766, it is the only really extensive area of accessible greenery in the centre of the city, and can be one of the pleasantest spots for a midday picnic or siesta. Some five million visitors annually, more than at any other Italian garden, take time out here. There's a café (the *Kaffeehaus*) with a panoramic view in the garden, but it's probably nicer to bring a picnic.

Aligned with the central block of the palazzo, the garden's **amphitheatre** was designed in the early seventeenth century as an arena for Medici entertainments. The site had previously been laid out by Ammannati in 1599 over an earlier stone quarry as a garden in the shape of a Roman circus. For the wedding of Cosimo III and Princess Marguerite-Louise, cousin of Louis XIV, twenty thousand guests were packed onto the stone benches to watch a production that began with the appearance of a gigantic effigy of Atlas with the globe on his back; the show got under way when the planet split apart, releasing a cascade of earth that transformed the giant into the Atlas mountain. Such frivolities did little to reconcile Marguerite-Louise to either Florence or her husband, and after several acrimonious

GIARDINO DI BOBOLI

years this miserable dynastic marriage came to an effective end with her return to Paris, where she professed to care about little "as long as I never have to set eyes on the grand duke again".

Of all the garden's Mannerist embellishments, the most celebrated is the **Grotta del Buontalenti** (1583–88), to the left of the entrance, beyond Giambologna's hideous and much-reproduced statue of Cosimo I's favourite dwarf astride a giant tortoise. Embedded in the grotto's faked stalactites and encrustations are replicas of Michelangelo's *Slaves* – the originals were lodged here until 1908. Lurking in the deepest recesses of the cave, and normally viewable only from afar, is Giambologna's lascivious *Venus Emerging from her Bath*, leered at by attendant imps.

Another spectacular set piece is the fountain island called the **Isolotto**, which is the focal point of the far end of the garden; from within the Boboli the most dramatic approach is along the central cypress avenue known as the **Viottolone**, many of whose statues are Roman originals. These lower parts of the garden are its most pleasant – and least visited – sections. You come upon them quickly if you enter the Boboli by the Porta Romana entrance, a little-used gate at the garden's southwestern tip. Birdwatchers might sample the special nature trail, laid out in 1994. Until 1772 the garden's wooded thickets were used for netting small birds for the Medici dinner table.

LA SPECOLA

Map 4, C6. Via Romana 17. Daily 9am–1pm, closed Wed; L6000/€3.10.

La Specola can reasonably claim to be the strangest museum in the city. A twin-sectioned museum of zoology, its popular name derives from the telescope (*specola*) on the roof. The first section is conventional enough, a mortician's ark of animals stuffed, pickled, desiccated and dissected. It includes a hippo given to Grand Duke Pietro Leopardo, which used to reside in the Boboli garden, and finishes with a display of wax models of animals and human joints.

This is a hint at what lies behind the door of the section called the **Cere Anatomiche** (Tues & Sat 9am–noon; closed Aug; free). Wax arms, legs and organs cover the walls, arrayed around satin beds on which wax cadavers recline in progressive stages of deconstruction, each muscle fibre and nerve cluster moulded and dyed with absolute precision. Most of the six hundred models were made between 1775 and 1814 by the artist Clemente Susini and the physiologist Felice Fontana, and were intended as teaching aids.

In a room on their own, however, are some **models** created by one Gaetano Zumbo, a cleric from Sicily, to satisfy the hypochondriacal obsessions of Cosimo III, a Jesuit-indoctrinated bigot who regarded all genuine scientific enquiry with suspicion. Enclosed in tasteful display cabinets, they comprise four tableaux of Florence during the plague – rats teasing the intestines from green-fleshed corpses, mushrooms growing from the mulch of fleshly debris, and the pink bodies of the freshly dead heaped on the suppurating semi-decomposed. The grisliest show in town, it's a firm favourite with school parties.

In 1883 poet Henry Longfellow wrote with relish of the Cere Anatomiche's "loathsome corpses... their blackening, the bursting of the trunk, the worm, the rat..."

Western Oltrarno

T he western Oltrarno is one of the city's earthier, more traditional districts. In recent years, though, it's been steadily colonized by the type of new bars, restaurants and shops that often spring up in previously low-rent working-class areas, providing a south-of-the-river equivalent of the lively area around Sant' Ambrogio. The area also houses one of the seminal works of the Florentine Renaissance: the famous fresco cycle in the church of Santa Maria del Carmine's Cappella Brancacci.

Some indication of the importance of the parish of **Santo Spirito**, the district's social and geographical heart, is given by the fact that when Florence was divided into four administrative *quartieri* in the fourteenth century, the entire area south of the Arno was given its name. The slightly run-down but busy Piazza Santo Spirito in front of Santo Spirito church, with its market stalls, cafés and restaurants, encapsulates the self-sufficient character of this part of the Oltrarno, an area not hopelessly compromised by the encroachments of tourism.

SANTO SPIRITO

Map 4, D4. Piazza Santo Spirito. Mon–Sat 8.30am–noon & 4–6pm (Wed 8am–noon only); free.

Designed in 1434 as a replacement for a thirteenth-century church, **Santo Spirito** was one of Brunelleschi's last projects, a swansong later described by Bernini as "the most beautiful church in the world". Many have concurred since, though the interior's measured monochrome of grey pietra serena and off-white *intaco* (plaster) can seem a trifle severe to modern eyes. Relief can be sought in the church's many chapels, however, nearly all of which are adorned by lavishly bright altar paintings.

Work on the church began in 1444, but only a single column had been raised by the time the architect died just two years later. Brunelleschi had wanted the church to enjoy an uninterrupted view of the Arno, but was thwarted by the aristocratic families whose homes would have to have been demolished. Many of the same families helped pay for the church, however, whose chief source of income was sponsorship of its many side chapels (see below). One Frescobaldi aristocrat donated 1000 florins, a huge sum at the time, as long as "no coat of arms other than that of the Frescobaldi were placed in the sepulchre" of his chapel. Funds were supplemented in more modest fashion by Augustinian monks from the neighbouring monastery, who sacrificed a meal a day as a money-raising example to others.

The church is so perfectly proportioned that nothing could seem more artless. Yet the plan is extremely sophisticated: a Latin cross with a continuous chain of 38 chapels round the outside and a line of 35 columns running without a break round the nave, transepts and chancel. The exterior wall was originally designed to follow the curves of the chapels' walls, creating a flowing, corrugated effect. As built, however, the exterior is a plain, straight wall, and even the main facade remained incomplete, disguised today by a simple plastering job. Inside the church, only the Baroque baldachin, about as nicely integrated as a garden gnome in a Greek temple, disrupts the harmony.

SANTO SPIRITO

●

A fire in 1471 destroyed most of Santo Spirito's medieval works, including famed frescoes by Cimabue and the Gaddi family, but as a result, the altar paintings in the many chapels comprise an unusually unified collection of religious works, most having been commissioned in the aftermath of the fire. For the first time, single painted panels replaced the gaudier medieval polyptychs, and there was a new emphasis on the so-called *Sacra Conversazione*, representing the Madonna and child surrounded by saints, each apparently lost in private meditation. Most prolific among the artists is the so-called **Maestro di Santo Spirito**, but some of the best paintings are found in the transepts.

In the south transept is Filippino Lippi's so-called **Nerli Altarpiece**, an age-darkened Madonna and Child with saints (second chapel from the left of the four chapels on the transept's south wall). The Nerli were the family who commissioned the chapel and the painting, the donors Tanai and Nanna dei Nerli being portrayed amidst the latter's saints: their Florentine home, the Palazzo dei Nerli near Porta San Frediano, is depicted in the background.

Across the church, in the north transept, is an unusual **St Monica and Augustinian Nuns** (1460–70), probably by Verrocchio or Francesco Botticini, that's virtually a study in monochrome, with black-clad nuns flocking round their black-clad paragon; it's in the second chapel on the right wall as you stand with your back to the high altar. Two chapels to the left, on the facing wall, the Cappella Corbinelli features a fine sculpted altarpiece (1492) by the young Andrea Sansovino.

A door in the north aisle leads through to Giuliano da Sangallo's stunning vestibule and **sacristy** (1489–93), the latter designed in conscious imitation of Brunelleschi's Pazzi chapel, though it would be impossible to build an octagonal chapel in Florence without thinking of the Baptistery. The meticulously planned proportions and soft grey and white tones create an atmosphere of extraordinary calm that is only disrupted by the exuberantly botanical carvings of the capitals, some of which were designed by Sansovino. Hanging above the altar is a wooden crucifix, attributed to **Michelangelo**. With its distinctive, tenderly feminized body, its existence had long been documented, but it was feared lost until discovered in Santo Spirito in 1963. For years it festered in the Casa Buonarotti until it was restored and returned to Santo Spirito in December 2000.

A glass door at the far end of the vestibule, usually locked, gives out onto the **Chiostro dei Morti**, the only cloister in the complex that is still part of the Augustinian monastery. The 1471 fire destroyed much of the rest of the monastery, with the exception of its refectory (entered to the left of the main church at Piazza Santo Spirito 29), which is now the home of the **Cenacolo di Santo Spirito** (Tues–Sat 9am–2pm, Sun 8am–1pm; L4000/€2.07). It's a one-room collection comprising an assortment of carvings, many of them Romanesque, and a huge fresco of *The Crucifixion* (1365) by Orcagna and his workshop.

CAPPELLA BRANCACCI

Map 4, B4. Piazza del Carmine. Mon & Wed–Sat 10am–4.30pm, Sun 1–4.30pm; L6000/€3.10.

Nowhere is the Florentine contrast of exterior and interior as stunning as in the plain brick box of **Santa Maria del Carmine**, a couple of blocks west of Santo Spirito in Piazza del Carmine. Outside it's a bleak mess; inside – in the frescoes of the separately entered **Cappella Brancacci** – it provides one of Italy's great artistic thrills. The **frescoes**, begun in the early fifteenth century by Masolino and Masaccio and completed towards its close by Filippino Lippi, are now as startling a spectacle as the restored Sistine

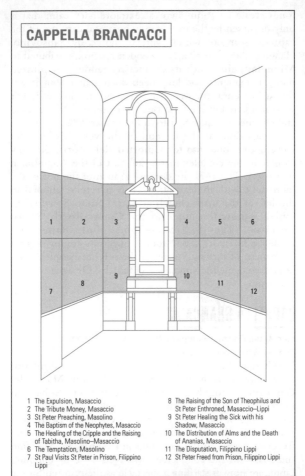

CAPPELLA BRANCACCI

1 The Expulsion, Masaccio
2 The Tribute Money, Masaccio
3 St Peter Preaching, Masolino
4 The Baptism of the Neophytes, Masaccio
5 The Healing of the Cripple and the Raising
   of Tabitha, Masolino–Masaccio
6 The Temptation, Masolino
7 St Paul Visits St Peter in Prison, Filippino
   Lippi
8 The Raising of the Son of Theophilus and
   St Peter Enthroned, Masaccio–Lippi
9 St Peter Healing the Sick with his
   Shadow, Masaccio
10 The Distribution of Alms and the Death
   of Ananias, Masaccio
11 The Disputation, Filippino Lippi
12 St Peter Freed from Prison, Filippino Lippi

Chapel, the brightness and delicacy of their colours and the solidity of the figures exemplifying what Bernard Berenson singled out as the "tactile quality" of Florentine art.

The Cappella Brancacci is barricaded off from the rest of the Carmine, and has to be entered through the cloister to the right of the main church entrance. Officially, you are allowed into the chapel, in a maximum group of thirty, for just fifteen minutes.

The small scene on the left of the entrance arch is the quintessence of Masaccio's art. Plenty of artists had depicted **The Expulsion of Adam and Eve (1)** before, but none had captured the desolation of the sinners so graphically: Adam presses his hands to his face in bottomless despair, Eve raises her head and screams. The monumentalism of these stark naked figures – whose modesty was preserved by strategically placed sprigs of foliage prior to the restoration – reveals the influence of Donatello, who may have been involved in the planning of the chapel. In contrast to the emotional charge and sculptural presence of Masaccio's couple, Masolino's almost dainty **Adam and Eve (6)**, on the opposite arch, pose as if to have their portraits painted.

St Peter is chief protagonist of all the remaining scenes. It's possible that the cycle was intended as propaganda on behalf of the embattled papacy, which had only recently resolved the long and bitter schism during which one pope held court in Rome and another in Avignon. By celebrating the primacy of St Peter, the rock upon whom the Church is built, the frescoes by implication extol the apostolic succession from which the pope derives his authority.

Three scenes by Masaccio are especially compelling. First off is the **Tribute Money (2)**, most widely praised of the paintings and the Renaissance's first monumental fresco. The narrative is complex, with no fewer than three separate

CAPPELLA BRANCACCI

THE BRANCACCI FRESCOES

The **Brancacci Chapel** frescoes were commissioned in 1424 by Felice Brancacci, a silk merchant and leading patrician figure, shortly after his return from a stint in Egypt as the Florentine ambassador. The decoration of the chapel was begun in the same year by **Masolino** (1383–1447), fresh from working as an assistant to Lorenzo Ghiberti on the Baptistery doors. Alongside Masolino was Tommaso di Ser Giovanni di Mone Cassai – known ever since as **Masaccio** (1401–28), a nickname meaning "Mad Tom". The former was aged 41, the latter just 22.

Two years into the project Masolino was recalled to Budapest, where he was official painter to the Hungarian court. Left to his own devices Masaccio began to blossom. When Masolino returned in 1427 the teacher was soon taking lessons from the supposed pupil, whose grasp of the texture of the real world, of the principles of perspective and of the dramatic potential of the biblical texts they were illustrating far exceeded that of his precursors. In 1428 Masolino was called away to Rome, where he was followed by Masaccio a few months later. Neither would return to the chapel.

Masaccio died the same year, aged just 28, but, in the words of Vasari, "All the most celebrated sculptors and painters since Masaccio's day have become excellent and illustrious by studying their art in this chapel." Michelangelo used to come here to make drawings of Masaccio's scenes, and had his nose broken on the chapel steps by a young

events portrayed within a single frame. The central episode shows Christ outside the gates of Capernaum being asked to pay a tribute owing to the city. To the left, St Peter fetches coins from the mouth of a fish in order to pay the tribute, Christ in the central panel having pointed to where

sculptor whom he enraged with his condescension. Any thought of further work on the frescoes ceased after 1436, when Brancacci (married to the daughter of Palla Strozzi, leader of the city's anti-Medici faction) was exiled by Cosimo de' Medici. The Carmelite monks in charge of the chapel and its frescoes had all portraits and other references to the disgraced donor quietly removed.

Work resumed between 1480 and 1485, some fifty years later, when the paintings were completed by **Filippino Lippi**. So accomplished were Lippi's copying skills that his work was only recognized as distinct from that of his predecessors in 1838. By then public taste had performed an about-face; back in the late seventeenth century, it had been seriously proposed that the frescoes with their "ridiculous men in their cassocks and old-fashioned outfits" be removed. That suggestion was overruled, but approval was given for building alterations that destroyed frescoes in the lunettes above the main scenes. The surviving scenes were blurred by smoke from a fire that destroyed much of the church and adjoining convent in 1771, and subsequent varnishings smothered them in layers of grime that continued to darken over the decades. When critic Bernard Berenson saw the frescoes in 1930 he described them as "dust-bitten and ruined". Then, in 1932, an art historian removed part of the altar that had been installed in the eighteenth century, and discovered areas of almost pristine paint; half a century later, work finally got under way to restore the chapel to the condition of the uncovered patch.

the money will be found. The third scene, to the right, depicts Peter handing over the money to the tax official.

Masaccio's second great panel is **St Peter Healing the Sick (9)**, in which the shadow of the stern and self-possessed saint (followed by St John) cures the infirm as it passes over them, a miracle invested with the aura of a solemn ceremonial. The third panel is **The Distribution of Alms and Death of Ananias (10)**, in which St Peter instructs the people to give up their possessions to the poor. One individual, Ananias, retains some of his wealth with the knowledge of his wife, Sapphira. Rebuked by Peter, Ananias dies on the spot, closely followed by a similarly castigated Sapphira.

Filippino Lippi's work included the finishing of Masaccio's **Raising of Theophilus's Son and St Peter Enthroned (8)**, which depicts St Peter raising the son of Theophilus, the Prefect of Antioch (apparently after he'd been dead for fourteen years). The people of Antioch, suitably impressed by the miracle, build a throne from which St Peter can preach, shown as a separate episode to the right. The three figures to the right of the throne are thought to be portraits of Masaccio, Alberti and Brunelleschi, who made a trip to Rome together. Masaccio originally painted himself touching Peter's robe, a reference to the enthroned statue of Peter in Rome, which pilgrims touch for good luck. Lippi considered the contact of the artist and saint to be improper and painted out the arm; at the moment, his fastidious over-painting has been allowed to remain, but you can clearly see where the arm used to be.

Lippi left another portrait in the combined scene of **St Peter before Agrippa** (or Nero) and his crucifixion **(11)**: the central figure looking out from the painting in the trio right of the crucifixion is Botticelli, the painter's teacher, while Filippino himself can be seen at the far right.

Eastern Oltrarno

O n the tourist map of Florence, the **eastern Oltrarno** immediately beyond the Ponte Vecchio is something of a dead zone: as on the opposite bank of the river, blocks of historic buildings were destroyed by mines left behind by the Nazis in 1944. Some characterful parts remain, however, notably the medieval Via de' Bardi and its continuation, Via San Niccolò. These narrow, palazzo-lined streets will take you past the eclectic **Museo Bardini** and the medieval church of **San Niccolò**, both perhaps best visited as part of the walk up to **San Miniato al Monte**, widely regarded as one of the most beautiful Romanesque churches in Tuscany. En route you'll pass the entrance to the **Forte di Belvedere**, a late Medici fortress now used mainly for temporary exhibitions and with some fine views of the city.

MUSEO BARDINI

Map 4, H5. Piazza de' Mozzi 1 ⓣ055.234.2427. Currently closed for restoration.

The **Museo Bardini** is one of Florence's more undervalued museums, and well worth a visit if you've still time after seeing the city's big-name galleries. It was closed for restoration at the time of writing but may reopen during the lifetime of this edition. The best way to reach it from the Ponte Vecchio and elsewhere in the Oltrarno is to take Via de' Bardi, known in the Middle Ages as the Borgo Pitiglioso – the "miserable" or "flea-bitten" street. Part way down the street on the left, beyond the small Piazza di Santa Maria Soprarno, you'll pass the tiny church of **Santa Lucia dei Magnoli**, founded in 1078: pop inside if you're lucky enough to find it open; the first altar on the left has a panel of *St Lucy* by the Sienese master, Pietro Lorenzetti. The Bardini itself stands in the piazza at the end of the street.

Like the Museo Horne just across the Arno (see p.105), this museum was built around the bequest of a private collector. Whereas Horne was a moderately well off connoisseur, however, his contemporary Sergio Bardini (1836–1922) was once the largest art dealer in Italy. His tireless activity, at a time when Renaissance art was relatively cheap and unfashionable, laid the cornerstone of many important modern-day European and North American collections. Determined that no visitor to his native city should remain unaware of his success, he ripped down a church that stood on the site and built a vast home, studding it with fragments of old buildings. Doorways, ceiling panels and other orphaned pieces are strewn all over the place: the first-floor windows, for instance, are actually altars from a church in Pistoia. The more portable items are equally wide-ranging: musical instruments, carvings, ceramics, armour, furniture, carpets, pictures – if it was vaguely arty and had a price tag, Bardini snapped it up. His artistic pot-pourri was bequeathed to the city on his death.

The museum

The Bardini may lack genuine masterpieces, but it's a far larger and more satisfying museum than the Museo Horne:

it's also crammed with a sufficiently wide variety of beautiful objects to appeal to most tastes. Displays spread over a couple of floors and some twenty numbered rooms, though only the more precious exhibits are fully labelled.

On the ground floor, beyond the open-plan spread of rooms in the vestibule, Tino da Camaino's *Charity* (Room 7) stands out. In Room 10, up the stairs past the first landing, there's a room of funerary monuments arranged as if in a crypt, with an enamelled terracotta altarpiece attributed to Andrea della Robbia. On the first floor, beyond several rooms of weapons, three pieces in Room 14 grab the attention: a polychrome terracotta of the *Madonna and Child* by Donatello; an extraordinarily modern-looking stucco, mosaic and glass relief of the *Madonna dei Cordai* (1443), also probably by Donatello; and a terracotta *Madonna and Child with San Giovannino* by Benedetto da Maiano. Room 16 has some lovely *cassoni*, or medieval chests, and several of the museum's many depictions of the Madonna and Child, a subject with which Bardini appears to have been obsessed.

Other highlights of the final rooms include some gorgeous carpets and Domenico Beccafumi's *Hercules at the Crossroads between Vice and Virtue* (Room 15); Michele Giambono's *St John the Baptist* (Room 16); a painted relief in terracotta from the workshop of Jacopo della Quercia (Room 17); a *St Michael* by Antonio del Pollaiuolo and a beautiful terracotta *Virgin Annunciate*, an anonymous piece from fifteenth-century Siena (Room 18).

SAN NICCOLÒ AND PIAZZALE MICHELANGELO

Beyond the Bardini museum, Via San Niccolò swings towards the **Forte di Belvedere** past **San Niccolò sopr'Arno (Map 4, I6)**, another of this quarter's interesting little churches. Restoration work after the 1966 flood uncovered several frescoes underneath the altars, but none is as appealing as the fifteenth-century fresco in the sacristy; known as *The Madonna of the Girdle*, it was probably painted by Baldovinetti.

In medieval times the church was close to the edge of the city, and two of Florence's fourteenth-century gates still stand in the vicinity: the dinky **Porta San Miniato (Map 4, J6)**, set in a portion of the walls, and the huge **Porta San Niccolò (Map 4, K6)**, overlooking the Arno. From either of these you can begin the climb up to San Miniato (see opposite): the path from Porta San Niccolò weaves up through **Piazzale Michelangelo (Map 4, K7)**, with its replica *David* and bumper-to-bumper tour coaches; the more direct path from Porta San Miniato offers a choice between the steep Via del Monte alle Croci or the stepped Via di San Salvatore al Monte, both of which emerge a short distance uphill from Piazzale Michelangelo.

FORTE DI BELVEDERE

Map 4, G7. Via di Belvedere. Closed for conversion into the Museo delle Arme (Armour and Weapons Museum), due to open in 2003.

The star-shaped **Forte di Belvedere**, at the crest of the hill above the Boboli Garden, was built by Buontalenti on the orders of Ferdinando I between 1590 and 1595. Its ostensible purpose was to protect the city – its actual function was to intimidate the grand duke's subjects. The urban panorama from here is superb, and added attractions are the exhibitions held in and around the shed-like palace in the centre of the fortress, and occasional summer evening film screenings.

In the past it has sometimes been possible to get up to the fort from the Boboli Garden, but if you want to be certain of the view, approach the fort from the Costa San Giorgio. This is a lane which you can reach by backtracking slightly from the Museo Bardini, or pick up directly from the rear of Santa Felìcita: whichever approach you take, look out for the villa at no. 19, home to Galileo between 1610 and 1631.

East from the Belvedere stretches the best preserved section of Florence's fortified walls, paralleled by Via di Belvedere. South of the Belvedere, Via San Leonardo leads past olive groves to the rarely open church of **San Leonardo in Arcetri**, site of a beautiful thirteenth-century pulpit brought here from a church now incorporated into the Uffizi. Dante and Boccaccio are both said to have preached from the spot.

SAN MINIATO AL MONTE

Map 4, K9. Via del Monte alle Croci. Daily: summer 8am–noon & 2–7pm; winter 8am–noon & 2.30–6pm; free.

Arguably the finest Romanesque structure in Tuscany, **San Miniato al Monte** is also the oldest surviving church building in Florence after the Baptistery. Its brilliant multicoloured facade lures troops of visitors up the hill from Oltrarno, and the church and its magnificent interior and works of art more than fulfil the promise of its distant appearance.

The walk up to San Miniato has some steep sections; if you don't fancy the climb, take the #12 or #13 bus as far as Piazzale Michelangelo and then continue on foot. After seeing the church and enjoying the views, you can either bus back or follow the easy downhill route into town.

The exterior

San Miniato's gorgeous marble **facade** alludes to the Baptistery in its geometrical patterning, and like its model

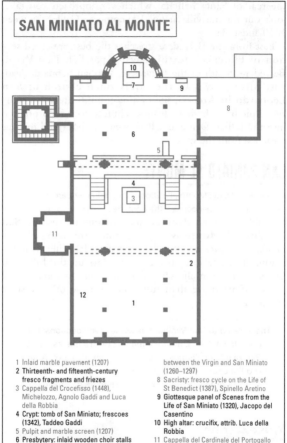

SAN MINIATO AL MONTE

was often mistaken for a structure of Classical provenance during the later Middle Ages. The lower five-arched register is simpler and probably earlier (eleventh-century) than the rest of the structure. No other facade in the city was to be as complete or accomplished until Alberti's frontage for Santa Maria Novella (completed in the fifteenth century), a work consciously modelled on San Miniato.

THE STORY OF SAN MINIATO

St Minias (San Miniato) was Florence's first home-grown martyr. Possibly a Greek merchant or the son of an Armenian king, he originally left home to make a pilgrimage to Rome. Around 250 he moved to Florence, where he became caught up in the anti-Christian persecutions of the emperor Decius. Legend has it that after martyrdom by decapitation – close to the present-day site of Piazza della Signoria – the saintly corpse was seen to carry his severed head over the river and up the hill to this spot, an area where he'd previously lived as a hermit: a shrine was subsequently erected on the slope.

The hill, the *Mons Fiorentinus*, was already the site of several pagan temples and a secret oratory dedicated to Peter the Apostle. A **chapel** to Miniato is documented on the site in the eighth century, though construction of the present building began in 1013. It was raised by Alibrando, bishop of Florence, and endowed by Emperor Henry II "for the good of his soul". Initially run as a Benedictine foundation, the building passed to the Cluniacs until 1373, and then to the Olivetans, a Benedictine offshoot, who reside here to this day. The monks sell their famous liquors, honeys and tisanes from the shop next to the church, as well as souvenirs and divers unguents, proof against complaints ranging from anxiety and depression to varicose veins and "lowering of the voice".

THE STORY OF SAN MINIATO

The angular upper levels date from the twelfth century onwards, and were financed in part by the Arte di Calimala (cloth merchants' guild), the body responsible for the church's upkeep from 1288: their trademark, a gilded copper eagle clutching a bale of cloth (1401), perches on the roof. The mosaic of *Christ between the Virgin and St Minias* dates from 1260. The original **bell-tower** collapsed in 1499 and was replaced in the 1520s by the present campanile, still unfinished. During the 1530 siege of Florence it was used as an artillery post, thus attracting the attention of enemy gunners. Michelangelo, no less, then advising on the city's defences, had it wrapped in woollen mattresses to protect it from cannon balls.

The interior

With its choir raised on a platform above the large crypt, the sublime **interior** of San Miniato is like no other in the city, and its general appearance has changed little since the mid-eleventh century. The main additions and decorations in no way spoil its serenity, though the nineteenth-century recoating of the marble columns is a little lurid: the columns' capitals, however, are Roman and Byzantine originals removed from older buildings. The intricately patterned panels of the pavement (1) are dated 1207, probably also the date of the church's eventual completion. Some claim the zodiac and strange beast motifs were inspired by Sicilian fabrics, others that they are of Byzantine origin, introduced into Italy through trade and the Crusades.

Works of special note are highlighted in green in the text and on the plan on p.204.

The Cappella del Crocefisso (see opposite) dominates the middle of the nave, blocking what would once have been an uninterrupted view of Miniatus's tomb in the **crypt (4)**. Steps either side of the cappella lead down to this crypt, the oldest part of the church, where the original high altar still contains the bones Bishop Alibrando confirmed as those of the saint in the eleventh century (ignoring a well founded belief that the real bones had been removed to Metz by a relic-obsessed German). The vaults, supported by 36 wonderfully mismatched pillars, contain gilt-backed frescoes (1341) of the saints, martyrs, prophets, virgins and Evangelists by Taddeo Gaddi.

Back in the main body of the church, steps beside the Cappella del Crocefisso lead to the raised **choir** and **presbytery (6)**, dominated by a magnificent Romanesque pulpit and screen (5) from 1207. The odd totem-like figures supporting the lectern may represent three of the four evangelists or, possibly, humanity placed in a middle state between the animal world (the lion) and the divine (the eagle).

The great mosaic (7) in the apse is dated 1297 – probably the year of one of the church's periodic restorations. It's likely it was executed by the same artist who created the facade mosaic, particularly as the works' themes are identical – *Christ Pantocrator* (the Universal Christ – note the alpha and omega symbols on either side of his head) enthroned between the Virgin and San Miniato. The **crucifix (10)** above the high altar is attributed to Luca della Robbia.

Off the presbytery to the right lies the sacristy (8), whose walls are almost completely covered in a superlative fresco cycle by Spinello Aretino, the first such complete cycle in Tuscany devoted to the *Life of St Benedict* (1387).

Cappella del Crocefisso

The lovely tabernacle, or Cappella del Crocefisso (3), between the choir stairs was designed in 1448 by Michelozzo.

SAN MINIATO AL MONTE

The date is significant, for the piece is one of the few works commissioned by Piero de' Medici, or Piero il Gottoso (the Gouty), during his brief tenure as head of the Medici dynasty. The marble medallion to the rear and other parts of the work are adorned with Piero's motto (*Semper*) and several Medici symbols – the eagle holding three feathers and an uncut diamond ring, the latter a symbol of durability and toughness.

The chapel originally housed the miraculous crucifix associated with San Giovanni Gualberto, moved to Santa Trìnita in 1671. Today the tabernacle contains painted **panels** by Agnolo Gaddi depicting the *Annunciation, Stories of the Passion* and *SS Giovanni Gualberto and Miniato* (1394–96). These were originally arranged in the form of a cross to act as a frame for the now vanished crucifix. Maso di Bartolomeo crafted the twin eagles (1449), symbols of the Calimala, who wished to stress that while Piero was the work's sponsor, the guild was responsible for overseeing all stages of its construction. The terracotta in the barrel vault is by Luca della Robbia.

For more about the story of San Giovanni Gualberto, see p.173.

Cappella del Cardinale del Portogallo

Back in the lower body of the church, the **Cappella del Cardinale del Portogallo (11)**, dating from a few years after the Cappella del Crocefisso, is one of the masterpieces of Renaissance chapel design and a marvellous example of artistic collaboration. Completed in 1473, it was built as a memorial to Cardinal James of Lusitania, who died in Florence in 1459, aged 25. The cultured nephew of King Alfonso V of Portugal, James was sent to study law in Perugia, later becoming archbishop of Lisbon, a cardinal, and subsequently the ambassador to Florence. Close to death in the city, he asked to be buried in San Miniato. The cardinal's aunt and his humanist friends and admirers jointly sponsored his tomb. Aside from that of Miniato himself, this is – remarkably – the church's only tomb.

The chapel's basic design was the work of Antonio di Manetto (or Manetti), a pupil and biographer of Brunelleschi, who borrowed heavily from his master's work in San Lorenzo's Sagrestia Vecchia (see p.111). The **tomb** itself was carved by Antonio and Bernardo Rossellino; their elder brother Giovanni oversaw the chapel's construction after Manetto's death. Antonio Rossellino's tondo of the *Mother and Child* keeps watch over the deceased.

Behind the effigy of the cardinal is a grille, probably a metaphor for the Gates of Paradise. The empty judge's throne is an allusion to and portent of the Last Judgement. Note, too, the angels flanking the tabernacle: the one holding a virgin's crown symbolizes the cardinal's presumed chastity, a virtue also suggested by the unicorns, more usually a symbol of female chastity after the ancient belief that the mythical creature could only be captured by a virgin; the angel holding a palm represents the subjugation of earthly passion.

The chapel's architectural and sculptural work was followed in 1466 by carefully integrated frescoes and **paintings**: an *Annunciation* (to the left) and the *Evangelists* and *Doctors of the Church* by Alesso Baldovinetti (lunettes and beside the arches). Antonio and Piero del Pollaiuolo produced the **altarpiece** depicting the cardinal's patron saint, St James, with SS Vincent and Eustace: the present picture is a copy, the original being in the Uffizi. The ceiling's tiled decoration and four glazed terracotta medallions, perhaps the finest such work in the city, were provided by Luca della Robbia.

All the decorative details were carefully designed to complement one another and create a unified artistic whole.

Thus Rossellino's tondo of the Madonna and Child, for example, echoes the round windows of the walls; the colours in Baldovinetti's *Annunciation* deliberately echo the tones of the surrounding porphyry and serpentine inlays; and the curtain held aside by angels on the cardinal's tomb is repeated in a similar curtain half-shielding the altar.

LISTINGS

Accommodation

Accommodation in Florence can be a problem: hotels are plentiful but prices are high and standards often less than alluring. Worse still, the tourist invasion has scarcely any slack spots. Between March and October you'd best book your room well in advance, or reconcile yourself to staying some way from the centre. If you're considering a package deal, check the location of your hotel carefully. A handful of **hostels** and a couple of **campsites** help out for budget travellers, but few are centrally located.

If you haven't booked ahead, the easiest solution is to queue up at the **Informazioni Turistiche Alberghiere** (ITA) next to the fast-food canteen, just inside the train sta-

---

FLORENTINE ADDRESSES

There is a double **address system** in Florence, one for businesses and one for all other properties. Business addresses are followed by the letter r, and are marked on the building with a red number on a white background. There's no connection between the two series – thus no. 20 might be several buildings away from no. 20r. The higher the number, the further you are from the river.

tion (daily 8.45am–9pm; ☎055.282.893, 🖷055.288.429). They make hotel reservations in return for a fee of €1.60 or more, according to the class of accommodation. Contact details for private booking agencies are listed on p.295. **Hotel touts** hang around the queues for this office, and around the station in general. Some of their hotels are genuine, but likely to be expensive or far from the centre, others are unlicensed private houses whose safety standards may be dubious. Only use them if you're desperate.

ACCOMMODATION PRICES

Throughout this section, accommodation is graded on a scale from ❶ to ❾. These codes indicate the cheapest double room in high season. The price bands to which the codes refer are as follows:

❶	under €50	❻	€150–200
❷	€50–75	❼	€200–250
❸	€75–100	❽	€250–300
❹	€100–125	❾	over €300
❺	€125–150		

HOTELS

Hotels are graded in Italy on a scale running from one to five stars: in Florence there's a dearth of decent places in the lower ranks. Our selection offers a choice of places over several price categories. All are central and within walking distance of the sights, and all, where possible, are free of the **noise** from busy streets that can blight many otherwise decent hotels. Even so, always ask for rear, garden or courtyard rooms where possible.

If you're trawling the streets looking for places on your own, there are two main concentrations of **lowish-cost**

hotels: one to the northeast of the station, centred on Via Faenza (**Map 3, E4/5**); the other to the south, centred on Via della Scala (**Map 3, C6**). Be warned that the whole station area, and especially the Via Faenza zone, has a sizeable night-time population of assorted lowlife. Note also that some of the places you come across in this area are unlicensed – if you're at all doubtful about a place, give it a miss. If you can afford to pay more for your accommodation, it's worth it, since there are plenty of colourful places to stay in the city's nicer districts.

Our **price codes** (see opposite) relate to high-season prices. Prices may be lower off-season (October to March), especially in expensive hotels, where rates often tumble in winter, and there are sometimes good deals to be found during July and August as well. Watch out for hidden extras, such as compulsory **breakfasts** – it's always cheaper and nicer to eat in a bar if you have the option. Better places include a decent breakfast in the room price. Some cheaper spots may charge for hot showers and towels, and some levy supplements for air-conditioning. Prices for rooms may vary within the same hotel, so if the first price you're quoted seems high, ask if there's anything cheaper; rooms without a private bathroom always cost less.

As ever in big cities, **single rooms** are at a premium – and you'll do well to pay less than two-thirds the cost of a double. The maximum cost of a room, plus any charge for breakfast, should be posted on the back of the door. Note that many hotels require a **deposit** to secure booking, which may involve sending cash or a eurocheque through the post.

The telephone code for Florence is ☏ 055, and must be used with all numbers, whether you're calling from within the city or from outside. Calling Florence from abroad, dial your international access code, then ☏ 39 (for Italy), then 055, followed by the subscriber's number.

HOTELS

BUDGET

Bavaria

Map 3, I8. Borgo degli Albizi 26
ⓣ & ⓕ 055.234.0313.
A budget delight in the city
centre, tucked away on the
second floor of a sixteenth-
century palazzo built for a
follower of Eleanor of Toledo.
Most of the eight monkishly
spartan rooms share one of
two simple bathrooms, but
the atmosphere makes up for
any lack of luxury. Be sure to
book as it's used by long-stay
language students. No credit
cards. Breakfast included. No
lift. ❷

Bretagna

Map 4, D2. Lungarno Corsini, 6
ⓣ 055.289.618, ⓕ 055.289.619,
ⓦ www.bretagna.it.
The grand rooms in this
converted palazzo are the
beautiful rococo-style
breakfast- and living rooms,
which overlook the Arno.
Only one bedroom has a
river view – book early – and
the rest of the hotel is slightly
tatty, but you can't fault the
location. ❸

Dali

Map 3, I8. Via dell Oriulo 17
ⓣ & ⓕ 055.234.0706,
ⓦ www.hoteldali.com.
One of the least expensive
one-star options close to the
centre. The ten rooms, five
with bath, are plain and
rather basic, but the location
– on the top floor of a
palazzo built in 1492 – helps,
as does the view from the
back rooms of the giant
magnolia in the garden
below. The friendly, young
owners speak good English.
❸

Firenze

Map 2, E4. Piazza dei Donati
4/Via del Corso ⓣ 055.214.203,
ⓕ 055.212.370.
The one-star *Firenze* may not
be particularly friendly, and it
is certainly devoid of old-
world character, but it is
clean, efficient, modern, well
fitted-out (nearly all rooms
have TVs and private
bathrooms) and superbly
located. With 61 rooms,
there's a better chance of
finding space here than in
some of the smaller budget
options, too. Rooms on top

floors enjoy a touch more daylight. Three-, four- and five-bed rooms are available. No credit cards. ❸

Maxim

Map 2, C3–D3. Entrances at Via dei Calzaiuoli 11 (with lift) and Via de' Medici 4 (stairs) ☎ 055.217.474.
Few hotels could ask for a more central location than the one-star *Maxim*, a friendly 32-room place located just a minute from the Duomo on the city's busy (but pedestrianized) main street. Half the rooms, all of which are clean and simple, have private bathrooms; the quietest look onto a central courtyard. ❸

Residenze Johanna

Map 3, H2. Via Bonifacio Lupi 14 ☎ 055.481.896, ⓕ 055.482.721, ⓔ lupi@johanna.it.
The genteel *Johanna* feels very much a "residence" rather than a hotel, hidden away in an unmarked apartment building (ring the bell on the brass plaque by the wrought-iron gates) in a

very quiet, leafy corner of the city, five minutes' walk north of San Marco. Rooms are cosy and well kept, there are books and magazines and the two *signore* who run the place are as friendly and helpful as you could hope for. ❷

Via Faenza 56

Map 3, E4. Via Faenza 56.
The upper three floors of this address contain no fewer than five one-star pensioni: the eight-room *Anna* (☎ 055.239.8322); seven-room *Armonia* (☎ 055.211.146); twelve-room *Azzi* (☎ & ⓕ 055.213.806); twelve-room *Marini* (☎ 055.284.824); and seven-room *Paola* (☎ 055.213.682). With most of its rooms overlooking the garden, the *Azzi* is probably the friendliest and most bohemian of the bunch; *Marini* has the nicest and priciest rooms, with private bathrooms; *Paola* is the scruffiest; *Anna* has some pleasant rooms at the back; while *Armonia* is well scrubbed and ordinary. Most rooms come in at around €50. ❷

HOTELS

MODERATE

Alessandra

Map 3, E9. Borgo SS Apostoli 17 ⓣ 055.283438, ⓕ 055.210619, ⓦ www.hotelalessandria.com. Noise shouldn't be a nuisance at this two-star hotel, thanks to a central position on a quiet back street between the Ponte Vecchio and church of Santa Trìnita. Rooms are bright and airy and have some nice touches such as wooden floors, but only around half have private bathrooms (for which you pay more): about the same proportion have TVs and air-conditioning. ❸

Annalena

Map 4, C6. Via Romana 34 ⓣ 055.222.402, ⓕ 055.222.403, ⓦ www.hotelannalena.it. Situated in the Oltrarno just beyond the Palazzo Pitti, this twenty-room three-star is heavy with history: once owned by the Medici, it passed to a young Florentine noblewoman (Annalena) who retired from the world after a disastrous love affair and bequeathed the building to the Dominicans. Today the place, with its partly frescoed main salon, has the feel of a delightful old-fashioned *pensione*. The rooms vary – the best open onto a gallery with garden views – but a sprinkling of antiques lends all a hint of old-world charm. ❺

Belletini

Map 3, F6. Via dei Conti 7 ⓣ 055.213.561, ⓕ 055.283.551, ⓦ www.firenze.net/hotelbelletini The warm welcome of owner Signora Gina counts for much in this 27-room two-star hotel close to San Lorenzo and Cappelle Medicee. So, too, do her copious breakfasts. Most of the simple rooms have private bathrooms, around half have TVs and all have air-conditioning; rooms in the more expensive annex (❺) have frescoes as well. ❹

Casci

Map 3, G5. Via Cavour 13 ⓣ 055.211.686, ⓕ 055.239.6461, ⓦ www.hotelcasci.com.

It would be hard to find a better two-star in central Florence than this 24-room hotel. Despite the busy Via Cavour location, only two (sound-proofed) rooms face the street; the rest, converted from a former convent, are wonderfully quiet, clean and fitted out in a manner that wouldn't disgrace a four-star. The welcome is warm and the owners – the multilingual Lombardi family – are unfailingly helpful and courteous. Free internet access and big buffet breakfasts in the vaulted and frescoed reception are major pluses. ❹

Cimabue

Map 3, H2. Via Bonifacio Lupi 7 ⓣ & ⓕ 055.471.989, ⓦ www.venere.it/firenze /cimabue.

Like the *Casci* (see above), this sixteen-room hotel offers much more than the usual two-star establishment, though its position, a ten-minute walk north of the Duomo, is not as good. Some of the double and triple rooms have frescoed ceilings, and all are kitted out with antiques and pleasant fabrics. All have (mostly small) private bathrooms. The family atmosphere is welcoming and the breakfasts more than generous. ❹

Gallery Hotel Art

Map 2, A7. Vicolo dell'Oro 5 ⓣ 055.27.263, ⓕ 055.268557, ⓦ www.lungarnohotels.com. Book in the UK through Design Hotels (ⓣ 0800 169 8817).

This newly opened and immensely stylish four-star is unlike any other hotel in central Florence. A member of the Design Hotels group, it has a sleek, minimalist and hyper-modern look – lots of dark wood and neutral colours – and tasteful contemporary art displayed in the reception and all 65 rooms. There is a small but smart bar, and an attractive lounge with art-filled bookshelves and comfortable sofas. The position is perfect – in a small, quiet square about ten seconds' walk from the Ponte Vecchio. ❺

HOTELS

219

Porta Rossa

Map 4, E2. Via Porta Rossa 19
Ⓣ 055.287.551, Ⓕ 055.282.179.
Florence has smarter three-star hotels, but none as venerable as the 81-room *Porta Rossa*, which has been a hotel since the fourteenth century and played host to, among many others, Byron and Stendhal. You come here for character and nineteenth-century ambience rather than luxurious modern touches – the rooms are vast and the corridors rambling. The two tower rooms are fabulous, but cost €247.90. ❺

Silla

Map 4, I5. Via dei Renai 5
Ⓣ 055.234.2888,
Ⓕ 055.234.1437,
Ⓦ www.hotel.silla@tin.it.
The *Silla* is unusual among hotels situated along the Arno in being neither overly noisy nor overpriced. The ambience of the fifteenth-century palazzo building is masked by a 1980s refit, but the rooms are in good shape and reasonably sized – and nine have a view over a small park and road to the river. ❹

EXPENSIVE

Benivieni

Map 2, E3. Via delle Oche 5
Ⓣ 055.238.2133,
Ⓕ 055.239.8248,
Ⓦ www.hotelbenivieni.it.
Most hotels in Florence advertise themselves as being near either the Duomo or Piazza della Signoria, but this small, friendly and family-run three-star is actually right between the two and, what's more, it's tucked away on a quiet backstreet. Fifteen smallish rooms are ranged around two floors of a former synagogue; the rooms on the first floor are brighter but all are simple, modern and in perfect condition. As they should be – the place only opened in 2001. ❻

Brunelleschi

Map 2, E3. Piazza Santa Elisabetta 3 Ⓣ 055.27.370,
Ⓕ 055.291.653,
Ⓦ www.hotelbrunelleschi.it.
The *Brunelleschi*'s main appeal is a position that's absolutely central while remaining pleasant and peaceful.

HOTELS

Designed by leading Italian architect Italo Gamberini, the four-star, 96-room hotel is built around a Byzantine chapel and fifth-century Pagliazza tower, the latter one of Florence's oldest buildings. A small in-house museum displays Roman and other fragments found during building work. Decor is simple and stylish, with the original brick and stone offset by lots of wood and the odd Art Nouveau touch. Rooms are spacious, comfortable and uniform: the best, on the fourth floor, have views of the Duomo and tower. **8**

Hermitage
Map 2, B8. Vicolo Marzio 1/Piazza del Pesce
Ⓣ055.287.216, Ⓕ055.212.208, Ⓦwww.hermitagehotelcom.
Pre-booking is essential to secure one of the 29 rooms in this superbly located three-star hotel right next to the Ponte Vecchio; book well in advance for the eight rooms with unbeatable views. The service is friendly, and rooms are cosy, intimate and decorated with the odd antique flourish; bathrooms are a touch small but nicely done. Rooms from the former *Archibusieri* hotel, now incorporated into the *Hermitage*, are slightly less appealing. **6**

Hotel J & J
Map 3, K7. Via di Mezzo 20
Ⓣ055.263.12, Ⓕ055.240.282, Ⓦwww.jandjhotel.com.
The bland exterior of this former fifteenth-century convent, quietly located in the Sant'Ambrogio district close to Santa Croce, conceals a wonderful and romantic eighteen-room four-star hotel. All the rooms vary in appearance and size – some are vast split-level affairs – but all have charm and are simply furnished with modern fittings, attractive fabrics and a scattering of antiques. The common parts are decked in flowers and combine touches of old and new, retaining frescoes and vaulted ceilings from the original building. In summer breakfast is served in the convent's lovely old cloister. **7**

HOTELS

Loggiato dei Serviti

Map 3, I5. Piazza Santissima Annunziata 3 ⊤ 055.289.592, ⓕ 055.289.595, ⓔ loggiato_serviti@italyhotel .com.

This simple, elegant and extremely tasteful three-star hotel, situated on one of Florence's most celebrated squares, is one of the most appealing in the city in its category. Its 29 rooms have been incorporated with an architect's finesse into a building originally designed by Brunelleschi. All vary considerably in size, and their relative plainness reflects something of the sixteenth-century convent that once occupied the palazzo. This said, all are decorated with fine fabrics and antiques and look out onto either the (pedestrianized) piazza or peaceful gardens to the rear; top floor rooms have glimpses of the Duomo. ⑥

Morandi alla Crocetta

Map 3, J5. Via Laura 50 ⊤ 055.234.4747, ⓕ 055.248.0954, ⓦ www.dada.it/hotel.morandi.

An intimate ten-room, three-star gem, whose small size and friendly ex-pat welcome – owner Katherine Doyle has lived in Florence since she was 12 – provide a nice home-from-home atmosphere. Rooms are individually and tastefully decorated with antiques, old prints and vivid carpets laid over polished parquet floors. Two rooms have small balconies opening onto a modest garden; the best room of all – with fresco fragments and medieval nooks and crannies – is the one converted from the chapel of the former convent on the site. ⑥

LUXURY

Excelsior

Map 3, B8. Piazza Ognissanti 3 ⊤ 055.264.201, toll-free in Italy ⊤ 1678.35035, ⓕ 055.210.278, ⓦ www.starwood.com.

This five-star, 168-room luxury hotel is marginally the better of the two grand old hotels on this less than prepossessing piazza. The

HOTELS

antique-filled rooms ooze old-world elegance and refinement, while the public areas are on the grandest imaginable scale – a vision of columns, marble floors and decorated wooden ceilings. This said, the atmosphere is unstuffy and the service impeccable. Some of the best rooms (fifth floor) have terraces and views, but you pay a supplement for a glimpse of the Arno. ❾

Helvetia & Bristol
Map 3, E8. Via de' Pescioni 2
ⓣ 055.287.814, ⓕ 055.288.353,
ⓦ www.charminghotels.it.
Florence's finest and most exclusive five-star luxury hotel has been in business since the eighteenth century. Previous guests have included Pirandello, Stravinsky and Bertrand Russell. Fully restored in 1989, the public spaces and 49 individually decorated rooms are faultless, the latter luxurious, elegant and beautifully appointed with antiques and period paintings. Facilities and bathrooms are modern – many have Jacuzzis – but the overall tone is traditional and hyper-tasteful. Service is also first-rate, but with a pleasantly informal edge. ❾

HOSTELS

Florence has only a handful of hostels and the best – the Ostello Villa Camerata – is some way from the centre, though it's one of the most pleasant hostels in Italy. Budget beds are also provided by a number of religious and other institutions, where rooms are plain but invariably spotless.

Istituto Gould
Map 4, B5. Via dei Serragli 49
ⓣ 055.212.576,
ⓔ gould.reception@dada.it.
Open for check-in Mon–Fri 9am–1pm & 3–7pm, Sat 9am–1pm; closed Sun; no curfew.

Reception is on the second floor of this recently renovated seventeenth-century palazzo – the doorbell is easily missed. The *Gould*'s ninety-odd beds are extremely popular, so it's wise to book in advance, especially during the academic year. Street-front rooms can be noisy – rear rooms are better – but the old courtyard, terracotta floors and stone staircases provide plenty of atmosphere throughout. Singles €33.60 with private bathroom (€28.40 without); doubles €23.20 per person (€20.20 without private bathroom); triples €19.60 per person (€17.10 without private bathroom); quads and quins are also available.

Ostello Archi Rossi

Map 3, E5. Via Faenza 94r
℡055.290.804,
℻055.230.2601,
📧 ostelloarchirossi@hotmail.com.
Open 6.30–11.00am for reservations in person – arrive early – and to deposit luggage; no reservations by phone. Closed 11am–2.30pm; 1am curfew.
A five-minute walk from the train station, this newish and privately owned hostel is spotlessly clean but decorated with guests' wall-paintings and graffiti. It's popular – the 96 places fill up quickly. Breakfast and evening meals are available at extra cost; spacious dining room with satellite TV and films shown on request in the evening. Single rooms €25.80. Dorm beds €15 and up to €23.30, depending on size of dorm – they vary from four to nine beds. No credit cards.

Ostello Santa Monaca

Map 4, B4. Via Santa Monaca 6
℡055.268.338, ℻055.280.185,
🌐 www.ostello.it.
Open for check-in 9.30am–12.30pm & 2pm–midnight; 12.30am curfew.
A former convent in Oltrarno, close to Santa Maria del Carmine, which was converted into a rather downbeat privately owned hostel in 1968. Kitchen facilities, 115 places (in fourteen rooms), free hot showers and no maximum length of stay. The noticeboard is useful for information on lifts. To get here from the station it's a

fifteen-minute walk: otherwise take bus #36 or #37 to the second stop after the bridge. Dorm beds €11.40. No credit cards.

Ostello Villa Camerata

Viale Augusto Righi 2–4
☏ 055.601.451, 🅕 055.610.300.
Doors open 2pm – phone for a reservation if you can't be there by then; 11.30pm curfew.
A half-hour journey on the #17b bus from the train station. Tucked away in a beautiful park, the *Villa Camerata* is one of Europe's loveliest-looking hostels, a sixteenth-century house with frescoed ceilings and a wide loggia, fronted by lemon trees in terracotta pots. If you don't have a Hostelling International card, you can buy a special guest card that's valid in other Italian youth hostels. There are 322 dorm places, and a few family rooms. Breakfast and sheets are included; optional supper from €7.20 (no kitchen facilities); films in English every night. Beds €12.40 per person; rooms €36.20–40.30.

Pio X – Artigianelli

Map 4, B6. Via dei Serragli 106
☏ 055.225.044 or 055.225.008.
Open all day throughout the year; midnight curfew; no reservations by phone.
One of the cheapest options in town, but often booked up by school groups. Don't be put off by the huge picture of Pope Pius X at the top of the steps – the management is friendly and the atmosphere relaxed. Get there by 9am as the 64 beds are quickly taken. Free showers. Doubles, triples, quads and quins at €13.40 per person per night; minimum stay two nights, maximum five.

Suore Oblate dell'Assunzione

Map 3, J7. Via Borgo Pinti 15
☏ 055.248.0583.
Open all year; 11.30pm curfew.
Not far from the Duomo, and run by nuns, but open to both men and women as long as rooms are not required by the nuns or their visitors; no breakfast. Singles €25.80, doubles €51.70, both with private bathrooms.

HOSTELS

225

Triple and quad rooms are also available.

Suore Oblate dello Spirito Santo

Map 3, E5. Via Nazionale 8
ⓣ 055.239.8202.
Open mid-June to Oct; 11pm curfew.

Run by nuns, this clean and pleasant hostel a few steps from the station is open to women, families and married couples only; minimum stay two nights. Beds are arranged in double, triple and quad rooms, all with private bathroom; breakfast included. Doubles €41.30, triples €46.50.

Youth Hostel Firenze 2000

Viale Sanzio 16

ⓣ 055.233.5558,
ⓦ www.florencegate.it.
Open all day throughout the year.

Bus #12 makes a fifteen-minute journey from the train station to Piazza Pier Vettori (a ten-minute walk west of Piazza del Carmine, in Oltrarno), just off which is this new, upmarket 76-bed hostel. Rooms have private showers and there's even a (small) heated swimming pool, though it'll cost you €5.20 per day to use it. Twins and doubles cost €28.40 per person, three- and four-bed rooms cost €23.20; prices drop by €2.60 from November to February, and in July and August.

CAMPSITES

The situation for campers in Florence is poor: summer arrivals are almost certain to find that the only available spaces are at the *Area di Sosta*, an emergency accommodation area set aside by the city authorities whose location varies most summers – it usually amounts to a patch of ground sheltered by a rudimentary roof, with a shower block attached. An alternative would be to try the campsite in Fiesole, to the north of the city.

CAMPSITES

Italiani e Stranieri

Map 4, L7. Viale Michelangelo 80 ☎ 055.681.1977.

Open April–Oct.

This 320-place site is always crowded, owing to its superb hillside location. Kitchen facilities and well stocked, if expensive, shop nearby. Take bus #13 from the station.

Villa Camerata

Viale Augusto Righi 2–4 ☎ 055.600.315.

Open all year

A more basic one-star site in the grounds of the hostel (see p.225), with 55 places. Take bus #17b from the station.

Eating

I n gastronomic circles, **Florentine cuisine** is accorded as much reverence as Florentine art, a reverence encapsulated in the myth that French eating habits acquired their sophistication in the wake of Catherine de' Medici's marriage to the future Henry II of France. In fact, Florentine food, like all Italian food, has always been characterized by modest raw materials and simple technique – beefsteak (*bistecca*), tripe (*trippa*) and liver (*fegato*) are typical ingredients, while grilling (*alla fiorentina*) is a favoured method of preparation.

The **location** of eating places is fairly arbitrary, with no well defined restaurant and nightlife district, though there's a slight preponderance of more interesting places in the Oltrarno and around Santa Croce. All our recommendations are within easy walking distance of the centre. They're spread across several **price ranges**: at those classed as inexpensive, you should be able to get a three-course meal with house wine for under €20 per head; at those classed as moderate you'll be charged between €20 and €40; while the expensive places will set you back upwards of €40. Remember, though, that a pasta and plate of salad at lunch won't break the bank even in some of the pricier places. Categorizing restaurants is difficult, for virtually all serve similar Tuscan food, and even self-styled pizzerias often offer a range of pastas and main courses.

EATING ITALIAN: THE ESSENTIALS

Working your way through an Italian menu (*la lista*, or sometimes *il menù*) is pretty straightforward. **Antipasto** (literally "before the meal") generally consists of cold cuts of meat, seafood or vegetables. Ham *(prosciutto)* – either cooked *(cotto)* or just cured *(crudo)* – is served alone or with melon, figs or mozzarella cheese. Also common are *crostini*, canapés of minced chicken liver or other savoury toppings.

The next course, **il primo**, consists of a soup, risotto, polenta or pasta dish. This is followed by **il secondo** – the meat or fish course, usually served alone, except for perhaps a wedge of lemon or tomato. Watch out when ordering fish or Florence's famous *bistecca alla fiorentina;* anything marked *S.Q.* or *hg* means you are paying by weight (250g is usually plenty for one person). Vegetables *(contorni)* or salad *(insalata)* are ordered and served separately. There's seldom much choice: the most common vegetables are beans *(fagioli)* or potatoes *(patate)*, while salads are either green *(verde)* or mixed *(mista)*.

For **pudding**, you nearly always get a choice of fresh fruit *(frutta)* and desserts *(dolci)*, invariably focused on ice cream or a selection of home made flans *(torta della casa)*.

At the end of the meal ask for the bill (**il conto**). In many trattorias this amounts to no more than an illegible – and illegal – scrap of paper; if you want to be sure you're not being ripped off, ask for a receipt *(ricevuta)*, which all bars and restaurants are legally bound to provide. Almost everywhere, you'll pay a cover charge *(coperto)* on top of your food. If service isn't included you may choose to tip about the same amount, but it's not expected.

Opening hours have been given for all restaurants; note that many are closed during August.

Angiolino

Map 4, D3. Via Santo Spirito 36r ☎ 055.239.8976. Daily 12.30–2.30pm & 7–10.30pm. Closed Mon in winter. Inexpensive to moderate.

Ambience alone makes *Angiolino* worth a visit – it's one of the city's prettiest old-fashioned trattorias. Dried flowers and chillies hang from the brick-vaulted ceiling, and colourful strings of tomatoes and pumpkins festoon the bar. The tablecloths are red check while dozens of wicker-clad Chianti bottles add another pleasant decorative cliché: there's even an old-fashioned iron stove in the centre of the main room. The menu is short and to the point, never venturing away from Tuscan classics such *crostini*, *bistecca*, *ribollita* and *pappa al pomodoro*. Quality is variable: some dishes are acceptable, others exceptional.

Baldovino

Map 4, K3. Via San Giuseppe 22r ☎ 055.241.773. Tues–Sun 11.30–2.30pm & 7–11.30pm. Moderate. *Baldovino* is run and owned by a charming young Scottish couple, which accounts for the pleasantly trendy, laid back look of the place, and for a relaxed and welcoming atmosphere that sees it packed with Italians and foreigners alike (be sure to book in the evening). It's especially known for its pizzas, but the menu is chock-full of other Italian dishes. For a devotedly Tuscan menu, head a few doors down towards the piazza to the new sister restaurant, *Francescano*, at Largo Bargellini 16 (☎ 055.241.773).

Beatrice

Map 2, G4. Via del Proconsolo

31r ⓣ 055.239.8762.
Tues–Sun 7pm–11pm. Closed
Aug. Expensive.

The Italian-international
food here doesn't attract
many plaudits – though it's
certainly not bad – but if
you're on a smoochy date or
just want to revel in the
extraordinary neo-Liberty
interior, it's hard to imagine a
more beautiful dining room
(it's been used as a location
for several films and TV
programmes). The medieval
painted wooden ceiling alone
is worth the price of a plate
of pasta. The restaurant is
entered through the lobby of
the *Hotel Cavour*.

Beccofino

Map 4, C3. Piazza degli
Scarlatti 1r, off Lungarno
Guicciardini ⓣ 055.290.076.
Daily 12.30–2.30pm &
7–11.30pm. Closed Aug.
Moderate to expensive.

The poshest venture from the
Baldovino stable (see opposite)
has quickly acquired celebrity
status. It may be the presence
of a well known Italian chef,
or perhaps the Glaswegian

sous chef who previously
worked under Gordon
Ramsay, or even the
persistent rumour that the
owner is Hugh Grant's cousin
(he isn't, but looks as if he
might be). Most likely,
however, it's the sharp, stylish
contemporary feel of the
place. The food is modern
European, with an emphasis
on Tuscan ingredients, and
there's an inexpensive but
limited bar menu, which is a
good way to sample the
atmosphere and the talent in
the kitchen.

Belle Donne

Map 3, E7. Via delle Belle
Donne 16r ⓣ 055.238.2609.
Mon–Fri 12.30–2.30pm &
7–10.30pm. Closed Aug.
Inexpensive.

A tiny trattoria lent a
distinctive touch by its banks
of fresh flowers, hanging legs
of ham and decorative
mounds of fruit and
vegetables. You sit at small
shared tables with paper
tablecloths and choose from
one of the day's specials
chalked up on the

EATING

blackboard. This may sound off-putting for non-Italian speakers, but the service and atmosphere are friendly.

Benvenuto
Map 4, H3. Via della Mosca 15r, corner Via de' Neri ⓣ055.214.833.
Mon, Tues & Thurs–Sat 12.30–2.30pm & 7.30–10.30pm. Inexpensive.
Benvenuto has been around for years and yet still manages to maintain its reputation for low prices. It's probably not going to offer a hugely memorable experience food-wise, but you can't go wrong here if all you want is a cheap and straightforward trattoria-quality meal just a couple of minutes' walk from Piazza della Signoria.

Birreria Centrale
Map 2, E5. Piazza dei Cimatori 2r, off Via Dante Aligheri ⓣ055.211.915.
Mon–Sat noon–4pm & 7pm–midnight. Inexpensive to moderate.
There's a dearth of decent places to eat (and drink) at a reasonable price right in the city centre. This spot, on a tiny piazza between the Badia and Orsanmichele, is an notable exception. It offers snacks, beers and light meals in a nicely dark, old-fashioned room scattered with big wooden cabinets and antiques. Inevitably the interior becomes uncomfortably cramped late on, but there's more room in summer when tables spill over onto the piazza outside.

Borgo Antico
Map 4, D4. Piazza di Santo Spirito 6r ⓣ055.210.437.
Daily 12.45–2.30pm & 7.30pm–11pm. Inexpensive to moderate.
The more traditional of two good restaurants on Oltrarno's trendy Piazza di Santo Spirito, *Borgo Antico* is often very noisy and crowded, though in summer the much sought-after tables outside on the piazza offer relative peace and quiet. Choose from around ten different pizzas, a daily set-price menu or a more

FLORENTINE CUISINE

The most important ingredient of Florentine cooking is **olive oil**, which comes into almost every dish – for frying, as a salad dressing, or poured into soups and stews just before serving. Soups are central to the cuisine. The most famous is **ribollita**, a thick vegetable concoction using left-over beans (hence "reboiled"). **Pappa al pomodoro** is a stodgy, sustaining broth made with bread, tomatoes and basil.

The city's most famous dish is **bistecca alla fiorentina**, a thick T-bone steak grilled over charcoal, usually served rare – at the time of writing a BSE scare had knocked beef on the bone off all Florence's menus, but the rule isn't likely to be maintained (or enforced) for long. Florentines are also fond of the unpretentious **arista**, roast pork loin stuffed with rosemary and garlic, and of **pollo alla diavola**, a grilled flattened chicken marinated with olive oil and lemon juice or white wine. "Hunters' dishes" (**cacciatore**) are common, especially *cinghiale* (wild boar) and *pollo* (chicken). Wild hare features as **lepre in dolce e forte** (cooked in wine and tomatoes with raisins, pine nuts, orange peel and herbs) or as **pappardelle con lepre** (fried with bacon and tomatoes on a bed of noodles).

White **cannellini beans** are the favourite vegetable, boiled with rosemary and eaten with olive oil, or cooked with tomatoes (*all'uccelletto*). Broad beans, peas, artichokes and asparagus are much used, but none is as typically Tuscan as **spinach**, often eaten cold with a squeeze of lemon.

Sheep's-milk **pecorino** is the most widespread Tuscan cheese. The most famous is the oval *marzolino* from the Chianti region, eaten either fresh or ripened, and often grated over meat. Desserts often include **cantuccini**, hard biscuits which are dipped in a glass of sweet Vinsanto, or **zuccotto**, a brandy-soaked sponge cake filled with cream mixed with chocolate powder, almonds and hazelnuts.

FLORENTINE CUISINE

expensive range of Tuscan standards. Salads here are particularly good, and there's often a selection of fresh fish and seafood pastas. Servings – on the restaurant's famous huge plates – are generous to a fault.

Caffè Italiano
Map 4, I2. Via Isole delle Stinche 11–13r ⓣ055.289.368.
Tues–Sun 10am till late.
Inexpensive to moderate.
This mini-restaurant "complex" consists of an informal wine bar serving cold meats, *crostini* and light meals (see p.248), a smarter and more expensive restaurant, and a smaller room for lunch round the corner at Via della Vigna Vecchia 2. All the rooms are prettily medieval in appearance – lots of beams, terracotta and old wood – with simple, tasteful decoration to match: the lunch spot, in particular, with its low ceilings and battered marble tables, looks the part of an old trattoria to perfection. Food is Tuscan and first-rate throughout, though the late menu offers a

more limited selection. Excellent wine list.

Casalinga
Map 4, D4. Via del Michelozzo 9r ⓣ055.218.624.
Mon–Sat noon–2.30pm & 8–10pm. Closed Aug.
Inexpensive.
Located in a small side street off the eastern side of Piazza di Santo Spirito, this famous, long-established and traditional family-run trattoria serves up some of the best low-cost authentic Tuscan dishes in town. Fills up with regulars and a good few outsiders seeking an alternative to the nearby *Borgo Antico* and *Osteria Santo Spirito* (see p.232 and p.238). The paper tablecloths, pine walls, jugs of wine and brisk service are all that you'd expect from this sort of place.

Cibreo
Map 4, L2. Via de' Macci 122r ⓣ055.234.1100.
Tues–Sat 12.50–2.30pm & 7–11.15pm. Closed Aug.
Moderate.
First Florentine port of call for all self-respecting Italian

and a fair few foreign foodies, *Cibreo* has achieved fame well beyond the city, the original restaurant having spawned a café, trattoria and deli despite what was – when it started out twenty years ago – an outlying and downbeat area. Since recent price rises, the more spartan trattoria is the section to head for, as the food – superb creative takes on Tuscan classics – is identical (though the selection of dishes is more limited), the atmosphere more relaxed and the prices significantly lower. You'll have to queue most nights, or pay the premium to book a table in the famed dining room at Via de'Macci 118r, where a three-course meal will set you back over €50.

Coco Lezzone

Map 4, D2. Via del Parioncino 26r, corner of Via del Purgatorio ☎ 055.287.178.
Mon–Sat 12.30–2.30pm & 7.30–10.30pm. Closed mid-July to mid-Aug. Moderate. Stumble on this back-street place and you'd swear you'd found one of the great

undiscovered old-world Florentine trattorias. The place certainly looks the part: tiny entrance, red check tablecloths, low ceilings, narrow dining room and utilitarian half-tiled yellow walls. The prices tell a different story, for the place is too classic and self-conscious for its own good, and has long attracted slumming politicians, actors and captains of industry. Don't let this put you off, as the food is good and about as thoroughly Florentine as you'll find: try the *zuppa di lampredotto*, for example, a soup made from a veal calf's stomach. Fresh fish is a feature on Fridays.

Enoteca Pinchiorri

Map 4, I2. Via Ghibellina 87 ☎ 055.242.777
Tues 12.30–2pm; Wed–Sat 12.30–2pm & 7.30–10pm. Closed Aug. Very expensive. No one seriously disputes the *Pinchiorri*'s claim to be Florence's most exclusive restaurant: Michelin have given it two of their coveted stars. The food is sublime and sophisticated, even if the

ceremony that surrounds it strikes many as excessive. As for wine, you've a choice of 80,000 different bottles from around the world, including some of the rarest and most expensive vintages on the planet. None of this comes cheap – you could easily drop €150 per person eating à la carte – but there's nowhere better for the never-to-be-repeated Florentine treat.

Garga

Map 3, D8. Via del Moro 48r ⓣ 055.239.8898. Tues–Sun 12.30–3pm & 7.30–11pm. Expensive. One look at the lurid, almost decadently frescoed walls tells you that this isn't your ordinary Florentine restaurant. That said, the cuisine follows the familiar pattern for Florence's more expensive establishments, of traditional, meat-heavy Tuscan dishes enlivened by some rather fancy modern techniques and combinations. The eccentric decor is set off by simple white tablecloths and courteous service. Don't

miss "Il cheesecake della Sharon", a popular creation from the chef's wife, who runs a cookery school in the house opposite.

I Ghibellini

Map 3, J8. Piazza San Pier Maggiore ⓣ 055.214.424. Tues–Sun 12.30–2.30pm & 7.30–10.30pm. Inexpensive to moderate. *I Ghibellini* sticks to a successful formula: it's a bustling, unpretentious ristorante-pizzeria with a bright, convivial atmosphere and good food (the pizzas are excellent). The menu is unadventurous but reliable Italian fare, while the daily specials often feature a homely Tuscan dish or two.

Latini

Map 3, D8. Via dei Palchetti 6r ⓣ 055.210.916. Tues 7.30–10.30pm, Wed–Sun 12.30–2.30pm & 7.30–10.30pm. Moderate. Once a trattoria of the old school, famous for its low prices and authentic atmosphere, the almost legendary *Latini* is now

EATING

something of a caricature. Everything still looks the part – hams hanging from the ceiling, the dreadful trattoria-quality paintings, family photos on the wall, simple tables and old rush chairs. Food quality, though, is now unexciting at best (the *bistecca* is an honourable exception), and prices well above what a genuine trattoria would be charging. Old regulars still eat here, but for the most part the inevitable queues in the evenings – booking is difficult – are full of misguided foreigners.

Mario

Map 3, F5. Via Rosina 2r, off Piazza del Mercato Centrale ☏ 055.218.550.
Mon–Sat 12.30–3pm. Closed Aug. Inexpensive.
Mario has been around for ever, serving generations of students and market workers with no-nonsense, high-quality Tuscan food (fish on Friday). It's as authentic as you please, but hasn't been tempted into putting up its prices just because foreigners now form part of the clientele. It has jazzed up its front, however, though the old wood ceiling and functional interior remain the same as ever. This said, you don't come here for ambience – you come to fill up at low cost at shared tables: try *Zà-Zà* a couple of doors to the right if you want something cosier (see p.240).

Oliviero

Map 2, A6. Via delle Terme 51r ☏ 055.212.421.
Mon–Sat 7.30–midnight. Closed Aug. Expensive
Like *Cibreo* and the rather snooty *Alle Muratte*, *Oliviero* currently enjoys a reputation for some of Florence's best food, albeit at a price. It has a welcoming and old-fashioned feel – something like an Italian restaurant of the Sixties, the period, in fact, when this long-established place last enjoyed anything like its present fame. The innovative food is predominantly Tuscan, but includes other Italian dishes, and puddings, for once, are a cut above the usual. The

EATING

237

menu includes fresh fish when available, something of a rarity in Florence.

Osteria de' Benci

Map 4, I3. Via de' Benci 13r
ⓣ 055.234.4923.
Mon–Sat 1–2.45pm & 8–10.45pm. Inexpensive to moderate.

Modern and reasonably-priced *osteria* with a pretty dining room underneath a wonderful brick-vaulted ceiling. The outside tables, too near the road, are less tempting. The short menu changes regularly, combining excellent rustic standards with innovative takes on Tuscan classics. Staff are young and friendly, the atmosphere busy, informal and urbane.

Osteria Santo Spirito

Map 4, C4. Piazza di Santo Spirito 16r-Via Sant' Agostino
ⓣ 055.238.2383.
Daily 12.30–2.30pm & 7.30pm–midnight. Inexpensive to moderate.

One of the new wave of relaxed, modern and informal Florentine restaurants, with

PIZZERIAS

Pizzerias are scattered across the city and offer an obvious source of cheap, filling meals. Many also serve pastas and main courses in restaurant-like surroundings – we've given full details of these in our listings. For the best central options at a glance, check out the list below.

Baldovino Via San Giuseppe 22r (see p.230).
Borgo Antico Piazza di Santo Spirito 6r (see p.232).
I Ghibellini Piazza San Pier Maggiore. Closed Wed (see p.236).
Danny Rock Via Pandolfini 13. Map 4, H1. Evenings only.
Pizzaiuolo Via de' Macci 113r (see opposite).
Uvafragola Piazza Santa Maria Novella 9. Map 3, D7. Closed Wed.

outdoor tables on one of Florence's trendier piazzas. Simple, hearty Tuscan dishes are cooked and presented with contemporary flair. Set menus and daily specials are served, and there's no problem ordering a snack or single course.

Pizzaiuolo

Map 4, L2. Via de' Macci 113r ℡ 055.241.171.

Mon–Sat 12.30–2.30pm & 7.30pm–11pm. Closed Aug. Inexpensive to moderate.

Many Florentines reckon the pizzas here are the best in the city, something not entirely unconnected with the fact that the owner is Neapolitan. Wines also have a Neapolitan flavour, as does the atmosphere, which is invariably friendly and high-spirited. The look of the place is simple – a low ceiling with two massive beams over a few tables and humble wooden chairs. Space is at a premium, so booking's a good idea. Stays open until 1am, though the kitchen shuts at 11pm.

Quattro Leoni

Map 4, E4. Via dei Vellutini 1r-Piazza della Passera.

Daily 12.30–2.30pm & 7.30–10.30pm. Closed Aug & Wed in winter. Moderate.

A contemporary take on the traditional trattoria, with red check-clad tables arranged around a softly lit, three-roomed medieval interior, its huge beams hung with dried flowers. In summer you can eat outdoors under vast canvas umbrellas in the quiet piazza just a minute or so from the Palazzo Pitti. Head for the little *Caffè degli Artigiani* across the square if all you want is a snack. The menu is very Florentine – the *antipasti* stand out – with some interesting seasonal variations.

I' tozzo di pane

Map 3, F4. Via Guelfa 94r.

Mon–Sat 12.30–2.30pm & 7.30–10.30pm. Inexpensive.

Florence is starting to do this sort of thing really well: an informal osteria with a young clientele and a relaxed soundtrack where you can sit and chat over a glass of good

EATING

ICE CREAM

Good **ice cream** is as much a part of the Italian experience as any number of museums and galleries. And in a *gelateria*, or ice-cream parlour, such as *Vivoli*, Florence can claim to have one of the best purveyors of the stuff in the country. First decide whether you want a cone (*un cono*) or a cup (*una coppa*). Then decide how much you want to pay – cone and cup sizes go up in 25 cent increments from around €1.50, though you may pay more in tourist hotspots. Unless you plump for the smallest you'll usually be able to choose a combination of two or three flavours. Finally, you may be asked if you want a squirt of cream (*panna*) on top – it's usually free.

Vivoli (Map 4, I2, Via Isole delle Stinche; Tues–Sun 8am–midnight) has been making sublime ice cream from its back-street base near Santa Croce for three generations. Most people rate it the best in Florence, many the best in Italy, as countless postcards and newspaper clippings tacked to the walls testify. *Crema*, *cioccolata*, *fragola* (strawberry) and *limone* are the all-time classics, but any of the many flavours should be a winner. Frozen yoghurts and the various *semi-freddi* (literally "half-colds") are also well worth a try. Those with more experimental tastes may want to head for **Festival del Gelato** (Map 2, D4, Via del Corso 75r; daily 9am–11pm), which has a vast range.

wine with excellent crostini, or dip into the simple, inexpensive menu of pastas and meaty Tuscan classics. Such a warm, local atmosphere is rare in this rather downmarket, touristy area close to the train station.

There's a small conservatory area at the back.

Zà-Zà

Map 3, F5. Piazza del Mercato Centrale 26r.
Mon–Sat noon–3pm & 7–11pm.
Closed Aug. Inexpensive.

The best and, unfortunately, best-known of several trattorias close to the Mercato Centrale. Despite the large canteen-type area downstairs and the sophisticated new dining room – all exposed brick and cosy lighting – there's often a queue for seats, especially for the tables on the piazza. The food is conventionally, successfully Florentine, and the menu at €12.90 offers excellent value with a choice of three or four pastas and main courses.

Drinking

Pavement **cafés** are not really part of the Florentine scene. Smaller and less ostentatious venues are more the city's style – one-room cafés and bars – though many of its central retreats, with one or two commendable exceptions, are expensive and characterless. Slightly peripheral areas – Santa Croce, San Marco and the Oltrarno in particular – are more rewarding. The listings below begin with cafés that you're likely to visit for breakfast, a snack lunch or drinks during the day.

Hole-in-the-wall and other **wine bars** – a Florentine tradition – come next, on p.248. The city is much better served for these: some are throwbacks to workers' bars where you can get a glass of rough red and a snack, others are smooth, sophisticated places where you can sample fine wines and try some superb Florentine speciality foods.

Many wine bars and restaurants stay open late, but the large tourist and student population is served by more dedicated drinking venues, listed under "**Bars and pubs**" on p.252. Florence has suffered even more than most Italian cities from the popularity of identikit "Irish pubs" and the like, and there are few venues that would pass muster in larger cities. Bars that are fashionable among the local population may be buzzing one night and deserted the next, and if you want to meet young people – foreigners and locals alike – the pub is probably your best bet.

Opening hours have been given for all cafés and bars; note that many are closed during August.

CAFÉS

Caffè Amerini

Map 3, D8. Via della Vigna Nuova 63r.

Mon–Sat 8.30am–8.30pm.

Amerini manages to be modern, intimate and out of the ordinary at the same time. The clientele – old ladies, students, shoppers and tourists – is eclectic, while the medieval brick arching contrasts with orange-yellow paint effect walls, modern furniture and Art Deco mirrors. There are seven or eight tables at the front and a less cosy room to the rear. Sandwiches, salads and snacks are particularly good – point out what you want from the bar and sit down to be served: there's only a small premium for sitting, and it's the sort of place you could happily linger for an hour or so.

Caffè Cibreo

Map 4, L2. Via Andrea del Verrocchio 5r, off Via Macci.

Tues–Sat 8am–1am.

It's a long way to come just for a drink, but worth the detour to visit the prettiest and most chic café in Florence. Though it only opened in 1989, the sensational wood-panelled interior looks at least two hundred years older. Tables are tucked cosily into corners; in summer there are a few outside on the (not so pretty) street. Cakes and other desserts are great; light meals at lunch and dinner bear the stamp of the famous sister restaurant opposite (see p.234).

Caffè Gilli

Map 2, C3. Piazza della Repubblica 36–39r.

Mon & Wed–Sun 8am–midnight.

The huge and soulless Piazza della Repubblica is redeemed by five large cafés, some of them historic: *Gilli*, *Giubbe Rosse*, *Fiorino d'Oro*, *Donnini* and *Paszkowski*. Of these, *Gilli* is the best, though rather like *Rivoire* (see opposite) it's the sort of place you visit for the historical associations and a one-off cocktail or aperitif experience. Founded in 1733, the café moved to its present site in 1910, and the staggering *belle époque* interior is a sight in itself. Most people, Florentines and visitors alike, however, choose to sit out on the big outdoor terrace. On a cold afternoon try the famous hot chocolate – it comes in five flavours: almond, orange, coffee, *gianduia* and cocoa. If you like the *Gilli* experience, the 1897 *Giubbe Rosse* is the next best of the piazza's cafés.

Caffè I Ricchi

Map 4, C4. Piazza di Santo Spirito 9r.
Summer Mon–Thurs 7am–1am, Fri–Sat 7am–2am; winter Mon–Sat 7am–8pm.
Piazza di Santo Spirito, with its trees and neighbourhood atmosphere, is one of the few places in Florence you can sit out and feel you're in a real old-fashioned Italian square. *Ricchi* is the most pleasant and relaxed of its handful of bars – the *Cabiria* a few doors down has more of an edge and is better after dark (see p.252). The interior is bright, modern and full of locals, with a room at the rear for meals; the real attractions are the outside tables and the excellent and reasonably priced lunches. Menus change daily, and if you don't want anything cooked there's a good selection of cakes, ice cream and sandwiches.

Caffè Italiano

Map 2, D5. Via della Condotta 56r.
Mon–Sat 8am–8pm. Closed Aug.
Given its position just a few paces off the teeming Via dei Calzaiuoli, *Caffè Italiano* is a revelation. Downstairs there's an old-fashioned stand-up bar with lots of dark wood, silver teapots and superb cakes, coffees and teas. Upstairs is a

relaxed and peaceful den with waiter service and red velvet banquettes – ideal for a wet afternoon or late-night assignation. Lunch is excellent, as you'd expect from a place owned by Umberto Montano, head of the *Caffè Italiano* restaurants (see p.234).

Caffèlatte

Map 3, J6. Via degli Alfani 39r.
Mon–Sat 8am–midnight.

A good pit-stop up around Santissima Annunziata, with a vaguely alternative feel. Newspapers and magazines are scattered on old tables, while the walls feature temporary exhibitions of paintings and photographs. A label outside sells the place as a "Health Food Bar" – there's a tremendous organic bakery on site which produces delicious breads and cakes, and inexpensive vegetarian meals are usually available as well. *Caffè latte*, served in big bowls, is as good as you'd expect given the café's name, a nod to its 1920 origins as a milk and coffee shop.

Caffè Rivoire

Map 2, D6. Piazza della Signoria 5r.
Tues–Sun 8am–midnight.

Virtually every city has its *Caffè Rivoire*, an historic café whose central position and traditional reputation has seen it swamped by mass tourism. This said, if you want to people-watch on Florence's main square, this is the place to do so: the vast spread of outside tables is invariably packed. Founded in 1872, the café started life specializing in hot chocolate, still its main claim to fame. The ice creams are also fairly good, but the sandwiches and other snacks are run-of-the-mill – this is the sort of place for one pricey beer, cappuccino or chocolate just to say you've done it.

Hemingway

Map 4, A3. Piazza Piattellina 9r, off Piazza del Carmine.
Tues–Thurs 4.30pm–1.30am, Fri & Sat 4.30pm–2.30am, Sun 11am–8pm.

The style of the place is rather self-consciously manufactured, but don't let

CAFÉS

CAFÉS: THE ESSENTIALS

Bar and café **procedure** is standard. You almost always pay a premium to sit, inside or out; if you buy a drink at the bar and then sit down, the waiters will be on you like a shot. Standing at the bar is cheaper. In some more traditional places you state your order and pay at the cash desk (*la cassa*), then take your receipt (*lo scontrino*) to the bar and repeat your order. It's increasingly common, however, to simply order your coffee then pay for it when you leave. If service is slow, a coin slapped down with your receipt can work wonders.

Coffee

The standard kick-start coffee is the small dark espresso, usually known simply as *un caffè*. Italians drink cappuccino only in the morning, *never* after a meal. A *caffè latte* is a slightly longer cappuccino without the froth. *Una doppia* is a double espresso, *un caffè lungo* an espresso with a touch more water. *Un caffè macchiato* is an espresso "stained" with a dash of milk, *un latte macchiato* a glass of warm milk with a dash of espresso. Decaffeinated is *un Hag* or *un caffè* (or *cappuccino*) *decaffeinato*. A *caffè correto* is an espresso with a shot of brandy or other spirit. A *caffè Americano* is an espresso topped up with hot water, something like filter coffee. Milky cold coffee, *caffè freddo*, is popular in summer.

Tea

Tea is usually drunk with lemon (*tè al limone*). Tea with milk (*tè con latte*) is rare; you have to ask for it specifically, and you're liable to end up with a tea bag suspended in a glass of hot milk. Cold lemon tea (*tè freddo*) is popular in summer, fresh or

that put you off – there's nothing else like it in Florence. Tea, coffee and chocolate are the main attractions: indulge in a cream tea, choose from one of countless speciality teas, sample over twenty coffees,

in tins and bottles. Infusions, especially camomile (*camomilla*), are popular after dinner.

Water

Tap water is perfectly drinkable everywhere unless marked *acqua non potabile*, though Italians invariably prefer bottled (*acqua minerale*). This comes still (*senza gas, naturale,* or *non gassata*) or sparkling (*con gas, frizzante* or *gassata*). Ask for a full bottle (*una bottiglia*), half-bottle (*mezza bottiglia*) or a glass (*un bicchiere*).

Soft drinks

Freshly squeezed fruit juice is *una spremuta*: orange (*arancia*), lemon (*limone*) and grapefruit (*pompelmo*) are the most common. Bottled fruit juice – popular at breakfast – is *un succo di frutta*; the most common flavours are pear (*pera*), peach (*pesca*) and apricot (*albicocca*). Bottled or tinned lemon soda is an excellent bitter lemon drink – the orange soda's not so good. Chinotto is a less sweet Italian version of Coke. In summer, be sure to try a freshly made milk shake (*un frullato* or *un frappé* if made with ice cream).

Aperitifs

Fortified wines such as Martini, Campari and Cinzano are all popular aperitifs (*un aperitivo*). Campari and lemon soda is a dangerously drinkable combination. Prosecco, a light, sparkling white wine from the Veneto is a popular aperitif across Italy. So, too, is the more bitter artichoke-based Cynar. Crodino, a lurid orange non-alcoholic aperitif, is also widely drunk. Gin and tonic is simply *un gin e tonica*. Ice is *ghiaccio*, a slice of lemon *uno spicchio di limone*.

or knock back tea cocktails such as Victoria Tea (milk, vanilla tea and Southern Comfort). Owners Paul de Bondt and Andrea Slitti are members of the Compagnia del Cioccolato, a chocolate appreciation society, and it

CAFÉS: THE ESSENTIALS

shows: the handmade chocolates are sublime, and there are even wines specially chosen to be drunk with them. You can also enjoy more conventional soft and alcoholic drinks and snacks in the small, elegant blue-walled interior. Vast buffet brunches (€15.50) are served on Sundays.

WINE BARS

Caffè Italiano
Map 4, I2. Via Isole delle Stinche 11–13r.
Tues–Sun 10am until late.
Not to be confused with the co-owned café of the same name (see p.244), this small complex near Santa Croce consists of a formal restaurant, lunch restaurant and wine bar. The last is a big, vaulted medieval room with a gargantuan wrought-iron chandelier and lined with lovely old bottle-filled wooden cabinets. It's pretty and very Florentine but not especially intimate, though on a hot afternoon or balmy evening the cool interior is

the next best thing to drinking outdoors.

Cantinetta dei Verrazzano
Map 2, D4. Via dei Tavolini 18–20r.
Mon–Sat 8am–9pm.
Owned by Chianti vineyard Castello dei Verrazzano, this excellent place manages to retain its character despite being just seconds from busy Via dei Calzaiuoli. The huge glass-fronted display oozes with outstanding pizza, focaccia and cakes – pay at the cash desk and then take out or eat inside. The pleasant wood-lined rooms to the rear and at the side are perfect for a midday or early evening glass of wine. Very busy at lunch.

Capocaccia
Map 4, E2. Lungarno Corsini 12–14r.
Tues–Sun 9am–3am.
The brainchild of a young businessman from fashion-conscious Milan, this is about as trendy as it gets for the sort of smartly dressed Florentines who tote mobile phones and

THE VINAIO

One of Florence's great – but sadly fast-disappearing – institutions is the tiny street-corner or hole-in-the wall wine shop or **vinaio**. Some of these are surprisingly central, and all make fine places for a glass of wine on the hoof. Most open 8am to 8pm and are closed on Sunday.

All' Antico Vinaio Via dei Neri 65r. Map 4, H3. Not quite a hole in the wall, more of a walk-in wardrobe. May ensure its survival by selling a growing range of snacks, including meats, cheeses and hot sandwiches – and then there's the wine.

Quasigratis Via dei Castellani/corner of Via di Ninna. Map 2, E7. Little more than a window in a wall and it doesn't say Quasigratis ("almost free") anywhere, just "Vini" and "Lampredotto Caldo". Rolls, nibbles and wine – in tiny glasses called *rasini* – are consumed standing up. Open on Sunday.

Vineria Via dei Cimatori 38r. Map 2, D5. A perfect *vinaio* whose survival is all the more remarkable given its location almost immediately off the high-rent Via dei Calzaiuoli.

never miss a chance to admire themselves in a convenient mirror. The handful of outside tables look onto a busy road, but the atmosphere in the wood and blue-tiled interior is lively and welcoming: there's lots of room and plenty of tables and stools. You'll be mixing it almost entirely with locals, especially later on. Expensive, American-style snack meals are served at lunch and until late at dinner.

Casa del Vino

Map 3, F5. Via dell'Ariento 16r. Mon–Sat 8.30am–8pm. Closed Aug.

Located just west of the Mercato Centrale, the "House of Wine" is passed by thousands of tourists daily but visited by only a handful. Florentines pitch up for a drink, a natter with wine devotee and owner Gianni Migliorini, and an assault on a fine range of panini, *crostini* and hunks of Tuscan bread and salami.

Enoteca Baldovino
Map 4, K3. Via San Giuseppe 18r.
Tues–Sun 10am–late.
An off-shoot of the excellent *Baldovino* restaurant and pizzeria across the road (see p.230). Bright, modern and painted in warm ochre tones, this is a stylish, friendly little place to buy a range of gastronomic goodies, indulge in light snacks (until 11pm), and drink wine by the bottle or glass at the small bar or handful of tables to the rear. The small menu of snacks, sandwiches, soups and excellent home made cakes changes daily. Very convenient for Santa Croce.

Fiaschetteria
Map 3, I5. Via degli Alfani 70r, corner of Via dei Servi.
Mon–Sat 8am–8pm.
The nearby university ensures that this deeply traditional,

low-key place heaves at lunch, when students pile in for the special (pasta and a salad for around €8) or one of the wide range of snacks and sandwiches. There's a reasonable variety of wines by the glass, for drinking seated at one of the wooden benches set against the tiled walls.

Fiaschetteria Nuvoli
Map 2, B1. Piazza dell'Olio 15.
Mon–Sat 8am–8pm.
It's something of a surprise to find such a traditional place this close to the Baptistery. A tiny, dark shop lined with bottles is dominated by a counter laden with cold meats, *crostini* and other snacks, and a number of open bottles. There's a room further inside for meals and a seat, but most of the customers – local workers – are here for a glass and a bite.

Fuori Porta
Map 4, J7. Via del Monte alle Croci.
Mon–Sat noon–12.30am.
Closed two weeks in Aug.
If you decide to climb up to

San Miniato and regret your decision halfway, console yourself at this superb wine bar-osteria, a traditional hang-out for Florence's trendy left-wing types. There are over four hundred wines by the bottle – the choice by the glass changes every few days – and a wide selection of grappas and malt whiskies. Bread, cheese, hams and salamis are available for snacks, together with a small choice of hot dishes at lunch for around €10.

Procacci
Map 3, E8. Via Tornabuoni, 64r. Mon–Sat 10.30–8pm.
It's extraordinary that, over a hundred years on, this delicatessen and wine bar still manages to keep going in this street of high-rent designer clothes shops. But then their sandwiches must, weight for weight, be among the most expensive in the world. However tiny – and they are minuscule – their *panini tartufati* (truffle rolls), are absolutely delicious, and won't break the bank at €1.30. The traditional

accompaniment is a glass of tomato juice, but there's an excellent and reasonably priced selection of wines by the glass. The decor is authentically nineteenth-century, all tiles, wood panelling and high ceilings, and there are just two tiny tables, for hushed conversations.

Le Volpi e L'Uva
Map 4, E4. Piazza dei Rossi 1r, off Piazza di Santa Felicita. Tues–Sat 10am–8pm. Closed one week in Aug.
This discreet little place just over the Ponte Vecchio has done good business for many years, thanks to its policy of concentrating on the wines of interesting small producers and providing high-quality snacks to help them down (the cheeses in particular are tremendous). Wines change every few days, but you should always be able to choose from twenty or more by the glass.

Zanobini
Map 3, F5. Via Sant'Antonino 47r.

WINE BARS

251

Mon–Sat 8am–2pm &
3.30–8pm.

Like the *Casa del Vino*, its
rival just around the corner
(see p.249), this is an
authentic Florentine place
whose genuine feel owes
much to the presence of
passing locals and traders
from the nearby Mercato
Centrale. Essentially a grocer's
shop, a small counter and a
few glasses draw locals in for
a chat over a *vino rosso*.

BARS AND PUBS

Art Bar

Map 3, D8. Via del Moro 4r.
Mon–Sat 7pm until late. Happy
hour 7–9pm.

A fine little bar in an unlikely
central location near Piazza di
Carlo Goldoni. Small and
cosy, the elegant interior
looks like an antique shop,
while its club-like
atmosphere attracts a chic set.
Happy hour is busy, with
low-priced cocktails; much
later, the after-hours
ambience is conducive to a
laid-back nightcap.

Cabiria

Map 4, D4. Piazza di Santo
Spirito 4r.
Mon & Wed–Sun 8am–2.30am.

Dark, cultish place, though
it's rather more laid-back
before dark. The main seating
area is in the modish room to
the rear, but plenty of punters
(locals and foreigners) sit out
on the piazza or crowd into
the narrow bar at the front.
DJs play most nights from
around 9pm. Serves decent
and very inexpensive meals at
lunchtime.

Caracol

Map 3, G5. Via Ginori 10r.
Tues–Sun 12.30–2.30pm &
5.30pm–1.30am. Happy hour
5.30–7pm.

When Florentines aren't
drinking in cod-Irish pubs,
they're posing in pseudo-
Latin American dives, of
which *Caracol* is by far the
best. A big wooden bar and
ranks of tequila bottles create
a Latin look, while a multi-
ethnic babble of punters
produces the requisite energy
level. Happy hour is the
busiest time, for the cheap

cocktails, and live music on Wednesday and Thursday can pull in the punters. The usual Tex Mex food can be had for around €10–15, and there are some cheaper snacks too.

A trio of good, trendy places for a late drink are *Cabiria* (see p.252), *Capocaccia* (see p.248) and *Rex* (see p.256).

Dolce Vita

Map 4, B3. Piazza del Carmine. April–Oct Mon–Sat 10.30am until late, Sun 4pm–midnight; Nov–March Mon–Sat 5pm until late.

A smart, modern-looking and extremely popular bar, but a little lacking in atmosphere unless you're in the mood for dressing up and don't mind the bright and gleaming interior, styled as a strange kind of modern rococo. In summer the action spreads onto the piazza; a good place to preen with (or pry on) Florence's beautiful things.

Fiddler's Elbow

Map 3, D7. Piazza di Santa Maria Novella. Daily 2pm–3am or later.

If you're homesick for this sort of thing and want to drink in a central location with lots of foreigners, this is the place. *Fiddler's Elbow* is remarkably close in look and feel to a real Irish dive – in both its good and bad points. The one dark, smoky wood-panelled room is invariably heaving, though there's extra seating out on the piazza. Women visitors are likely to find themselves the object of concerted attention from Guinness-sozzled Italians. Shows UK football and other sports events on satellite TV.

Kikuya

Map 4, I3. Via de' Benci 43r ☎ 055.234.4879. Mon & Wed–Sun 7pm till late. Happy hour 7–10pm.

Kikuya affects the look and feel of a pub with brick-vaulted ceiling and red velvet bar stools and banquettes. It's

BARS: THE ESSENTIALS

Bars with an emphasis on night-time action occasionally differ from their day-time equivalents in that you may be able to pay for your drinks directly at the bar. Otherwise there's likely to be little difference other than in the sort of things you'll probably be drinking.

Beer

Italian beer (*una birra*) is usually a yellow, lager-type brew, though occasionally you'll come across darker beers (*birra scura*, *rossa* or *nera*) which are closer to British bitters and stouts. The cheapest way to buy beer in a bar is draught (*alla spina*). The three basic measures are *piccola* (roughly 30cl), *media* (50cl) or *grande* (70cl). The key Italian brands – always the cheapest – are Peroni and Dreher: ask for them by name or for *una birra nazionale*. Most are also usually available in bottles; the little 25cl bottle of *Peroni* – ask for *un Peroncino* – is a good instant thirst-quencher. More exotic and most foreign-brand beers are usually only available in bottles.

Wine

All wine bars and the better ordinary bars should have a reasonable selection of Tuscan and other wines, the former having moved on a long way from the days of the wicker-wrapped flask of Chianti. However, ask for a plain glass of wine (*un bicchiere di vino*) in most bars and you'll end up with something fairly ropey – but very cheap. House wine in restaurants is *vino della casa*, and should usually be available by the bottle (*un bottiglia*) or carafe, the latter ordered by litre, half litre or "a little

also tiny, which is why it wisely restricts its live music mainly to solo and acoustic acts. Fashionable with a young international crowd, it's a good place for a beer close to Santa Croce. If the music doesn't take your fancy, head for the *Lochness*, a few doors down, which has pool tables.

quarter" (*un litro, un mezzo or un quartino*). House wine in a large jug is usually the leftovers from lunch.

Spirits

Bars and cafés stock most popular spirits. The key Italian brandy is Vecchia Romagna, though the best-known Italian firewater is grappa, a clear spirit distilled from the mulch of skins, stalks and pips left over from the wine-making process. Usually drunk as a *digestif* after a meal, it may come flavoured with a grotesque medley of herbs and other unlikely substances. Purists stick to the plain version, the best examples of which in Florence are likely to be from Montalcino or Montepulciano.

Liqueurs

Your average Italian is more likely to take *un amaro* (literally "a bitter") after dinner than a grappa. The locals' belief in the digestion-aiding properties of this cough-medicine-like syrup are probably misplaced, but once the taste's been acquired, it's difficult to resist. Fernet-Branca is the best-known and most bitter variety available: it's great for hangovers and any form of upset stomach, but not for drinking for its own sake. Far less bitter, and probably the most widely drunk brand, is Averna, closely followed by Montenegro and the lighter Ramazzotti. Other popular liqueurs include the sweet almond-based amaretto, the syrupy, lemon-based limoncello, and the aniseed-flavoured sambuca, the last often ignited before drinking and accompanied by a floating coffee bean.

The Lion's Fountain

Map 3, I8. Borgo degli Albizi 34r.
Daily 4pm–2am.

If you want to drink in one of Florence's pseudo-Irish pubs, this small place towards Santa Croce is probably the one to go for. Background music isn't usually traditional, but it's invariably inoffensive;

BARS: THE ESSENTIALS

●

255

the decor is more pleasant than in other such places and the bar staff are generally friendly. Food is simple and good – lots of snacks, salads and sandwiches – and you can catch big sporting events on the TVs. Drinks are reasonably priced, and include a good range of cocktails as well as Guinness.

Maramao
Map 4, L2. Via de' Macci 79r. Fri & Sat 10pm–2am.

The much-patronized *Maramao* is as trendy as you'd expect in happening Sant'Ambrogio: not the sort of place to turn up in a T-shirt and trainers. The decor is as slick and self-conscious as the punters, who are generally here as much to dance as to drink – this is a self-styled "discobar", with good DJs and a dance floor that cranks up from about 11pm.

Monte Carla
Map 4, G4. Via de' Bardi 2r. Mon, Tues, Thurs–Sun 6pm–2am.

An ex-brothel, *Monte Carla* is almost a pastiche of itself, with its exotic bordello fabrics, coloured lighting, divan beds and atmosphere of decadence. These days, it's a great place to chill out with a long, expensive cocktail, and there are even board games if you fancy them. If unaccompanied, you may need to sign up as a "member" on first walking in.

Rex
Map 3, J7. Via Fiesolana 25r. Daily 5pm–2.30am. Happy hour 5–9.30pm. Closed July & Aug.

Rex is probably the Florentine bar to visit if you visit no other. One of the city's long-established night-time fixtures, it's friendly, has a varied clientele, and an eye-catching look: vast curving lights droop over an oval bar studded with Gaudí-inspired turquoise stone and mirror mosaics. Cocktails are good and the tapas-like snacks excellent. The background music is usually impeccable, and on some nights you may catch the odd live show; DJs provide the sounds at weekends.

Zoe

Map 4, I5. Via de'Renai 13r.
Mon–Sat 6pm–1am.
One of the cool bars where the beautiful people have *un aperitivo* and a chat before going on to dinner and a night out. The atmosphere is stylish but not aggressively so, and it's often quieter later, except on weekend nights, when a young Florentine pre-club crowd swarms in the street outside.

Nightlife

Florence has a reputation for catering primarily to the middle-aged and affluent, but like every university town it has its pockets of activity, not to mention the added nocturnal buzz generated by thousands of summer visitors. Full details of the city's dependable club and live music venues are given below, but for up-to-the-minute information about what's on, call in at the tourist office in Via Cavour (see p.8) or at **Box Office**, which has outlets at Via Alamanni (**Map 3, B4**, ☏055.210.804) and Chiasso dei Soldanieri 8r, off Via Porta Rossa at the corner with Via de' Tornabuoni (**Map 4, E2**, ☏055.219.402). Tickets for most events are available at Box Office; otherwise, keep your eyes peeled for advertising posters, or pick up monthly magazines such as *Firenze Spettacolo*.

The streets of central Florence are generally safe at night, but women should be wary of strolling through the red-light districts alone – the station area and Piazza Ognissanti have a particularly dodgy reputation, and kerb-crawling is not unknown. Unaccompanied tourists of either gender should stay well clear of the Cascine park at night: if you're going to one of the several clubs located there, get a taxi there and back.

CLUBS AND DISCOS

Put together balmy summer evenings, a big student population and Florence's huge summer surge of young travellers,
and you have a recipe for a massive **club scene**.
Unfortunately, those same ingredients don't necessarily add
up to produce the most sophisticated of venues, and in any
case, clubs in Italy don't resemble their equivalents in
London or other big cities. For one thing, most Florentines
aren't in clubs to dance or drink – they're there to see and
be seen and dress up to the nines. Foreigners are a different
matter, and one or two – mostly central – clubs have a
slightly more sweaty and familiar atmosphere as a result.

Faced with a low income from the bar, most clubs charge
a fairly stiff **admission** – reckon on €12.90 and up for the
bigger and better-known places. This is not quite as bad as
it sounds, for the admission often includes one or two
drinks. Prices at the bar after that are usually pretty steep.
Other more insidious admission procedures include a card
system, where you're given a card on (usually free) entry
that gets stamped every time you spend money at the bar.
By the end of the night you have to have spent a minimum
sum – if not you have to pay the difference before the
bouncers will let you out. And of course everyone loses
their card. Alternatively, the card may be used just to keep
tabs on your drinks, with the bill settled at the end of the
evening. Payment always has to be in cash – credit cards are
not accepted.

Opening and closing times for clubs are rarely set,
though the weekly closing day, if there is one, doesn't usually vary. Clubs are also prone to closure, or to closing and
then opening up under a different name. We've listed the
ones that are currently worth recommending, but consult
Firenze Spettacolo (€1.60), available from news-stands, for
details of the best individual nights.

CHAPTER SEVENTEEN

Central Park

Off map. Parco delle Cascine.
No phone.
Midnight till late.

Currently one of the city's best clubs, with adventurous, wide-ranging and up-to-the-minute music from DJs who know what they're doing and have access to a superb sound system. A card system operates for drinks, but the minimum spend – currently €7.80 – is more reasonable than most places. It's unsafe to wander around the park outside, especially for women.

Full Up

Map 4, H2. Via della Vigna Vecchia 21r ⓣ055.293.006.
Closed Sun, Mon & June–Sept.
Situated close to the Bargello, this is another of the city's major central clubs, and has been going so long it's become something of a night-time institution. Popular with foreigners, local students and a slightly older Florentine set. Music is usually fairly anodyne dance stuff with occasional hip-hop nights, the decor standard disco mirrors and flashing

lights. Admission is usually free until around midnight and €5 after that. Reckon on around €8 for most drinks.

Meccanò

Off map. Viale degli Olmi 1/Piazzale delle Cascine ⓣ055.331.371.
Closed Sun, Mon & Wed, plus two weeks in Aug.
Florence's most famous disco and also one of its longest-running. People flock here for a night out from across half of Tuscany. The place is labyrinthine, with a trio of lounge and bar areas, and a huge and invariably packed dance floor. In summer, when the action spills out of doors, you can cool off in the gardens bordering the Parco delle Cascine. The stiff €15.50 admission (usually less during the week) includes your first drink.

Pongo

Map 4, J2. Via Giuseppe Verdi 59r ⓣ055.234.7880.
Bar opens 4.30pm; happy hour 7pm; club 10.30pm till late.
Closed Sun & June–Sept.
Located close to Santa Croce,

within staggering distance of the city centre. In the afternoon you can sit in the bar and watch satellite TV or fiddle around for free on the Internet. On weekday evenings there's often a theme night or, more often, live music. DJs are some of the city's best and closest to current trends – you may not find speed garage, but drum 'n' bass nights have a serious following. Admission is €5.20, which includes a drink.

Space Electronic
Map 3, B6. Via Palazzuolo 37
℡055.293.082.
Daily 10pm till late. Closed Mon in winter.
Space Electronic claims to be the largest disco in Europe. True or not, it's got all the disco clichés you'd expect of a massive Continental club – lasers, glass dance floors and mirrored walls – though the music is surprisingly good. Cooler than thou clubbers might be sniffy about the place, but it's popular with American students and fine if all you want to do is dance.

Foreign women, be warned, are seen as fair game by the resident Latin Lotharios. Admission is €12.90.

Tenax
Off map. Via Pratese 46
℡055.308.160.
11pm till late. Closed Mon. Bus #29 or #30.
You'd hardly come to Florence for its cutting-edge dance scene, but if you're missing a serious club, this is the place to go – it even pulls in the odd big-name house and garage DJ. Given its location in the northwest of town, near the airport (take a taxi), you'll escape the hordes of *internazionalisti* in the more central clubs. It's a major venue for concerts earlier on. Later, or when there's no band playing, Thursday is student night, anything goes on Friday, and Saturday is four-to-the-floor Euro-house. Admission is steep (for Florence) at €15.50.

Yab
Map 3, E8. Via Sassetti 5r
℡055.215.160.
9pm–4am. Closed Wed & Sun.

CLUBS AND DISCOS

Yab doesn't have the most up-to-the-minute playlist in the world, and is crammed into a basement, but it's currently enjoying something of a vogue; a reliable night's clubbing with a relaxed, mostly Italian clientele. You are given a card and pay on leaving if you've spent less than €12.90.

LIVE MUSIC

Clubs and discos often lay on **live bands** during the week or before the DJs take over later in the evening. Check listings magazines for such events, but don't expect much more than some small-time local outfit running through its repertoire. Venues below include places that present either bigger names or brands of music such as jazz where the performers' fame – or lack of it – is less critical.

Auditorium Flog
Off map. Via Michele Mercati 24
℡ 055.490.437.
Opening times vary depending on the event.
Flog is one of the city's best-known mid-sized venues, and a perennial student favourite – with a suitably downbeat studenty look and feel – for all forms of live music (and DJs), but particularly local indie-type bands. It's usually packed, despite a position way out in the northern suburbs at Il Poggetto – to get here take buses #8, #14, #20 or #28.

Be Bop
Map 3, H6. Via dei Servi 28r.
No phone.
Opening times vary.
A nice and rather classy rock, jazz and blues bar with bow-tied bar staff and faux Art Nouveau decor. Handily placed close to the university district, between the Duomo and Santissima Annunziata, and often full of local students as a result. No dance floor as such – this is more a place to sit and chill out to the music.

Chiodo Fisso

Map 2, E4. Via Dante Alighieri 16r ⓣ 055.238.1290.

Open nightly 9pm till late.

This small, dark cave of a place is an oddly understated sort of venue to find at the high-rent heart of the city centre. In fact, it's a well known venue for left-wing singer-songwriters – still a force in the Italian music scene – and at any time it's a good and very central spot for listening to folk, solo guitarists and the occasional jazz musician – the wine's decent as well.

Eskimo

Map 3, C6. Via dei Canacci 12r, off Via della Scala. No phone.

Tues–Sun 9.30pm–3.30am.

A small but well established club close to Santa Maria Novella with live music every night. Its long-standing status as *the* lefty student bar is reflected in the music, which tends to be Italian solo singers or trios. The atmosphere is welcoming and you may catch the odd theatre and other cultural event. Punters are occasionally let loose to try their hand on stage – you have been warned.

Places listed elsewhere in the guide where you might also occasionally hear live music include *Kikuya* (see p.253), *Pongo* (see p.260) and *Rex* (see p.256).

Girasol

Map 3, J7. Via del Romito 1 ⓣ 055.474.948.

8pm–2.30am. Closed Mon.

It may be a fashion which has passed its peak, but Florence's liveliest Latin bar is still hugely popular. Rather than relying on salsa classes, cocktails and the usual vinyl suspects – although it does all these – *Girasol* draws in some surprisingly good live acts, with different countries' sounds each day of the week, from Brazilian bossa nova to Cuban son; Friday is party night.

Jazz Club

Map 3, J7. Via Nuova de' Caccini 3 ⓣ 055.247.9700.

LIVE MUSIC

GAY FLORENCE

Florence's history is scattered with the names of some of history's greatest gay and bisexual artists – Michelangelo, Leonardo and Botticelli, among others – and *Florenzer* was, during the seventeenth century at least, German slang for gay. The city remains, for the most part, tolerant and welcoming for gay and lesbian visitors. The leading gay bar is the men-only **Crisco**, Via Sant'Egidio 43r (Map 3, I7; ☎055.248.0580), which is open to members only, though temporary membership is usually available on the door (Mon & Wed–Sun 10pm till late). **Il Piccolo Caffè**, Borgo Santa Croce 23r (Map 4, I3; 055.241.704) has a more chilled-out atmosphere and is a good place to make contacts, while **Y.A.G. Bar**, Via de' Macci 8r (**Map 4, K3**; ⓦwww.yagbar.com) is stylish, new and draws a trendy, mixed crowd. The key disco-bar is the long-running **Tabasco**, Piazza Santa Cecilia 3r (Map 2, C6; 055.213.000; daily 10pm till late), or you could try **Flamingo Disco**, Via Pandolfini 26r (Map 3, I8; ☎055.243.356; Mon–Sat 11pm till late), which is more devoted to dance.

For more information and contacts, log on to ⓦwww.gay.it/pinklily. For lesbian contacts, check the noticeboard at the women's bookshop Libreria delle Donne, Via Fiesolana 2b (Map 3, J8; ☎055.240.384; Mon 3.30–7.30pm, Tues–Sat 9am–1pm & 3.30–7.30pm).

Tues–Fri 9.30pm–1.30am; Sat till 2.30am.

Florence's foremost jazz venue has been a fixture for years. The €5.20 "membership" fee gets you down into the medieval brick-vaulted basement, where the atmosphere's informal and there's live music most nights (and an open jam session on Tuesdays). Cocktails are good, and you can also snack on bar nibbles, focaccia and desserts. Located in a tiny side street a block south of Via degli Alfani at the corner with Borgo Pinti.

Tenax

Off map. Via Pratese 46
☎ **055.308.160.**
Tues–Sun 9pm–4am. Bus #29 or #30.

Way out northwest near the airport at Peretola, *Tenax* is a heck of a trek – but it's the city's leading venue for new and established bands as well as big-name international acts. Keep an eye open for posters around town or call at the tourist office for upcoming gigs. The place is enormous but easy-going, and doubles as a club after hours. There are ranks of bars, pool tables, computer games and plenty of seating.

LIVE MUSIC

●

Culture and entertainment

Florence has no shortage of cultural and other **entertainment**, offering everything from world-class orchestras and Italy's oldest music festival to classic films in dingy cinemas and the chance to watch one of Serie A's leading soccer teams. Classical music presents few language barriers, unlike theatre and cinema, where only Italian-speakers will be able to make the most of what the city offers – and a couple of cinemas lay on undubbed English-language films.

For a fuller list of exhibitions, shows, festivals and other events, ask at tourist offices for the annually updated Firenze Avvenimenti/Events pamphlet.

CLASSICAL MUSIC

Classical music abounds in Florence. The famous Maggio Musicale, Italy's oldest and most prestigious music festival, is only the most high-profile of several festivals and concert seasons – other concerts and events are held year-round at venues across the city. The orchestras and musical associations listed below organize concerts, as do churches and theatres such as the Teatro Comunale. As well as the better known orchestras you'll see adverts for recitals at churches and other venues throughout the city, some by student orchestras, others by touring chamber groups; turning up a little early should guarantee a ticket at the door. Organ recitals are held in the Lutheran church on Lungarno Torrigiani (Wed; free).

For information on all events contact the tourist offices (see p.8), and consult listings at Ⓦ www.boxoffice.it, in the *La Nazione* newspaper and in *Firenze Spettacolo* (see p.8), or keep your eyes peeled for posters outside theatres, churches and elsewhere. **Tickets** for most events can usually be bought from individual venues or the **Box Office** agency, which has outlets at Via Alamanni (**Map 3, B4**, Ⓣ055.210.804) and Chiasso dei Soldanieri 8r, off Via Porta Rossa at the corner with Via de' Tornabuoni (**Map 4, E2**, Ⓣ055.219.402).

Amici della Musica

Off map. Via G. Sirtori 49
Ⓣ055.607.440,
Ⓦ www.amicimusica.fi.it.
The "Friends of Music" – one of Florence's leading musical associations – organizes a season of chamber concerts with top-name international performers from January to April and October to December. Most concerts take place on Saturday or Sunday at 4pm or 9pm. The vast majority are held in the Teatro della Pergola, built in 1656 and believed to be Italy's oldest theatre. Beautiful and intimate, it's perfectly suited to the type of concerts organized by the association. Tickets (€7.20–18) and information from Box Office or Teatro della Pergola, Via della Pergola 18 Ⓣ055.247.9651.

CLASSICAL MUSIC

FLORENTINE FESTIVALS

Florence's cultural festivals are covered on p.270: what follows is a rundown on the best of its folkloric events.

Scoppio del Carro

The first major folk festival of the year is Easter Sunday's Scoppio del Carro (Explosion of the Cart). A cartload of fireworks is hauled by six white oxen from the Porta a Prato to the Duomo, where, during the Gloria of the midday Mass, the whole lot is set off by a "dove" (representing the Holy Spirit) that whizzes down a wire from the high altar. The ceremony goes back to the time when crusader Pazzino de' Pazzi, entrusted with the flame of Holy Saturday, rigged up a ceremonial wagon to transport it round the city. His descendants managed the festival until the 1478 Pazzi Conspiracy (see p.28) lost them the office. Since then the city authorities have taken care of the business. A satisfactory outcome is supposed to presage a good harvest.

Festa del Grillo

On Candlemas, the first Sunday after Ascension Day, the Festa del Grillo (Festival of the Cricket) is held in the Cascine park. Among stalls and picnickers, people sell tiny wooden cages of crickets, which are then released for good luck. The ritual may hark back to the days when farmers had to scour their land for locusts, or to the tradition of men placing a cricket on their lovers' doors to serenade them.

Saint John's Day and the Calcio Storico

The saint's day of Florence's patron, John the Baptist (June 24) is marked by a public holiday and I Fochi di San Giovanni,

Live rock, jazz and other music, plus clubs and discos, are dealt with in Chapter 17 on pp.258–265.

a parade and massive fireworks display up on Piazzale Michelangelo. It's also the occasion of the first game of the Calcio Storico, a three-match series staged in this last week of June. Played in sixteenth-century costume, this uniquely Florentine mayhem commemorates a game that took place during the siege of 1530. Fixtures are usually held in Piazza Santa Croce (scene of that first match) and Piazza della Signoria. Each of the four historic quarters fields a team, Santa Croce playing in green, San Giovanni in red, Santa Maria Novella in blue and Santo Spirito in impractical white. The prize is a calf, which gets roasted in a street party after the tournament. For more information call ☏ 055.295.409.

Festa delle Rificolone

The Festa delle Rificolone (Festival of the Lanterns) takes place on the Virgin's birthday, September 7, with a procession of children to Piazza Santissima Annunziata. Each child carries a coloured paper lantern with a candle inside it – a throwback to the days when people from the surrounding countryside would troop by lantern-light into the city for the Feast of the Virgin. The procession is followed by a parade of floats and street parties.

Festa dell'Unità

October's Festa dell'Unità is part of a nationwide celebration run by the Italian communists, or what's left of them. Florence's is the biggest event after Bologna's, with loads of political stalls and restaurant-marquees. News about the *Feste* can be found in supplements published with Friday's edition of the left-wing daily *L'Unità*.

Associazione Giovanile Musicale

Off map. Via della Piazzuola 7r
☏ 055.580.996.

This association (A.GI.MUS for short) is devoted to young musicians and holds concerts throughout the year, often in wonderful settings: two of the best are the Concerti di Pasqua, a series of Easter concerts usually held in the church of Orsanmichele, and a summer series – in 2002, for example, concerts take place every Wednesday of September in Fiesole's Castello di Poggio. Tickets (€7.80) and information from the Box Office agency (see p.267).

Estate Fiesolana

Slightly less high-profile and exclusive than the Maggio Musicale, the Estate Fiesolana is a festival that concentrates more on chamber and symphonic music. It's held in Fiesole every summer, usually from June to late August. Films and theatre groups are also featured, and most events are held in the open-air Teatro Romano. Information ℡055.597.8423.

Filarmonica di Firenze G. Rossini

The main concert season of this Florence-based orchestra is in January and February, but it also performs a series of outdoor concerts in June in Piazza della Signoria. Information on ℡055.280.236.

Maggio Musicale Fiorentino

Ⓦ www.maggiofiorentino.com
The highlight of Florence's cultural calendar, the Maggio Musicale Fiorentino is one of Europe's leading festivals of opera and classical music; confusingly, it isn't limited to May (*maggio*), but lasts from late April to early July. The festival has its own orchestra, chorus and ballet company, whose performances alternate with guest appearances from foreign ensembles. Events are staged at the Teatro Comunale (or its Teatro Piccolo), the Teatro della Pergola, the Palazzo dei Congressi (by the train station), the Teatro Verdi and occasionally in the Boboli Garden. Information and tickets (€12.90–103.30) can be obtained from the Teatro Comunale (see opposite).

Orchestra da Camera Fiorentina

Map 3, F2. Via Enrico Poggi
Ⓣ 055.783.374,
Ⓦ www.orcafi.it.

The Florence Chamber Orchestra performs a season of concerts and also organizes performances by visiting chamber orchestras, quartets, trios and soloists between March and October. Performances are held two or three times weekly at 9pm, and usually take place in the church of San Jacopo Soprarno, off Borgo San Jacopo, in Oltrarno (Map 4, E3), or San Stefano al Ponte, immediately north of the Ponte Vecchio (Map 2, B8). Tickets (€10.30) are available from Box Office (see p.267) or from the venues themselves up to an hour before each performance.

Orchestra Regionale Toscana

Map 4, I3. Via Ghibellina 101
Ⓣ 055.280.670 or
Ⓣ 055.281.993,
Ⓦ www.dada.it/ort.

Tuscany's regional orchestra has its headquarters in Florence, and plays one or two concerts a month in the city during its main December to May season. Performances are held in the Teatro Verdi at 9pm, usually on a Saturday or Thursday. Tickets (€6.20–15.50) from Box Office (see p.267) or the Teatro Verdi, Via Ghibellina 99–101 Ⓣ 055.212.320.

Teatro Comunale

Map 3, A7. Corso Italia 16
Ⓣ 055.213.535 or
Ⓣ 055.211.158.

The dreary-looking Teatro Comunale is Florence's main municipal theatre, and as such hosts many of the city's major classical music, dance and theatre productions. It hosts performances by fine world-class names, as well as its own orchestra, chorus and dance company. The main season (concerts, opera and ballet) runs from January to April and September to December, with concerts usually held on Friday, Saturday and Sunday evenings.

CLASSICAL MUSIC

CINEMA

Florence has a large number of **cinemas**, but very few show subtitled films, and nearly all English-language films are dubbed. See *Firenze Spettacolo* or the listings pages of *La Nazione* for locations and latest screenings. A handful of cinemas have regular English-language screenings – promoted as *versione originale*.

Florence has two major **film festivals**: *Under Florence* (first two weeks of December), which shows Tuscan and other Italian independent films and videos, and the more worthy *Festival dei Popoli* (two weeks in November or December), concerned with social documentaries – though it does have less earnest programmes on for example, François Truffaut, or jazz in the cinema. For information on both events contact the Cinema Alfieri Atelier, Via dell'Ulivo 6 (℡055.240.720).

From June to September there are often seasons of open-air cinema, at varying locations: ask at the tourist office for the latest venues.

Astra Cine Hall – Original Sound

Map 2, B1. Via Cerratani 54r, ℡ 055.294.770, ⓦ www.cinehall.it.
Closed mid-June to Aug.
By far the most arty of Florence's cinemas showing original language films, with one drawback: the emphasis is on non-anglophone productions and the subtitles are in Italian. Screenings are every Thursday, usually just in the early afternoon and late evening only. Good central location, a step west of the Duomo.

Fulgor

Map 3, B7. Via dei Maso Finiguerra ℡ 055.238.1881, ⓦ www.cinemafulgor.it.
Another Thursday-only cinema, offering a familiar diet of easily digested

Hollywood productions. Located a little way west, beyond Ognissanti, but reasonably handy if you're in the vicinity of the train station.

Odeon Cine Hall – Original Sound

Map 2, A4. Piazza Strozzi/Via de' Sassetti 1 ⓣ 055.214.068,

Ⓦ www.cinehall.it.

Closed mid-June to Aug.

The grandest and plushest of Florence's cinemas, packing in the international students, with three original language films weekly, usually on Mondays, Tuesdays and Thursdays. Very close to Piazza della Repubblica.

THEATRE

If your Italian is up to a performance of the plays of Machiavelli or Pirandello in the original, Florence's **theatres** offer year-round entertainment, some of it riskier than the generally conservative repertoire of the city's concert halls and musical associations. In addition to the places listed below, various halls and disused churches are enlisted for one-off performances – keep an eye out for posters, or drop in to Box Office (see p.267) or the tourist offices (see p.8) for the latest information.

Teatro Comunale

Off map. Corso Italia 16 ⓣ 055.277.9236.

Florence's principal performance space hosts theatre as well as dance and performances of classical music (see p.271). Productions here are usually

mainstream and uncontentious. Located west of Ognissanti off Lungarno Amerigo Vespucci.

Teatro della Pergola

Map 3, I7. Via della Pergola 18 ⓣ 055.226.4316, Ⓔ teatro@pergola.firenze.it.

THEATRE

FOOTBALL

Florence's soccer team, **Fiorentina** – or the *Viola*, after their natty purple shirts – is usually one of Italy's glamour sides. In the early 1990s they produced one of Italy's most lavishly talented players, the mercurial Roberto Baggio, transferred to Juventus for what was then a world record transfer fee of £7,700,000 amid scenes of fervent protest in Florence. Fiorentina last won the league title in 1969, however, and in 1993 – the year Baggio was voted European Footballer of the Year – they suffered the ultimate ignominy. Halfway through the season they sacked their coach, went on to win just three games out of nineteen, and were relegated for the first time in 55 years, despite the services of such world-class players as Brian Laudrup and Stefan Effenberg.

But they returned to the top flight, thanks in part to the services of Argentinian wonderboy Gabriel Batistuta (aka "Batigol"), and even won the Italian cup in 1996. But Batistuta left Fiorentina in 2000 and despite the presence of international stars such as Nuno Gomes and Rui Costa – who helped capture the Italian cup once more, in 2001 – the team are

Box office Tues–Sat 9.30am–1pm & 3.45–6.45pm, Sun 9.45am–noon.

The beautiful little Pergola is Florence's main classical theatre, its intimate seventeenth-century interior hosting some of the best-known Italian companies. Productions are usually Italian or foreign classics in translation. The season runs from October to May.

Teatro Verdi
Map 4, I2. Via Ghibellina 99–101 ℡055.263.8777, Ⓔ info@teatroverdi.firenze.it. Box office daily 10am–noon & 4–7pm.

Theatre productions at the

probably a couple of players short of the squad needed to beat the mighty Juventus and top the league. Moreover, as the 2001/2 season got underway, the club's future rested on its accounts rather than its score sheet, with bankruptcy threatened. That said, it would be a brave bank that called in the club's debt.

Games are played at the **Stadio Artemio Franchi** between August and May on alternate Sundays. To check on ticket availability and fixtures, call ☏ 055.292.363, ☏ 055.572.625 or ☏ 055.587.858, or contact the tourist office (see p.8). Tickets cost from around €15 to €90 and can be bought at the ground itself, in theory at least. You can sometimes obtain tickets from the Toto booth on Piazza della Repubblica, on the Tuesday before the game (arrive before 9am), but casual visitors are likely to be forced to deal with the illegal touts outside the game, who charge a hefty mark-up. To get to the ground, take bus #17 from the station. The classic fans' bar is the *Maresi*, on Via della Manfredo Fanti, just opposite the main stand.

Teatro Verdi, another of the city's premier venues, are similar to the mainstream fare of the Teatro Comunale, though you may occasionally catch the odd musical.

FOOTBALL

●

Kids' Florence

Florence is not the best city for a holiday with the **kids**. An endless round of galleries and museums is going to exhaust – and probably bore – most children. Hot weather will make already tired kids even more fractious, while crowds and busy streets mean you need to keep an eagle eye on your offspring.

On the plus side, though, the Italians' famous fondness for children helps offset the relative shortage of child-friendly attractions. Any toddler – the younger and blonder the better – will also ease the way in dealings with waiters, hotel staff and Italian bureaucracy. **Hotels** and **restaurants**, even smart ones, are usually happy to make special provisions for children (though be warned that there's no such thing as a smoke-free environment). Hotels normally charge around thirteen percent extra to put a child's bed or cot in your room.

The only **hazards** are the summer heat and sun. Sunblock can be bought at any chemist, and bonnets or straw hats in most markets. Take advantage of the less intense periods – mornings and evenings – for travelling, and use the quiet of siesta time to recover flagging energy. The rhythms of the southern climate soon modify established patterns, and you'll find it more natural carrying on later into the night past normal bedtimes. In summer, it's not unusual to see Italian children out at midnight, and not looking much the worse for it.

A number of bookshops in the city (see p.280) stock **books** aimed at opening up the city to bored children or teenagers. *Florence for Kids* (€11.40) is quite a useful general guide with questions to answer and plentiful illustrations, but it's not quite sure what age it's aiming at – 12-year-olds may find the tone patronizing. *Florence for Teens* (€9.30) won't convince many adolescents, but has useful facts presented by Florentine "pen pals". Other books focus on art and may help sustain interest during gallery visits.

SIGHTS

Certain **museums** hold out more than usual allure, notably the Palazzo Vecchio (see p.46), with its multimedia screens and workshops dedicated to children (Ⓦ www.museoragazzi.it). The Museo di Storia della Scienza (see p.57), La Specola (see p.188) and the Museo Archeologico (see p.146) may also prove popular, and the odd **gallery** is likely to be a winner. Many children will be familiar with Michelangelo's *David*, and will probably be tickled by seeing it in the flesh (see p.125), while the enormous sculpted face/mask in the Giardino di Boboli is perennially popular (see pp.186 and 278). Fun and narrative-filled frescoes such as those in the Palazzo Medici-Riccardi should also appeal (see p.120). The suits of armour and Giambologna's bronze menagerie in the Bargello (see p.77) are another possibility.

Among other sights, the novelty of the Ponte Vecchio (see p.177) makes it one of the more obvious for kids, closely followed by anywhere which offers views – the Campanile and the Duomo (see pp.21 and 20) are obvious high points to make for, though coaxing younger children up all the steps will be a tall order. Don't forget the famous

Porcellino, the little bronze boar with a much polished snout in the Mercato Nuovo (see p.290). The sights and sounds of the Mercato Centrale (see pp.123 and 290) and San Lorenzo market (see p.291) may also appeal.

PARKS AND POOLS

Children will probably relish the **open spaces** of the Giardino di Boboli (see p.186), and its giant sculpture of a broken face, which stands near the top of the main section's westernmost avenue. Reasonably central is the playground in Piazza Massimo d'Azeglio, on Via Niccolini (**Map 3, L6**). Further afield, the Cascine park to the west of the city centre (bus #1, #17 or #B) has plenty of swings, slides and a small, tree-shaded central swimming pool, Le Pavoniere, on Viale Catena (daily May–Sept 10am–6pm; ☏055.333.979).

A better **pool complex** for small children, by virtue of its range of shallower paddling pools, is the Piscina di Bellariva on Lungarno Colombo (daily May–Sept 10am–6pm; ☏055.677.541): bus #31/32 drops you nearby. Much the largest pool in the city, with slides, games and so on, is the municipal Piscina Costoli (daily 9am–6pm; ☏055.670.812), in the sports stadium east of the centre, on Viale Paoli; bus #10 connects with the station and Piazza San Marco.

FOOD AND DRINK

There are few greater culinary treats than an Italian ice cream – see p.240 for more. Fresh milk shakes (*frullati* or *frappè*) and slices of pizza (*pizza taglia*) should also appeal, while older children may enjoy the novelty of breakfast in a bar. If Italian food fails, then there are several fast-food outlets, including branches of *McDonald's* by the Ponte Vecchio and inside and just outside the train station.

Shopping

I f you're after high-quality clothes and accessories, paintings, prints and marbled paper, or any number of other beautiful or luxury objects, then you'll find them in Florence. Your credit may be stretched to the limit, though – this is no city for bargain-hunters.

Its best-known area of manufacturing expertise is **leather**

OPENING HOURS

Usual **opening hours** for most shops are Monday 3.30–7.30pm, Tuesday–Saturday 8.30/9am to 1pm and 3.30 to 7.30pm. Afternoon opening and evening closing may vary by an hour so, especially in summer, when many shops open and close later – typically from 4 to 8pm. Some shops also close all of Saturday afternoon in summer, and many establishments will close down for a summer break of up to a month in either July or August.

Food shops are a notable exception to the general rule – most close on Wednesday morning throughout the year. So, too, are department stores, which tend to be open throughout the day with no lunchtime closing, a practice increasingly being taken up by clothes shops and other forward-looking stores.

goods, with top-quality shoes, bags and gloves sold across the city. The main concentration of quality outlets is around **Via de' Tornabuoni** – the city's premier shopping thoroughfare – and the tributaries of Via degli Strozzi and Via della Vigna Nuova, also home to the shops of virtually all Italy's top fashion designers. If their prices are too steep, passable imitations (and outright **fakes**) can be unearthed at the various **street markets**, of which San Lorenzo is the most central. If you want everything under one roof, there's a handful of upmarket department stores. **Marbled paper** is another Florentine speciality, and, as you'd expect from this arty city, it has some of the best places in the country to pick up **books** on Italian art, architecture and general culture.

BOOKS

- - - - - - - - - - - - - - - - - - - -

BM

Map 3, C8. Borgo Ognissanti 4r Ⓣ 055.294.575, Ⓔ bmbookshop@dada.it. April–Oct daily 9.30am–7.30pm, Nov–March Mon–Sat 9am–1pm & 3.30–7.30pm.

A comfortable English-language bookshop with a wide selection of guidebooks and general English and American titles, with particular emphasis on Italian literature in translation and art, cookery and travel books connected with Italy.

Edison

Map 3, D1. Piazza della Repubblica 27r Ⓣ 055.213.110. Daily 9am–midnight, Sun 10am–midnight.

American-style book buying comes to Italy. It may not have necessarily the largest selection in the city, despite the three spacious floors arranged around a large building in the northwest corner of Piazza della Repubblica. It does boast, however, internet connection (expensive at €5.20 per hour), coffee and home-made cakes, and swarms of studenty types.

Feltrinelli
Map 2, B1. Via Cerretani 30r
ⓣ 055.238.2652.
Mon–Sat 9am–7.30pm.
Part of a modern Italy-wide chain, and the city's best overall bookshop. You'll find most Italian titles here, and an excellent selection of maps, guides and other English-language titles downstairs; the sister store (see below) specializes in foreign-language material.

Feltrinelli International
Map 3, G6. Via Cavour 12r
ⓣ 055.219.524.
Mon–Sat 9am–7.30pm.
Bright, modern and well staffed, this is by far the best organized of the large central shops. The first port of call for any English or other foreign language books, newspapers and videos, as well as posters, cards and magazines.

Libreria delle Donne
Map 3, J8. Via Fiesolana 2b
ⓣ 055.240.384.
Mon 3.30–7.30pm, Tues–Sat 9am–1pm & 3.30–7.30pm.
A specialist women's bookshop, though most of the titles are in Italian. The noticeboard here is an excellent point of reference for information and contacts regarding women's and lesbian groups in Florence.

Paperback Exchange
Map 3, K7. Via Fiesolana 31r
ⓣ 055.247.8154,
ⓦ www.papex.it.
Mon–Fri 9am–7.30pm, Sat 9am–1pm & 3.30–7.30pm.
A little outlying (north of Santa Croce), but the staff are informative and friendly, and there's a good stock of English and American books, particularly Italian-related titles. The shop also operates an exchange scheme for secondhand books.

Seeber
Map 3, E8. Via de' Tornabuoni 68–70r ⓣ 055.215.697,
ⓔ lib_seeber@libero.it.
Mon–Sat 9.30am–7.30pm.
Long regarded by many as the best general bookshop in the city, it's certainly the most handsome. The art and antiques section alone has over 10,000 titles, there are

BOOKS

scores of guidebooks and the foreign language department is also highly renowned. High rents in the Via de' Tornabuoni will soon be forcing the bookshop out, however; its new destination was undecided at the time of writing.

CLOTHES

There are **clothes shops** all over Florence, many of them selling the sort of "classics" you might well find cheaper at home. We've listed some of the principal designer outlets in case you're planning to make a special purchase while still in free-spending holiday mode. Most other big names have outlets in the city on or near Via de' Tornabuoni: Prada, Trussardi, Valentino, Versace, Louis Vuitton…

Armani

Map 4, D1. Via della Vigna Nuova 51r ⓣ 055.219.041. Mon 3.30–7.30pm, Tues–Sat 10am–7.30pm.

Gorgeous clothes from the most astute designer in Italy, at prices that make you think you must have misread the tag.

Emporio Armani

Map 3, E8. Piazza Strozzi 14–16r ⓣ 055.284.315. Mon 3.30–7.30pm, Tues–Sat 10am–1pm & 3.30–7.30pm.

The lowest-priced wing of the Armani empire, this is really only a place to go if you're desperate to get Italy's number one label on your back – you're paying a fair premium for the name, and the quality isn't all it could be at the price.

Enrico Coveri

Map 4, D1. Via della Vigna Nuova 27–29r & Via de' Tornabuoni 81r ⓣ 055.211.263. Mon–Sat 10am–7.30pm.

Born in nearby Prato, Coveri specialized in bold multicoloured outfits that contrast sharply with the prevailing sobriety of

Florentine design. The designs produced by his firm since his death continue along the founder's path.

Ferragamo

Map 3, E8. Via de' Tornabuoni 14r Ⓣ 055.292.123.
Mon 3.30–7.30pm, Tues–Sat 9.30am–7.30pm.

Salvatore Ferragamo emigrated to the US at the age of 14 to become the most famous shoemaker in the world, producing everything from pearl-studded numbers for Gloria Swanson to gladiators' sandals for Cecil B. de Mille's blockbusters. Managed by Salvatore's widow and children, Ferragamo has expanded to occupy the entire grand floor of Palazzo Spini, and now produces complete ready-to-wear outfits. But the firm's reputation still rests on its beautiful, comfortable and expensive shoes.

Gucci

Map 3, E8. Via de' Tornabuoni 73r & Via della Vigna Nuova 11r Ⓣ 055.264.011.
Mon 3–7pm, Tues–Sat 10am–7pm, Sun 2–7pm.

The Gucci empire was founded at no. 73, which remains the company's flagship showroom; everything is impeccably made, but even if it weren't the demand for the linked Gs would probably keep going under its own momentum.

Pucci

Map 3, G6. Showroom at Via dei Pucci 6.
Map 3, D8. Shop at Via della Vigna Nuova 97r Ⓣ 055.294.028.
Mon 3.30–7.30pm, Tues–Sat 9am–1pm & 3.30–7.30pm.

Marchese Emilio Pucci first stunned the catwalk shows in the 1950s with his vividly dyed, swirling-patterned silks. After a lull, Pucci suddenly became the London clubland uniform in 1990, and their £400 shirts were selling so fast that supply couldn't keep up. The wave may have broken, but the name still carries some clout in fashion circles.

CLOTHES

DEPARTMENT STORES

Coin

Map 2, D4. Via dei Calzaiuoli 56r ⓣ 055.280.531.
Mon–Sat 9.30am–8pm, Sun 11am–8pm.

This mid-market chainstore in an excellent central position has a wide variety of branded and own-brand clothes. Quality is generally high, though styles are fairly conservative except for one or two youth-oriented franchises on the ground floor. Also a good place for linens and other household goods.

Rinascente

Map 2, C4. Piazza della Repubblica 1 ⓣ 055.239.8544.
Mon–Sat 9am–9pm, Sun 10.30am–8pm.

Like Coin, Rinascente is part of a countrywide chain, though this newish store, opened in 1996, is definitely a touch more upmarket than its nearby rival. Sells clothes, linens, cosmetics, household goods and other department store staples.

HOUSEHOLD GOODS

Bartolini

Map 3, H6. Via dei Servi 30r, corner of Via Bufalini
ⓣ 055.289.223,
ⓦ www.dinobartolini.it
Mon 3.30–7.30pm; Tues–Sat 9am–1pm, 3.30–7.30.

Bartolini was founded in 1921 and has since become such a fixture of Florentine life that the spot on which it stands is known locally as the *angolo Bartolini*, or "Bartolini corner". It offers a tremendous range of porcelain and glassware from Italian and international specialists, including Wedgwood and Spode, as well as a staggering range of kitchenware.

Mazzoni

Map 2, C4. Via Orsanmichele 14r ⓣ 055.215.153.
Tues–Sat 9.30am–1pm, 3.30–7.30pm; closed Saturday afternoon in summer.

One of three Mazzoni stores in the city, a small chain that has been renowned for its fabrics, linens, towels, pyjamas and similar products for over a century.

La Ménagère
Map 3, G5. Via de' Ginori 8r
℡ 055.213.875.
Mon 3.30–7.30, Tues–Sat 9am–1pm.
This shop behind the Palazzo Medici-Riccardi was founded in 1911 and has been in the same family since 1921. Over several floors you'll find a host of china, ceramics, glassware and

contemporary and traditional design items.

Mesticheria Mazzanti
Map 3, L8. Borgo La Croce 101r ℡ 055.248.0663.
Mon–Fri 9am–1pm, 3.30–7.30pm, Sat 9am–1pm.
Northwest of Santa Croce, the Mesticheria Mazzanti store has, since 1930, sold a bewildering variety of items – anything from screws, lightbulbs and cutlery to seeds, saucepans and coffee-makers.

FOOD AND DRINK

Excellent little **delicatessens** and general food shops (*alimentari*) can be found on virtually every street. These are more than adequate for picnic supplies, but like the city's street markets – notably the Mercato Centrale – they can also be used to purchase that special bottle of oil or hunk of parmesan to take home.

Brunori
Map 3, J7. Borgo Pinti 16r
℡ 055.248.0809.
Mon–Tues & Thurs–Sat 8am–1pm, 3.30–8pm; Wed 8am–1pm; closed Saturday afternoon in summer.
This wonderful bakery sells one of Florence's best selections of bread, foccacia and pizza by the slice, making

it a great source of picnic provisions.

Pegna
Map 2, F3. Via dello Studio 26r
℡ 055.282.701 or
℡ 055.282.702,
Ⓦ www.pegna.it.
Mon–Tues & Thurs–Sat 9am–1pm, 3.30–7.30pm; Wed 9am–1pm; closed Saturday afternoon in summer.

FOOD AND DRINK

Florentines have flocked to this superb delicatessen a few steps south of the Duomo since it opened in 1860. Over 7000 items are stocked from Italy and the rest of the world, including top-quality cheeses, hams, wines, cakes, preserves and other gourmet products.

Procacci

Map 3, E8. Via Tornabuoni, 64r.
Mon–Sat 10.30–8pm.

Certainly not the place to pick up a bargain, but if you're looking for luxury goods such as truffles, wine and fine olive oils you could hardly do better. Try a *panino tartufato* while you're here (see p.251).

Stenio del Panta

Map 3, F5. Via Sant'Antonino 49r ⊤ 055.216.889.
Summer: Mon–Fri 7am–7.30pm, Sat 7am–1pm; winter Mon 4–7.30pm, Tues–Sat 8am–7.30pm.

Generations of Florentines have patronized this food store close to the Mercato, known above all for its many types of preserved fish (salt cod, tuna, sardines and anchovies). You can also buy good sandwiches to take away – the staff will make up orders with your choice of filling.

JEWELLERY

The whole Ponte Vecchio is crammed with **jewellers' shops**, most of them catering strictly to the financial stratosphere. Those of more limited means could either take a chance on the counterfeits and low-cost originals peddled by street vendors on and around the bridge, or check out the places below.

Bijoux Cascio

Map 3, E8. Via de' Tornabuoni 32r.
Map 2, B8. Via Por Santa Maria 1r.

Mon 3.30–7.30pm, Tues–Sat 9.30am–1pm & 3.30–7.30pm.

Cascio has made a name for itself over the last thirty years as a maker of imitation jewellery; it takes a trained eye to distinguish its work from the window displays on the Ponte Vecchio.

Gatto Bianco

Map 4, E2. Borgo SS. Apostoli 12r ⓣ055.282.989.
Mon 3–7pm, Tues–Sat 9.30am–1pm & 3–7pm.
Combinations of precious and everyday materials are the signature of this outlet, one of the city's more adventurous workshops.

Torrini

Map 3, G7. Piazza del Duomo 10r ⓣ055.230.2401.
Mon 3.30–7.30pm, Tues–Sat 9.30am–1pm & 3.30–7.30pm.
Torrini registered its trademark – a distinctive half clover-leaf with spur – as early as 1369. More than seven centuries later this store remains one of the premier places to buy Florentine jewellery: gold still predominates, but all manner of classic and modern pieces are available – at a price.

PAPER AND STATIONERY

Giannini

Map 4, E5. Piazza Pitti 37r ⓣ055.280.814.
Mon–Sat 9am–7.30pm.
Established in 1856, this paper-making and book-binding firm was once the only place in Florence to make its own marbled papers; now its exclusivity is more an economic one. They also sell diaries, address books and stationery made from the paper.

Pineider

Map 2, D6. Piazza della Signoria 13r & Via de' Tornabuoni 76r ⓣ055.284.655 or ⓣ055.211.605.
Mon 3.30–7.30pm, Tues–Sat 10am–7.30pm, Sun 10am–2pm & 3.30–7.30pm.
Founded in 1774, this is Italy's ultimate stationer's: Florence's gentry would rather die than use anything except Pineider's colour-coordinated calling cards, handmade papers and envelopes. Napoleon,

PAPER AND STATIONERY

Stendhal, Byron, Shelley, Puccini and Maria Callas are just a few past customers. Another, Elizabeth Taylor, ordered Pineider visiting cards in purple to match her eyes.

Il Torchio

Map 4, F4. Via de' Bardi 17
℡ 055.234.2862.
Mon–Fri 9am–1pm & 3.30–7.30pm, Sat 9.30am–1pm.
A marbled paper workshop that scores over some of its competitors by charging slightly lower prices. Several of the colouring and manufacturing techniques are known only to Signora Anna, the business's owner. Desk accessories, diaries, albums and other items in paper and leather are also available.

Zecchi

Map 2, F3. Via dello Studio 19r
℡ 055.211.470.
Mon–Fri 8.30am–12.30pm, 3.30–7.30pm; Sat 8.30am–12.30pm
Just the sort of shop you would expect in an artistic city like Florence, Zecchi is a haven for artists, filled with paints, pigments, papers, brushes and any other artist's material you care to mention: it's worth a look even if you don't intend to buy anything.

PERFUMES AND TOILETRIES

Farmacia Santa Maria Novella

Map 3, D7. Via della Scala 16
℡ 055.216.276.
Mon–Sat 9.30am–7.30pm, Sun 10.30am–6.30pm.
Occupying the virtually unaltered pharmacy of the Santa Maria Novella monastery – formerly a thirteenth-century chapel – the shop's as famous for its wonderful interior as for its wares. It was founded in the sixteenth century by Dominican monks as an outlet for elixirs, potions and ointments from their gardens and workshops. Many of these are still available, including countless extracts and distillations of flowers and herbs, together with face creams, shampoos and soaps.

PRINTS AND ENGRAVINGS

Giovanni Baccani

Map 3, D8. Via della Vigna Nuova 75r ☎055.214.467.
Mon 3.30–7.30pm, Tues–Sat 9am–1pm & 3.30–7.30pm.
A beautiful old shop established in 1903 that's crammed with all manner of lovely prints, frames and paintings. Prices range from a few Euros (a few thousand lire) into the realms of credit-card madness.

SHOES AND ACCESSORIES

Beltrami

Map 3, E8. Via de' Tornabuoni 48r ☎055.287.779.
Mon 3.30–7.30pm, Tues–Sat 9.30am–1pm & 3.30–7.30pm.
Beltrami is a chain with outlets across Italy, though few of its shops are as spectacular as this one, selling high-fashion, high-priced shoes, bags, leather, and clothes for men and women.

Cellerini

Map 3, D7. Via del Sole 37r ☎055.282.533.
Mon 3.30–7.30pm, Tues–Sat 9.30am–1pm & 3.30–7.30pm.
Bags, bags and more bags. Everything is made on the premises, under the supervision of the founders. Bags don't come more elegant, durable – or costly. Over 600 styles to choose from.

Francesco da Firenze

Map 4, C3. Via Santo Spirito 62r ☎055.212.428.
Mon–Sat 8.30am–1pm & 3–7.30pm.
Handmade shoes for men and women at remarkably reasonable prices. Designs combine classic footwear with more striking designs: the workshop supplies UK chain Hobbs.

Pusateri

Map 2, D5. Via Calzauoli 25r ☎055.212.614.
Mon 3.30–7.30pm, Tues–Sun 9am–7.30pm.
Gloves: fur-lined, silk- and string-backed, beige, cream, tan, yellow, driving, ladies'

PRINTS AND ENGRAVINGS • SHOES AND ACCESSORIES

and gents'. From €15.50 and a long way up.

Madova

Map 4, E4. Via Guicciardini 1r
☎ 055.239.6526.
Mon–Sat 9am–7pm.
The last word in gloves: every colour, every size, every shape… though mostly in the upper price bracket.

Peruzzi

Map 4, I2. Borgo de' Greci 8–20r ☎ 055.289.039,
Ⓦ www.peruzzispa.com.
Mon–Sat 9am–7pm.
Cavernous leather goods store with stock ranging from ties to trousers, as well as the obligatory shoes, bags and wallets. The quality and the prices aren't necessarily the very best but are certainly good enough, and it's useful to find such a variety of styles under one roof.

STREET MARKETS

- -

Cascine

Parco del Cascine.
Tues 8am–1pm.
Biggest of all Florence's

markets is the Tuesday morning one at the Cascine park near the banks of the Arno on the west side of the city (bus #1, #9, #12 or #17c), where hundreds of stallholders of all descriptions set up an alfresco budget-class department store. Few tourists make it out here, so prices are keen. Clothes and shoes (including secondhand clothes) are the best bargains, though for the cheapest clothes in Florence you should check out the weekday morning stalls at Piazza delle Cure, just beyond Piazza della Libertà (bus #1 or #7).

Mercato Centrale

Map 3, F5. Piazza del Mercato Centrale.
Mon–Fri 7am–2pm, plus Sat afternoon in winter.
Europe's largest indoor food hall is situated at the heart of the stall-filled streets around San Lorenzo. Great for picnic supplies, as well as people-watching. See also p.123.

Mercato Nuovo

Map 2, B6. Loggia del Mercato

Nuovo.

Mon–Sat 9am–7pm.

Just to the west of Piazza della Signoria, this is the main emporium for straw hats, plastic *Davids* and the like.

Mercato dei Pulci

Map 4, K2. Piazza dei Ciompi.

Mon–Sat 9am–7pm.

A bric-a-brac market is pitched every day near the Sant'Ambrogio food market; more professional antique dealers swell the ranks on the last Sunday of each month, from 9am to 7pm.

The name refers to *pulci* – fleas.

San Lorenzo

Map 3, F6. Piazza di San Lorenzo.

Daily 9am–7pm.

The market around the church of San Lorenzo is another open-air warehouse of cheap clothing. Huge waterproof awnings ensure that the weather can't stop the trading, and some of the stallholders even accept credit cards.

Fakes of well known brands account for much of the turnover at San Lorenzo. Some big-name companies have gangs of counterfeit-busters to root them out – and to their embarrassment, they've not always been able easily to distinguish the fake from the real thing.

STREET MARKETS

Directory

AIRLINES Air France, Borgo SS. Apostoli 9 (℡ 055.284.304); Alitalia, Piazza dell' Oro 1r (℡ 055.27.881, 🌐 www.alitalia.it); British Airways, Pisa Airport (free phone 147.812.266); Lufthansa, Via Lamberti 39r (℡ 055.217.936); Meridiana, Lungarno Vespucci 28r (℡ 055.230.2314).

AIRPORT INFORMATION Aeroporto Galileo Galilei, Pisa (℡ 050.500.707, 🌐 www.pisa-airport.com); information also from the check-in desk at Santa Maria Novella train station, platform 5 (daily 7am–8pm). Peretola-Amerigo Vespucci airport (℡ 055.306.1700, flight information ℡ 055.373.498, 🌐 www.safnet.it).

BANKS AND EXCHANGE Florence's main bank branches are on or around Piazza della Repubblica (Map 2, F5), but exchange booths (*cambio*) and ATM cash-card machines (*bancomat*) for Visa, Mastercard and Eurocheque advances are found across the city. Banks generally open Mon–Fri 8.30am–1.30pm and 2.30–4pm, but increasingly open longer. American Express is on Via Dante Alighieri 22r (Mon–Fri 9am–5.30pm, Sat 9am–12.30pm ℡ 055.50.981, 🖷 055.509.8240); and Thomas Cook at Lungarno Acciaiuoli 6–12r (℡ 055.289.781; Mon–Sat 9am–6pm, Sun 9am–2pm).

BIKE RENTAL Alinari, Via Guelfa 85r (℡ 055.280.500;

Mon–Sat 9am–1pm & 3–7.30pm, Sun 10am–1pm & 3–7pm). Rates are €2 hourly, €6.20 per five hours, €10.30 daily and €18 for a weekend (Fri pm–Sun). The same rates are charged by Florence by Bike, Via Zanobi 120r (☎055.488.992, ⓦwww .florencebybike.it; daily 9am–7.30pm). In summer, the municipality rents more basic bikes for €1.60 per hour from stalls outside the train station and on Piazza Strozzi.

BUSES Most buses to destinations outside the city (including SITA services to Florence airport) depart from the bus station immediately west of the train station at Via Santa Caterina da Siena 17 (city services: ATAF ☎800.424.500; services to Peretola airport ☎055.214.721; state-run services all over Italy: SITA, Via Santa Caterina di Siena 15 ☎800.373.760 or ☎055.214.721, ⓦwww .sita-on-line.it). The offices for

most other private bus companies, for other destinations in Tuscany and beyond, are found near around the bus and train station; contact the tourist office for details.

CAR RENTAL Avis, Borgo Ognissanti 128r (☎055.239.8826, airport ☎055.315.558); Europcar, Borgo Ognissanti 53r (☎055.290.438, airport ☎055.236.0073, ⓦwww .europcar.it); Excelsior, Via Lulli 76 (☎055.321.5397 or ☎055.321.6947); Hertz, Via Maso Finiguerra 33r (☎055.239.820 or ☎055.282.260, ⓦwww.hertz.it); Maggiore, Via Maso Finiguerra 31r (☎055.282.260 or ☎055.422.343); airport ☎055.307.370; Program/Thrifty, Borgo Ognissanti 135r (☎055.282.916); Thrifty, Borgo Ognissanti 134r (☎055.287.161).

More information on getting to and from Florence, airports, trains, buses and city transport, as well as details of tourist information can be found on pp.4–12.

CONSULATES UK, Lungarno Corsini 2 (☎ 055.284.133); US, Lungarno Amerigo Vespucci 38 (☎ 055.239.8276). Travellers from Ireland (☎ 06.697.9121), Australia (☎ 06.685.2721), New Zealand (☎ 06.440.2928) and Canada (☎ 06.445.981) should contact their Rome consulates.

CONTRACEPTION Condoms (*preservativi* or *profilattici*) are available over the counter from pharmacies and some supermarkets.

DISABLED TRAVEL Florence, with its narrow, often cobbled streets crowded with parked cars, is not an easy city to negotiate in a wheelchair. More generally, neither Florence nor Italy in general is particularly well equipped to help travellers with disabilities. Pisa and Florence airports, the train station and one or two major sights have special toilets. Most city buses have special low seats close to the front, while the newest buses are fully wheelchair-accessible: there are lifts at the rear and space for wheelchairs on board. Newer trains have wheelchair provisions in carriages (look for

the wheelchair sign) but rarely any means of getting a wheelchair into the carriage save by clumsy manhandling. Taxis should be able to deal with wheelchairs, but tell them when booking a car that you might need help.

DOCTORS The Tourist Medical Service (IAMAT) is a private service used to dealing with foreigners and can also dispatch a doctor within 90 minutes 24 hours a day (☎ 055.475.411 or 0335.692.2781); a visit will cost from about €46.50 upwards. Alternatively you can visit their clinic for a consultation at Via Lorenzo il Magnifico 59 (Mon–Fri 11am–noon & 5–6pm, Sat 11am–noon), or call in at the hospital, Piazza Santa Maria Nuova 1 (☎ 055.27.581), where you'll find most medical staff speak at least competent English.

ELECTRICITY The supply is 220V AC (50 cycles) and compatible with all UK (but not US) appliances. A two-pin adaptor is required; buy one before travelling as they're hard to come by in Italy. A few older plugs may still have three-pin or slightly different two-pin arrangements, in which case you'll need to borrow an adaptor from your hotel or buy one from an electrical shop.

EMERGENCIES Police ⓣ112; ambulance ⓣ118; fire ⓣ115; any emergency ⓣ113; car breakdown ⓣ116. Lost or stolen passports: report to police and contact your consulate (see p.294). Central police station ⓣ055.49.771 (see p.296). Lost credit cards: Amex ⓣ1678.64.046; Diners Club ⓣ1678.64.064; Mastercard ⓣ1678.70.866; Visa ⓣ1678.77.232.

HOSPITALS Florence's most central hospital is Santa Maria Nuova, Piazza Santa Maria Nuova 1 (ⓣ055.27.581). Call 118 for an ambulance.

HOTEL BOOKING AGENCIES The Informazioni Turistiche Alberghiere (ITA), just inside the train station (daily 8.45am–9pm; ⓣ055.282.893) can book rooms on the spot (see p.213). For advance booking through private agencies, try Family Hotels, Viale Fratelli Rosselli 39r (ⓣ055.333.403, ⓕ055.324.7058) or Florence

Promhotels, Viale Volta 72 (ⓣ055.570.481, ⓕ055.587.189). For private rooms, Prenotazioni Afittacamere, Piazza San Marco 7 (ⓣ & ⓕ055.284.100). The internet is another resource: ⓦwww.firenze.turismo.toscana.it and ⓦwww.comune.firenze.it have listings and links to individual hotels.

INTERNET ACCESS The presence of so many students and visitors means you can hardly stir hand or foot without coming across an internet café, or *internet point*, as they're known in Italian. Most don't serve coffee but do stay open late. Prices hover around €5 per hour, mostly subdivided into quarter or half hours, but offers for students, "happy hours" and the like make it possible to spend as little as €2.60 an hour, and the price drops the longer you stay on. The two biggest companies, with branches all over the city, are Net Gate and Internet Train, both of which operate a rechargeable card-based system. Central internet points can be found: near the Duomo, at Via Sant' Egidio 10r, Via degli Alfani 11r and Via dell' Oriuolo 40r; near Piazza Signoria,

DIRECTORY

●

295

at Via dei Cimatori 17r and Via dei Neri 37r; near Santa Croce at Via de' Benci 30r, Via Ghibellina 98r and Via de' Macci 8r; near San Lorenzo at Via dei Conti 22r; near San Marco at Via delle Ruote 14r; in the train station itself and its underground arcade, and nearby at Via Nazionale 156r and Via Guelfa 24; in Oltrarno, at Via de' Serragli 76r, Borgo San Jacopo 30r and Via Santa Monaca 6r.

LAUNDRY Florence has plenty of self-service *lavanderie* which cost around €3.10 for a complete wash and are mostly open all day. Some even have internet access. Ask at your hotel for the nearest, or head for one of the following: Guelfa, Via Guelfa 106r; Self Service, Via Faenza 26r; Wash & Dry, Via dei Servi 105r, Via della Scala 52r, Via del Sole 29r, Via Ghibellina 143r, Via dei Serragli 87r, Via Nazionale 129r.

LEFT LUGGAGE The left-luggage desk at the main Santa Maria Novella train station, between platform 15 and the exit, is open 24 hours.

LOST PROPERTY ATAF city buses: Via Circondaria 19 (Mon–Wed & Fri–Sat 9am–noon; ☎055.328.3942); take bus #23 to Viale Corsica. Trains: Santa Maria Novella station; the office is on platform 16 next to left luggage; open daily 4.15am–1.30am (☎055.235.2190). Peretola airport: call ☎055.308.023.

PHARMACIES The main all-night pharmacy (*farmacia*) is the Comunale della Stazione (☎055.289.435) on the main train station concourse (no credit cards). Another central late-opening option is Molteni, Via dei Calzaiuoli 7r (☎055.289.490). Normal opening hours for pharmacies are Mon–Sat 9am–1pm and 3.30–8pm. All pharmacies, which are indicated by a green (or red) cross sign outside, display the late-night roster in their windows; or you can consult the listings pages of the local *La Nazione* newspaper; or call free 800.420.707.

POLICE Emergency 112 or 113. The Questura, for passport problems, reporting thefts and so on, is at Via Zara 2 (daily 8.30am–12.30pm; ☎055.49.771; dedicated foreigners' office ☎055.497.7235). The special

Tourist Aid Police may be useful if you're having communication problems: Via Pietrapiana 50 (Mon–Fri 8.30am–7.30pm, Sat 8.30am–1.30pm; ℡055.203.911). If you do report a theft or other crime, you will have to fill out a form (*una denuncia*): this may be time-consuming, but it's essential if you want to make a claim on your travel insurance on returning home.

POST The most central post office is near Piazza della Repubblica at Via Pellicceria 8 (Mon–Fri 8.15am–7pm, Sat 8.15am–noon; telegram office open 24hr); poste restante (*fermo posta*) is through the door immediately on the left as you enter from the street. Florence's main post office is at Via Pietrapiana 53–55 (same hours). If all you want are stamps (*francobolli*), then the easiest places to buy them are tobacconists (*tabaccaio*), which are often annexed to bars and marked by a sign outside with a white "T" on a blue background.

PUBLIC HOLIDAYS Most shops, banks, offices and schools close on the following holidays: 1 January (New Year's Day); 6 January (Epiphany); Good Friday; Easter Sunday; Easter Monday; 25 April (Liberation Day); 1 May (Labour Day); June 24 (Feast of St John); 15 August (Assumption); 1 November (All Saints' Day); 8 December (Immaculate Conception); Christmas Day; 26 December (Santo Stefano). Accommodation is in short supply around public holidays, and roads and railways will be especially busy. When a holiday falls on a Tuesday or a Thursday Italians often make a *ponte* (bridge) to the weekend and take the Monday or Friday off as well.

TAXIS The main ranks are by the train station, Piazza della Repubblica, Piazza del Duomo, Piazza Santa Maria Novella, Piazza San Marco, Piazza Santa Croce and Piazza Santa Trinita. To telephone a cab call ℡4798, 4242, 4499 or 4390.

TELEPHONES Local or international calls can be made easily from Telecom Italia's public phone boxes, most of which take cash and phone cards (*schede* or *carte telefoniche*). The latter are available from tobacconists and some newsstands for €2.60, €5.20 and €7.80; tear off the perforated corner before using them. The €10.30 Scheda Unica contains €7.80 of pre-paid calls which can be used from any private phone, plus €2.60 for callboxes.

TIME Italy is always one hour ahead of UK time. Italian time is seven hours ahead of US Eastern Standard Time and ten hours ahead of Pacific Time.

TOURIST OFFICES There are three tourist offices, at Via Cavour 1r, just north of the Duomo (Mon–Sat 8.15am–7.15pm, Sun 8.30am–1.30pm; closed Nov–Feb; Ⓣ 055.290.832/3); at Borgo Santa Croce 29r, just off Piazza Santa Croce (Mon–Sat 9am–7pm, Sun 9am–1pm; Ⓣ 055.234.0444); and outside the train station in Piazza della Stazione (Mon–Sat 8.30am–7pm, Sun 8.30am–1.30pm; Ⓣ 055.212.245). The Santa Croce and Piazza della Stazione offices keep shorter hours in winter.

TRAIN INFORMATION Toll-free Ⓣ 8488.88088, Ⓦ www.trenitalia.com.

EXCURSIONS

Fiesole and around

Fiesole (295m) spreads over a cluster of hilltops above the Mugnone and Arno valleys, some 8km northeast of Florence. A long-established retreat from the city's summer heat and crowds, its attractions are unfortunately so well advertised that these days it's hardly less busy than Florence itself. This said, Fiesole offers a grandstand view of the city, and bears many traces of its long history. First settled in the Bronze Age, then by the Etruscans, then absorbed by the Romans, it rivalled its neighbour until the early twelfth century, when the Florentines overran the town. From that time it became a satellite of Florence, being especially favoured as a semi-rural second home for its wealthier citizens.

The #7 ATAF **bus** runs roughly every 20 minutes from Florence train station, through San Domenico (see p.305) to Fiesole's central square, Piazza Mino da Fiesole; the journey takes around twenty-five minutes and costs €0.80 (ticket valid for sixty minutes). The town itself is small enough to be explored in a morning, but the country lanes of its surroundings invite a more leisurely tour. The **tourist office** (March–Oct Mon–Sat 8.30am–7.30pm, Sun 10am–7pm; winter hours vary; ☎055.597.8373 or 055.598.720) is next to the entrance of the Theatro Romano, just off the main square. This is the place to pick up the joint APT and

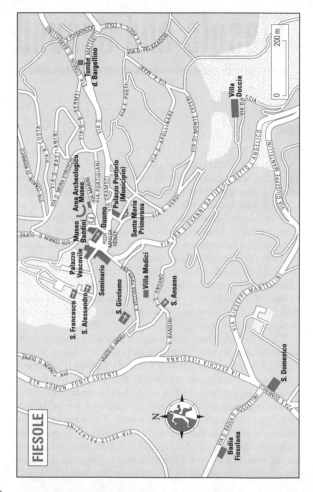

Comune di Fiesole pamphlet of pretty local **walks**, *Itinerari Fiesolani*, complete with map and itineraries: walks take between three and eight hours and are indicated on the ground with purple and blue markers.

THE TOWN

Nineteenth-century restoration has ruined the exterior of the **duomo** (daily 7/8am–noon, 2/3–7/8pm), founded in 1028 on the central piazza. The interior is something like a stripped-down version of Florence's San Miniato, though there's relief from the overall austerity in the **Cappella Salutati**, to the right of the choir: it contains two fine pieces carved by Mino da Fiesole in the mid-fifteenth century – a panel of *The Madonna and Saints* and the tomb of Bishop Leonardo Salutati (1465). The **high altarpiece** in the apse is a polyptych painted in the 1440s by Bicci di Lorenzo. Be sure to walk down into the charming four-columned crypt, whose lunettes are frescoed with episodes from the life of St Romulus.

Around the back of the duomo, in Via Marini, is the entrance to the **Museo Fiesole** (or Museo Civico/Archeologico) **e Teatro Romano** (Easter–Sept daily 9.30am–7pm, Oct–Easter Mon & Wed–Sun 9am–6pm; €6.20 including admission to Museo Bandini and Cappella di San Jacopo). Built in the first century BC, the 3000-seater Teatro Romano, or Roman theatre, was excavated towards the end of the last century and remains in good enough repair to be used for performances during the Estate Fiesolana festival. Most of the museum exhibits were discovered here, and encompass pieces from the Bronze Age to the Roman occupation. The other ruins – Etruscan and Roman temples and fragments of baths and old defensive walls – lie amidst olive groves dappled with plenty of pleasant shady spots for a picnic or siesta.

THE TOWN

Behind the duomo at Via Dupré 1, the **Museo Bandini** (same hours & ticket) possesses a collection of glazed terracotta in the style of the della Robbias, the odd case of Byzantine ivory work and a few thirteenth- and fourteenth-century Tuscan pictures – all very worthy but rather uninspiring.

Fiesole's other major churches, Sant'Alessandro and San Francesco, are reached by the steep Via San Francesco: en route, at Via San Francesco 4, stop off at the **Cappella di San Jacopo** if you're here at the weekend (Sat & Sun 10am–7pm; €5.20 with combined ticket to Museo Civico-Teatro Romano and Museo Bandini). It houses a collection of gold and silverware and a fifteenth-century fresco of the *Coronation of the Virgin* attributed to Bicci di Lorenzo.

Below the churches, Via San Francesco widens into a terrace giving a remarkable panorama of Florence. **Sant'Alessandro** (currently open only for special exhibitions) was founded in the sixth century on the site of Etruscan and Roman temples; recent repairs have rendered the outside a whitewashed nonentity, but the beautiful *marmorino cipollino* (onion marble) columns of the basilican interior make it the most atmospheric building in Fiesole. Again, restoration has not improved the Gothic church of **San Francesco** (daily 9.30am–12.30pm, 3–6/7pm), which probably occupies the site of the old Etruscan acropolis. Across one of the convent's tiny cloisters there's a chaotic museum of pieces brought back from Egypt and China by missionaries. An alternative descent back to the main square is through the public park, entered by a gate facing San Francesco's facade.

AROUND FIESOLE

The haul up to San Francesco may be enough exercise for one day in high summer, but if you've time to spare wander down the narrow Via Vecchia Fiesolana past the **Villa**

Medici, built for Cosimo il Vecchio by Michelozzo in 1458. The villa building is generally closed (call ℡055.239.8994 for details of opening), but the beautiful gardens, some of the earliest Renaissance gardens of their kind, are usually open (Mon–Fri 8am–1pm; €5.20).

Continuing past the villa, you eventually reach the hamlet of **San Domenico**, 1500m southwest of Fiesole. Fra' Angelico was once prior of the Dominican monastery in San Domenico, and the **church** (daily 8.30am–noon, 3.30–5.30pm; free) retains a 1430 *Madonna with Saints and Angels* by him (first chapel on left); the chapter-house also has a Fra' Angelico fresco of *The Crucifixion* and a detached fresco of the *Madonna and Child* with its *sinopia*.

Five minutes' walk northwest from San Domenico brings you to the sublime little **Badia Fiesolana** (Mon–Fri 9am–5pm, Sat 9am–noon; free), Fiesole's cathedral until 1028. Cosimo il Vecchio had the church altered in the 1460s, a project which left the magnificent Romanesque facade intact – now marvellously inset in a larger fifteenth-century frontage – while transforming the interior into a superb Renaissance building.

EATING AND DRINKING

Fiesole's many shady nooks make it ideal picnic country. Otherwise a couple of pizzerias and busy bars in the main Piazza Mino da Fiesole are reasonable enough – the busy *Pizzeria Etrusia* does takeaway. *I Polpi*, just up Via Gramsci away from the main square (℡055.59.485; closed Wed and Aug), is the best place for a more formal meal, while the touristy restaurants on the south side of the square have views over the city – *Aurora*, at no. 45, has a pleasant vine-shaded terrace. If you are still in town in the evening, try the pleasant and relatively tranquil *Reggia degli Etruschi*, Via San Francesco 18 (℡055 59.385; closed Tues).

Siena

It's a little over an hour by bus to **Siena** – a touch longer by train – a city that definitely merits a day trip on anything but the shortest visits to Florence. For a hundred or so years, in the twelfth and thirteenth centuries, the city was one of the major centres of Europe. Apotheosis came with the defeat of a much superior Florentine army at the battle of Montaperti in 1260. The city then built its cathedral and the extraordinary Campo, the greatest medieval square in Italy. The building boom was cut short by the Black Death, which reached Siena in May 1348; the city went into decline, eventually becoming part of Cosimo I's Grand Duchy of Tuscany. This explains Siena's astonishing state of preservation. Little was built and still less demolished, and only since the last war has Siena again become prosperous, thanks in large part to tourism.

The centre of Siena is its great square, the **Campo**, built at the convergence of the city's principal roads, the Banchi di Sopra, Banchi di Sotto and Via di Città. Each of these roads leads out across a ridge, straddled by one of the city's three medieval terzi, or districts: the Terzo di Città to the southwest, the Terzo di San Martino to the southeast, and the Terzo di Camollia to the north. A day-trip is enough to take in the key sights: the Campo and **Palazzo Pubblico**, the latter home to the outstanding Museo Civico; the **Piazza**

del Duomo, site of the Duomo, Ospedale di Santa Maria della Scala and Museo dell'Opera del Duomo; the **Pinacoteca Nazionale** – the city's principal art gallery; and a roster of **churches** of which San Domenico, San Francesco and Santa Maria dei Servi are the most outstanding.

The easiest way to **reach Siena from Florence** is by **bus** from the bus station in Via di Santa Caterina da Siena (**Map 3, A5**). The journey takes 1hr 15min by express bus (every 30min) and 1hr 30min by ordinary bus (every 20min). In Siena buses drop you on Viale Curtatone (**Map 5, A2**), a few minutes' walk from the Campo and cathedral. Trains from Florence are less convenient and no faster (12 daily; 1hr 30min). The station in Siena is 2km from the centre – you'll need to take one of the town buses up to the centre from the far side of the station forecourt: tickets are sold inside the station foyer and buses drop at different points depending on the service. The **tourist office** (**Map 5, F5**) is at no. 56 on the Campo (Mon–Sat 8.30am–7.30pm, Sun 9am–3pm; ☎0577.280.551).

MUSEUM PASSES

Siena has several **museum passes**, though if you are visiting just for the day you will have to work hard and see several sights to make them worthwhile. The "Musei dell'Opera Metropolitana" costs €7.20 and is valid for five days, for entry to the Battistero di San Giovanni, Museo dell'Opera del Duomo, Sant'Agostino, Oratorio di San Bernardino and Libreria Piccolomini. The seven-day "Siena Itinerari d'Arte" (€15.50) is valid in the summer only for seven days and provides admission to the same sights plus the Museo Civico, Santa Maria della Scala and Palazzo delle Papesse (an exhibition of mostly modern art). A joint ticket valid for two days is available for the Museo Civico and Santa Maria della Scala for €8.80.

MUSEUM PASSES

CHAPTER TWENTY-THREE

> The telephone code for Siena is ☎ 0577, and must be used
> with all numbers whether you're calling within or from
> outside the city.

THE CAMPO

The **Campo** might seem an organic piece of city planning, but when Siena's ruling body, the Council of Nine, began its construction in 1347 they were building on the only possible land – the old marketplace, which stood at the convergence of the city quarters but belonged to none. At its highest point the Renaissance makes a fleeting entry with the Fonte Gaia (Gay Fountain), designed and carved by Jacopo della Quercia in the early fifteenth century. Its panels are reproductions; the originals, badly eroded, can be seen on the rear loggia of the **Palazzo Pubblico** whose vertiginous bell-tower, the **Torre del Mangia**, dominates the Campo.

> Siena's Campo is the scene of Italy's most spectacular – and controversial – horse race, the Palio, held twice a year on July 2 and August 16. Each horse is sponsored by one of the ancient quarters (contrade) of the city; competition is fierce, and allegations of bribery, drugs and cruelty are not infrequent.

The Palazzo Pubblico

Map 5, F6. Mid-March to Oct 31 daily 10am–7pm except July & Aug 10am–11pm; Nov to mid-March 15 daily 10am–6.30pm; €6.20, combined ticket with Torre del Mangia €9.30.

This palace remains in use as Siena's town hall, but its principal rooms have been converted into the **Museo Civico**, entered to the right of the palace courtyard. Off to the left there is separate access to the **Torre del Mangia** (same summer hours, including late opening in July and Aug; winter daily 10am–4pm; €5.20), with its fabulous views across town and countryside.

The museum visit begins on the first floor, with a rather miscellaneous picture gallery and the Sala del Risorgimento, painted with nineteenth-century scenes of Vittorio Emanuele. The medieval interest begins as you reach the **Sala di Balìa**, frescoed by Spinello Aretino in 1407 with episodes from the life of Pope Alexander III and his conflict with Emperor Frederick Barbarossa, and, beyond it, the **Cappella del Consiglio**, frescoed by Taddeo di Bartolo a year later, and with a majestic wrought-iron screen by Jacopo della Quercia.

These rooms are little more than a warm-up, however, to the **Sala del Mappamondo**, dominated by the fabulous *Maestà* (Virgin in Majesty) of Simone Martini on the left end wall. The richly decorative style is archetypal Sienese Gothic, and the work forms a fascinating comparison with the Maestà by Duccio, with whom Martini perhaps trained, in the Museo dell'Opera (see p.313). The picture on the opposite wall, the wonderful *Equestrian Portrait of Guidoriccio da Fogliano*, a motif for medieval chivalric Siena, was until recently unanimously credited to Martini. Depicting the knight setting forth from his battle camp to besiege a walled hill-town, it would, if it were by Martini, be accounted one of the earliest Italian portrait paintings. The newly revealed fresco below the portrait, of two figures in front of a castle, is variously attributed to Martini, Duccio and Pietro Lorenzetti.

The Palazzo Pubblico's most important frescoes are to be seen in the adjacent **Sala della Pace** (Room of Peace). These are Ambrogio Lorenzetti's *Allegories of Good and Bad Government*, commissioned in 1338 to remind the councillors of their civic responsibilities. The paintings include the first known panorama in western art, and their moral theme is expressed in a complex iconography of allegorical virtues and figures. Good Government is dominated by a throned figure representing the comune, flanked by the Virtues and with Faith, Hope and Charity buzzing about his head. To the left, Justice (with Wisdom in the air above) dispenses rewards and punishments, while below her throne Concordia advises the Republic's councillors on their duties. Bad Government is ruled by a horned demon, while over the city flies the figure of Fear, whose scroll reads: "Because he looks for his own good in the world, he places justice beneath tyranny. So nobody walks this road without Fear: robbery thrives inside and outside the city gates." Within a decade of the frescoes' completion, Siena was engulfed by the Black Death – Lorenzetti and his family were among the victims – and the city was under tyrannical government.

THE PIAZZA DEL DUOMO

Just to the west of the Campo, the Piazza del Duomo is the focus of some of Siena's most important monuments: the awe-inspiring, black and white striped **Duomo** with its subterranean **Baptistery**, and the **Ospedale di Santa Maria della Scala** with its marvellous frescoes. Few buildings reveal so much of a city's history and aspirations as the Duomo. Complete to virtually its present size around 1215, it was subjected to constant plans for expansion throughout Siena's years of medieval prosperity. At the north end of the square stand the huge remains of an extension that would have created the largest church in Italy outside Rome; its unfinished arcades now house the **Museo dell'Opera del Duomo**.

The Duomo

Map 5, C7.

The **Duomo** as it stands, however, is a delight. Its style is an amazing conglomeration of Romanesque and Gothic, its lineaments picked out in bands of black and white marble, an idea adapted from Pisa and Lucca – though here with much more extravagant effect. The facade was designed in 1284 by the Pisan sculptor Giovanni Pisano, who with his workshop created much of the statuary – philosophers, patriarchs, prophets (now replaced by copies). In the next century a Gothic rose window was added. The mosaics in the gables, however, had to wait until the nineteenth century, when money was found to employ Venetian artists.

The use of black and white decoration is continued in the sgraffito marble **pavement**, which begins outside the church and takes off into a startling sequence of 56 panels within. They were completed between 1349 and 1547, with virtually every artist who worked in the city trying his hand on a design. To protect the stone surface from visitors' feet, most of the pavement is currently carpeted. Under the present regime at least, if you're determined to see the whole floor revealed you'll have to visit in September.

The rest of the interior is equally arresting, with its line of popes' heads – the same scowling, hollow-cheeked faces cropping up repeatedly – set above the multistriped pillars. Among the greatest individual artistic treasures are Nicola Pisano's **pulpit** – completed after his commission at Pisa (see pp.321–2) and more elaborate in its high-relief details of the *Life of Jesus* and *Last Judgement* – and, in the north transept, a bronze Donatello statue of *St John the Baptist*.

Midway along the nave, on the left, the entrance to the **Libreria Piccolomini** (daily: mid-March to Oct 9am–7.30pm; Nov to mid-March 10am–1pm & 2.30–5pm; €1.60 or combined tickets) is signalled by Pinturicchio's brilliantly coloured fresco of the Coronation of Pius II. Within the library a further ten frescoes by Pinturicchio and his pupils (who included Raphael) illustrate scenes from Pius's life – his travels to Scotland, canonization of St Catherine, and officiation at the marriage of Emperor Frederick III and Eleonora of Portugal outside Siena's Porta Camollia.

The Baptistery

Map 5, D6. Daily: mid-March to Sept 9am–7.30pm; Oct 9am–6pm; Nov–mid-March 10am–1pm & 2.30–5pm; €2.10.

The cathedral's magnificent subterranean **Baptistery** is reached down a flight of steps behind the cathedral. The elaborately frescoed space is fronted by an unfinished Gothic facade and houses a font – one of the masterpieces of Renaissance sculpture – with panels illustrating the Baptist's life by Jacopo della Quercia (The Angel Announcing the Baptist's Birth), Lorenzo Ghiberti (Baptism of Christ and John in Prison) and Donatello (Herod's Feast).

Museo dell'Opera del Duomo

Map 5, D7. Daily: mid-March to Sept 9am–7.30pm; Oct 9am–6pm; Nov–mid-March 9am–1.30pm & 2.30–5pm; €5.20.

After the Museo Civico, the best art in Siena is to be seen in the **Museo dell'Opera del Duomo**, which occupies the projected, re-oriented nave (**Map 5, D7**). Downstairs are Pisano's original statues from the facade. Upstairs, amid a comprehensive display of cathedral treasures, is a fine array of panels, including works by Simone Martini, Donatello, Pietro Lorenzetti and Sano di Pietro, and the cathedral's original altarpiece, the stark, haunting icon known as the Madonna degli Occhi Grossi (Madonna of the Big Eyes).

The painting that merits the museum admission, however, is the cathedral's second altarpiece, Duccio's *Maestà*. On its completion in 1311 this painting was taken in a ceremony that processed from Duccio's studio, then around the Campo to a special Mass in the duomo; everything in the city was closed and virtually the entire population attended. This is possibly the climax of the Sienese style of painting, its iconic spirituality heightened by Duccio's attention to narrative detail in the panels of the *Life of Christ and the Virgin*, originally on the reverse but now displayed opposite.

While visiting the museum, don't miss the chance to climb up onto the top of the "new nave", arguably a better vantage point for views of the city than the Torre di Mangia. Follow signs to the Ingresso al Panorama.

Ospedale di Santa Maria della Scala

Map 5, D8. Daily: April–Oct 10am–6pm; Nov–March 10am–5pm; €5.20.

Opposite the cathedral is the amazing **Ospedale di Santa Maria della Scala**, which for around eight hundred years served as the city's principal hospital. Today its wonderful interiors are gradually being converted into a major arts complex, revealing staggering works of art that have been out of bounds to all but the most determined of visitors for centuries. Chief of these is the fresco cycle (1440) in the **Sala del Pellegrinaio** by Domenico di Bartolo and Vecchietta, a vast series of panels depicting the history of the hospital, in its early days concerned principally with the care of orphans.

The **Sagrestia Vecchia** contains another outstanding cycle by Vecchietta illustrating the *Articles of the Creed*, while the highlight of the former hospital church, **Santissima Annunziata**, is a marvellous bronze high-altar statue by Vecchietta of the *Risen Christ*. Be sure to descend into the bowels of the building, where the spooky **Oratorio di Santa Caterina della Notte**, former meeting place of a medieval confraternity, contains a plethora of decoration and a sumptuous triptych by Taddeo di Bartolo. The Ospedale is also home to Siena's **Museo Archeologico**, a small but well presented collection of mostly Etruscan artefacts from sites around Siena.

Pinacoteca Nazionale

Map 5, E9. Mon 8.30am–1.30pm, Tues–Sat 8.15am–7.15pm, Sun 8.15am–1.15pm; €4.10.

After exploring the Piazza del Duomo, cut down to Via di Città, a street fronted by some of Siena's finest private palazzi. Off to the left at the end of the street, Via San Pietro leads to the outstanding **Pinacoteca Nazionale**, housed in a fourteenth-century palace. Although few individual works here can measure up to the Martini and Lorenzetti in the Palazzo Pubblico, or the Duccio in the cathedral museum, the collection provides a superb overview of Sienese painting, from the hieratic, gilt-encrusted Byzantine images of the twelfth century to the Mannerist extravagance of the sixteenth.

TERZO DI SAN MARTINO

Behind the top end of the Campo, marking the start of Banchi di Sotto – the main thoroughfare through the Terzo di San Martino – stands the fifteenth-century **Loggia di Mercanzia (Map 5, E5)**, designed as a tribune house for the merchants to do their deals. Following the Banchi di Sotto east, you pass the **Palazzo Piccolomini (Map 5,**

E7), a Renaissance building by Bernardo Rossellino. It now houses the fascinating but little-visited **Archivio di Stato** (Mon–Fri 9am–1pm; free), which displays the painted covers of the Tavolette di Biccherna, the city accounts. Take the door in the left corner of the palace courtyard and climb the stairs to the reception, where someone will guide you through the archives to the gallery. The earlier paintings depict religious themes, but they soon move towards images of the city's life: the monks doing the audits, victories against the Florentines, the demolition of the Spanish fortress, the entry of Cosimo I.

Heading south along the parallel Via Salicotto or Via San Martino will eventually bring you to **Santa Maria dei Servi** (**Map 5, L9**), the Servites' massive monastic church. Inside, there are two contrasting frescoes of the *Massacre of the Innocents* – a Gothic version by Lorenzetti, in the second chapel to the right of the high altar, and a Renaissance treatment by Matteo di Giovanni (1492) in the fifth chapel on the right. The church has fine altarpieces, too, by Giovanni di Paolo – a *Madonna della Misericordia* (1431) in the left transept – and Coppo di Marcovaldo's so-called *Madonna di Bordone* (1261) above the first altar on the right (south) wall. The latter artist was a Florentine captured at the Battle of Montaperti and reputedly forced to paint this picture by the Sienese as part of the terms for his ransom and release.

SAN DOMENICO

Map 5, A4.

Siena's last major churches and the lesser sights sprinkled across the northern half of the city are best left until you turn tail for the buses back to Florence or the railway station. **San Domenico**, founded in 1125, is closely identified with St Catherine of Siena. On the right of the entrance is a kind of raised chapel, with a contemporary portrait of her by her friend Andrea Vanni; below are steps and a niche, where she received the stigmata. Her own chapel, midway down the right (south) side of the church, has frescoes of her in ecstasy, by Sodoma, and a reliquary containing her head.

St Catherine's family house, the **Casa Sanctuario di Santa Caterina** (**Map 5, B2**; daily: summer 9am–12.30pm & 2.30–6pm; winter 9am–12.30pm & 3.30–6pm; free), where she lived as a Dominican nun, is a short distance to the south, near the Fontebranda on Via Santa Caterina. The building has been much adapted, with a Renaissance loggia and a series of oratories – one on the site of her cell – as is only fitting for Italy's patron saint and the first-ever canonized woman. Her career, encompassing innumerable miracles, was pretty extraordinary in secular terms, too, reconciling Tuscan cities to each other and persuading the pope, Gregory XI, to return to Rome from Avignon.

SAN FRANCESCO

Map 5, I1. Church free. Oratorio mid-March to Oct daily 10.30am–1.30pm & 3–5.30pm; €1.60

Catherine died in 1380, the year of the birth of Siena's other great saint, St Bernardino, who began preaching at the monastic church of **San Francesco**, across the city to the east. His **Oratorio**, with an appealing upper chapel frescoed by Sodoma, stands beside the church, which, like that of the Dominicans, is vast, Gothic and austere. Highlights here are the **tomb of the Tolomei** – a major Sienese banking dynasty – at the end of the right aisle, the best of the church's many funerary monuments, and paintings by Pietro and Ambrogio Lorenzetti in the first and third chapels to the left of the high altar.

EATING AND DRINKING

Prices in the Campo's **cafés** are predictably elevated if you want to sit down, but worth paying to enjoy one of Europe's great urban set pieces. Away from the square, the city's best-known café is *Nannini* at Banchi di Sopra 22–24 (**Map 5, E3**), good for snacks and sandwiches on the hoof though rather too functional to linger long. The city's best delicatessen is the amazing *Maganelli* at Via di Città 73 (**Map 5, E7**), though *Gastonomia Morbidi* (founded in 1925) at Via Banchi di Sopra 73–75 runs it a close second. Both are great for gifts to take home.

Avoid the restaurants in the Campo, which, with the exception of the odd pizzeria, are poor and overpriced. Nearby alternatives for a more memorable meal are *Le Logge*, Via del Porrione 33 (**Map 5, G5**; closed Sun), a lovely but well known old-fashioned place, or *Nello*, a friendly and slightly cheaper spot almost opposite Le Logge at Via del Porrione 28–30 (**Map 5, G6**; closed Sun); expect to pay around €25 or more per head at both places for three courses.

Good lunch places further from the Campo are the tiny, very traditional and cheap *La Taverna del Capitano*, close to the duomo at Via del Capitano 8 (**Map 5, D8**; closed Tues); the tasteful *Osteria del Fico Mezzo*, Via dei Termini 71 (**Map 5, D2**; closed Sun), which offers excellent and very reasonable lunches; and – for a treat – *Ai Marsili*, Via del Castoro 3, corner of Via di Città (**Map 5, E8**; closed Mon), the best of Siena's more formal **restaurants**. Alternatively, you might want to splurge at the most atmospheric of the city's restaurants, the *Antica Osteria da Divo*, just below the Duomo at Via Fanciosa 25 (**Map 5, C6**; open daily); the cosy vaulted stone rooms are excavated from the ancient city walls. Don't be put off by the English menu outside which promises, among other treats, "revisited beans" and a "garnish of grass".

Pisa

Since the beginning of the age of the tourist brochure, Pisa has been known for just one thing – the **Leaning Tower** – a freakishly beautiful building whose impact no amount of prior knowledge can blunt. Yet it's just a single component of the city's amazing religious core – the **Campo dei Miracoli** – where the **Duomo**, **Baptistery** and **Camposanto** complete an unrivalled quartet of medieval masterpieces. These, and a dozen or so churches and palazzi scattered about the town, belong to Pisa's "Golden Age", from the eleventh to the thirteenth centuries, when the city, then still a port, was one of the maritime powers of the Mediterranean.

Pisa is just an hour by train from Florence, and if you're flying in or out of the city's airport (see p.5) it doesn't take much effort to take in the main sights. Trains are very frequent; the ones on the hour and at 25 minutes past the hour are the fastest (1hr). You arrive at the Piazza della Stazione (**Map 6, C9**), about twenty minutes' walk or a five-minute taxi or bus ride (#1) from the Campo; local bus tickets are sold from a kiosk just outside the station. From the airport railway station you'd be best advised to take a taxi.

Tourist offices are located outside the station and in the northeast corner of the Campo dei Miracoli (**Map 6, C2**), close to the Leaning Tower (both Mon–Sat 9am–6pm, Sun 10.30am–6.30pm, summer 8am–8pm; station ☎050.42.291, Duomo ☎050.560.464). The station also has a left-luggage office, while the main **post office** is 100m away in Piazza Vittorio Emanuele (**Map 6, D8**).

The telephone code for Pisa is ☎ 050, and must be used with all numbers whether you're calling within or from outside the city.

THE CAMPO DEI MIRACOLI

Since it was first laid out, Pisa's ecclesiastical centre has been known as the **Campo dei Miracoli** (Field of Miracles), and the sight of it is as stunning today as it must have been to medieval travellers. Nowhere in Italy are the key buildings of a city arrayed with such precision, and nowhere is there so beautiful a contrast of stonework and surrounding meadow.

The five key museums and monuments in and around Campo dei Miracoli – the Duomo, Baptistery, Museo dell'Opera, Camposanto and Museo delle Sinopie – are all open April–Sept Mon–Sat 8am–8pm, Sun 1–8pm; Oct & March Mon–Sat 10am–6pm, Sun 1–6pm; Nov–Feb Mon–Sat 9am–12.45pm & 3–5pm, Sun 3–5pm. Ticket prices are on a complex sliding scale, from €1.60 for the cathedral alone, through €7.80 for the cathedral and two other sights to €9.80 for entrance to everything there is to see. Tickets are available from the office behind the north side of the leaning tower, the office just south of the Museo delle Sinopie and in the Museo dell'Opera.

CHAPTER TWENTY-FOUR

The Leaning Tower

Map 6, C2.

Underneath the pavements and the turf of the Campo dei Miracoli lies a platform of saturated sandy soil, whose instability accounts for the crazy tilt of the **Leaning Tower** (Torre Pendente); Galileo exploited the Leaning Tower's overhang in one of his celebrated experiments, dropping metal balls of different mass to demonstrate the constancy of gravity. Begun in 1173, the tower started to subside when it had reached just three of its eight storeys. Over the next 180 years a succession of architects continued to extend it upwards, until in 1350 Tomasso di Andrea da Pontedera completed the stack by crowning it with a bell-chamber.

Eight centuries on, the tower leans nearly 5m from the upright, and in 1990 was declared off limits to visitors. Steel bands have been wrapped round the tower to prevent the base from buckling, and steel cables have been attached, with 1000 tonnes of lead weighted to the far end, in an attempt – successful, to date – to correct the tilt by half a degree, or 8.5cm, back towards the vertical. Once the project is complete, as it should be by the time this book is published, the angle of lean will stand at roughly that of three hundred years ago. The difference will scarcely be visible to the eye, however, as the current angle is as much as ten degrees.

From early 2002, the Leaning Tower will be open to pre-booked groups (max 30 at a time so you'll need to book; phone ⓣ050.560.547 for information). Later in the year, it's proposed that it may be opened up to the public, but queues are likely to be long – and ticket prices steep.

The Duomo

Map 6, B2.

The **Duomo** was begun a century before the campanile, in 1064. With its four levels of variegated colonnades and subtle interplay of dark grey marble and white stone, it's the archetype of the Pisan Romanesque style, a model often imitated but never surpassed. The original bronze doorway, the Portale di San Ranieri, stands opposite the Leaning Tower, and was cast around 1180 by Bonnano Pisano, first architect of the Leaning Tower. Inside, the impact of the crisp black and white marble of the long arcades is diminished by the redecorations carried out after a fire in 1595, but a notable survivor from the medieval building is the apse mosaic of *Christ in Majesty*, completed by Cimabue in 1302. The acknowledged highlight, however, is the **pulpit** sculpted by Giovanni Pisano. This was packed away after the fire, sixteenth-century Pisans evidently no longer concurring with the Latin inscription around the base, which records that Giovanni had "the art of pure sculpture... and would not know how to carve ugly or base things, even if he wished to". Only in 1926 was it rediscovered and put back together in the nave.

The Baptistery

Map 6, B2.

The third building of the Miracoli ensemble, the circular **Baptistery**, is a bizarre mix, its three storeys of Romanesque arcades peaking in a crest of Gothic pinnacles and a dome shaped like the stalk end of a lemon. Begun in the mid-twelfth century and finished in the latter half of the thirteenth by Nicola and Giovanni Pisano, this is the largest baptistery in Italy, and the plainness of the vast interior is immediately striking, with its unadorned arcades and bare dome. Overlooking the massive raised font is Nicola

Pisano's **pulpit**, sculpted in 1260, half a century before his son's work in the cathedral. This was the sculptor's first major commission and manifests a classical spirit in part attributable to the influence of the court of Emperor Henry II, whose Italian power base was in Nicola's native Puglia.

The Camposanto

Map 6, B1.

The screen of sepulchral white marble running along the north edge of the Campo dei Miracoli is the perimeter wall of what has been called the most beautiful cemetery in the world – the **Camposanto**. According to Pisan legend, at the end of the twelfth century the city's archbishop brought back from the Crusades a cargo of soil from Golgotha, in order that eminent Pisans might be buried in holy earth. The building enclosing this sanctified site was completed almost a century later.

Incendiary bombs dropped by Allied planes on July 27, 1944, destroyed most of the cloister's famous frescoes: the most important survivors are the remarkable fourteenth-century cycle by the painter known as the Maestro del Trionfo della Morte, the Master of the Triumph of Death. These have been detached from the wall and put on show in a room on the opposite side of the cloister, beyond a photographic display of the Camposanto before the bombing. Painted within a few months of the Black Death of 1348, the Triumph is a ruthless catalogue of horrors. The *sinopie*, or sketches for the frescoes, now hang in the high-tech if rather over-scholarly **Museo delle Sinopie** on the south side of the Campo.

Museo dell'Opera del Duomo

Map 6, C2.

A vast array of statuary from the Duomo and Baptistery,

plus ecclesiastical finery, paintings and other miscellaneous pieces, are displayed in the **Museo dell'Opera del Duomo**, at the southeast corner of the Campo. Sculptures by the various Pisanos are the high points of the museum, but the first pieces you encounter – Nicola and Giovanni's figures from the Baptistery – are too eroded to give much of an idea of their power. **Room 7**, however, which is given over to works by Giovanni Pisano, contains the most affecting statue in Pisa, the *Madonna del Colloquio*, so called because of the intensity of the gazes exchanged by the Madonna and Child.

Nino Pisano – no relation to Nicola and Giovanni – is the subject of **Room 7**, where his creamy marble monuments show the increasing suavity of Pisan sculpture in the late fourteenth century. Giovanni Pisano returns in the **treasury**, two rooms beyond, his ivory *Madonna and Child* showing a remarkable ingenuity in the way it exploits the natural curve of the tusk from which it's carved. The other priceless object here is the Pisan Cross, which was carried by the Pisan contingent on the First Crusade.

Upstairs, big and witless altarpiece paintings take up a lot of room, as do cases of ecclesiastical clothing and lavish examples of intarsia, the art of inlaid wood, much practised here in the fifteenth and sixteenth centuries.

THE REST OF THE CITY

Away from the Campo dei Miracoli, Pisa takes on a very different character. Few tourists penetrate far into its squares and arcaded streets, with their Romanesque churches and – especially along the Arno's banks – ranks of fine palazzi. Despite the large student population it's generally quiet, except during the summer festivals and the monthly market, when the main streets on each side of the river become one continuous bazaar.

The **Piazza dei Cavalieri** (**Map 6, D4**) is an obvious first stop from the Campo, a large square that opens unexpectedly from the attractive narrow backstreets. Perhaps the site of the Roman forum, it was the central civic square of medieval Pisa, before being remodelled by Vasari as the headquarters of the Knights of St Stephen – their palace, the curving Palazzo dei Cavalieri, covered in sgraffiti and topped with busts of the Medici, adjoins the order's church of Santo Stefano, designed by Vasari and housing banners captured from the Turks. On the other (western) side of the square is the Renaissance-adapted **Palazzo dell'Orologio**, in whose tower the military leader Ugolino della Gherardesca was starved to death in 1208, with his sons and grandsons, as punishment for his alleged duplicity with the Genoese enemy.

The tragic story of Ugolino is recounted in Dante's *Inferno*, Chaucer's *The Monk's Tale* and Shelley's *Tower of Famine*.

Heading from Piazza dei Cavalieri towards the Arno, Via Dini swings into the arcaded Borgo Stretto, Pisa's smart street, its windows glistening with desirables that seem slightly out of tune with the city's unshowy style. More typically Pisan is the **market** just off Via Dini (**Map 6, E4**; weekday mornings and all day Sat), its fruit, vegetable, fish, meat and clothing stalls spilling south onto the lanes around Piazza Vettovaglie.

Past the Romanesque-Gothic facade of **San Michele in Borgo** (**Map 6, E5**) – built on the site of the Roman temple to Mars – the Borgo meets the river at the traffic-knotted Piazza Garibaldi and Ponte di Mezzo, the city's central bridge. A left turn along Lungarno Mediceo takes you to the **Museo Nazionale di San Matteo** (**Map 6, G6**; Tues–Sat 9am–7pm, Sun 9am–1pm; €4.10), where most of the major works of art from Pisa's churches are now gathered. Fourteenth-century religious paintings make up the meat of this collection, though there's also a panel of *St Paul* by Masaccio, Gozzoli's strangely festive *Crucifixion* and Donatello's reliquary bust of the introspective *St Rossore*.

To the west of the Ponte di Mezzo on the more down-at-heel south side of the Arno, the rather monotonous line of palazzi is suddenly enlivened by the spry turreted oratory of **Santa Maria della Spina** (closed Mon; **Map 6, C6**). Rebuilt in 1323 by a merchant who had acquired one of the thorns (*spine*) of Christ's crown, it's the finest flourish of Pisan Gothic. Originally built closer to the river, it was moved here for fear of floods in 1871. The interior is a disappointment that visitors are usually spared by extremely erratic opening hours.

EATING AND DRINKING

Restaurants near the Leaning Tower are not good value, but head a few blocks south to the area around Piazza Cavalieri and Piazza Dante, and you find more local places, many with prices reflecting student custom. For cakes and snacks try the *Caffè Pasticceria Salza* at Borgo Stretto 44 (**Map 6, E5**; closed Mon and after 8.30pm). The most atmospheric place to eat is in and around the central Piazza delle Vettovaglie (**Map 6, E5**), a delightful arcaded market in a warren of side streets. The tiny *La Mescita*, Via Domenico Cavalca 2, on the corner of the piazza, is excellent, while on the piazza itself, *Vineria di Piazza* at no. 13 is a good cheap alternative, with outside tables and simple snack meals. For first-rate and inexpensive pizzas, pastas and simple starters and desserts, try *Le Scuderie*, Via Sancasciani 1: pizza can be ordered by length – 50cm (ten slices) should do two people. A touch bigger and more expensive is the fine *Osteria dei Cavalieri*, Via San Frediano 16 (**Map 6, D4**; ☎050.580.858; closed Sat lunchtime and Sun).

Pisa's student life can be found milling around the lively traffic-free Piazza Dante (**Map 6, D4**), where *Caffeteria Betsabea* is one of many cafés serving coffees, sandwiches and drinks at tables on the square.

CONTEXTS

History

F lorence was only one of many players among Italy's medieval and Renaissance city states – albeit one that quickly emerged as a dominant force – and any history of the city is therefore also a history of the broader entanglements of the groups who vied for power in Tuscany and central Italy.

Etruscans and Romans

There may have been an **Etruscan** settlement where Florence now stands, but it would have been subservient to their more easily defended base in the nearby hill town of **Fiesole**. The substantial development of Tuscany's chief city began with the **Roman colony** of **Florentia**, established following a decree by Julius Caesar in 59 BC which set aside land for army veterans. Expansion of Florentia itself was rapid, with a steady traffic of trading vessels along the Arno providing the basis of accelerated growth in the second and third centuries AD.

Barbarians and margraves

The comparative tranquillity of the Roman regime was shattered in the fifth century by the invasions of the **Goths** from the north, though the scale of the destruction in this first barbarian wave was nothing compared to the havoc of the following century. Before the fall of Rome, the empire had split in two, with the western half ruled from Ravenna and the eastern from Constantinople (Byzantium). By the 490s Ravenna was occupied by the Ostrogoths, and forty years later the Byzantine emperor Justinian launched a campaign to repossess the Italian peninsula.

The ensuing mayhem between the Byzantine armies of Belisarius and Narses and the fast-moving Goths was probably the most destructive phase of central Italian history, with virtually all major settlements ravaged by one side or the other – and sometimes both. In 552 Florence fell to the hordes of the Gothic king **Totila**, whose depredations so weakened the province that less than twenty years later the **Lombards** were able to storm in, subjugating Florence to the duchy whose capital was in Pavia, though its dukes preferred to rule from Lucca.

By the end of the eighth century Charlemagne's **Franks** had taken control of much of Italy, with the administration being overseen by imperial **margraves**, again based in Lucca. These proxy rulers developed into some of the most powerful figures in the Holy Roman Empire and were instrumental in spreading Christianity even further, founding numerous religious houses. Willa, widow of the margrave Uberto, established the Badia in Florence in 978, the first monastic foundation in the centre of the city.

In 1027 the position of margrave was passed to the **Canossa** family, who took the title of the counts of Tuscia, as Tuscany was then called. The most influential figure produced by this dynasty was **Matilda**, daughter of the first Canossa margrave. When her father died she was abducted by the German emperor Henry III, and on her release and return to her home territory she began to take the side of the papacy in its protracted disputes with the empire. Later friction between the papacy, empire and Tuscan cities was assured when Matilda bequeathed all her lands to the pope, with the crucial exceptions of Florence, Siena and Lucca.

Guelphs and Ghibellines

Though Lucca had been the titular base of the imperial margraves, Ugo and his successors had shown a degree of favouritism towards Florence, and over the next three hundred years Florence gained pre-eminence among the cities of Tuscany, becoming especially important as a religious centre. In 1078 Countess Matilda supervised the construction of new fortifications for Florence, and in the year of her death – 1115 – granted it the status of an independent city. The new **comune of Florence** was essentially governed by a council of one hundred men, the great majority drawn from the rising merchant class. In 1125 the city's increasing dominance of the region was confirmed when it crushed the rival city of Fiesole. Fifty years later, as the population boomed with the rise of the textile and then banking industries, new walls were built around what was now one of the largest cities in Europe.

Throughout and beyond the thirteenth century, Florence and much of central Italy were torn by conflict between the **Ghibelline** and **Guelph** factions. The names of these two political alignments derive from Welf – the family name of the emperor Otto IV – and Waiblingen – the name of a castle owned by their implacable rivals, the Hohenstaufen. Though there's no clear documentation, it seems that the terms Guelph and Ghibelline entered the Italian vocabulary at the end of the twelfth century, when supporters of Otto IV battled for control of the central peninsula with the future Frederick II, nephew of Otto and grandson of the Hohenstaufen emperor Barbarossa (1152–90).

Ghibelline and Guelph divisions corresponded roughly to a split between the **feudal nobility** and the rising **business classes**, but this is only the broadest of generalizations. By the beginning of the thirteenth century the major cities of Tuscany were becoming increasingly self-sufficient and inter-city strife was commonplace. Affiliations were often struck on the basis that "my enemy's enemy is my friend", and allegiances changed at baffling speed – if, for instance, the Guelphs gained the ascendancy in a particular town, its neighbours might switch to the Ghibelline camp to maintain their rivalry. Nonetheless, certain patterns did emerge from the confusion: Florence and Lucca were generally Guelph strongholds, while Pisa, Arezzo, Prato, Pistoia and Siena tended to side with the empire.

Medieval Florence before the Medici

In this period of superpower manoeuvring and shifting economic structures, city governments in Tuscany were volatile. In 1207 Florence's governing council was replaced by the **Podestà**, an executive official who was traditionally a non-Florentine, in a semi-autocratic form of government then common throughout the region. Around this time, the first *Arti* (**Guilds**) were formed to promote the interests of the traders and bankers. In 1215 Florence was riven by a feud that was typical of the internecine violence of central Italy at this period. On Easter Sunday one **Buondelmonte de' Buondelmonti** was stabbed to death at the foot of the Ponte Vecchio by a member of the Amidei clan, in revenge for breaking his engagement to a young woman of that family. The prosecution of the murderers and their allies polarized the city into those who supported the *comune* – which regarded itself as the protector of the commercial city against imperial ambitions – and the followers of the Amidei, who aligned themselves against the *comune* and with the emperor.

These Ghibellines eventually enlisted the help of Emperor Frederick II to oust the Guelphs in 1248, but within two years they had been displaced by the Guelph-backed regime of the **Primo Popolo**, a quasi-democratic government drawn from the mercantile class. The *Primo Popolo* was in turn displaced in 1260, when the Florentine army marched on Siena to demand the surrender of some exiles who were hiding out in the city. Though greatly outnumbered, the Sienese army and its Ghibelline allies overwhelmed the aggressors at **Montaperti**, after which the Sienese were prevented from razing Florence only by the intervention of Farinata degli Uberti, head of the Ghibelline exiles.

By the 1280s the balance had again moved back in favour of Florence, where the Guelphs were back in control through the **Secondo Popolo**, a regime run by the *Arti Maggiori* (Great Guilds). In 1293 it passed a programme of political reforms known as the *Ordinamenti della Giustizia*, excluding the nobility from government and investing power in the **Signoria**, a council drawn from the *Arti Maggiori*.

Strife between the virulently anti-imperial "Black" and more conciliatory "White" factions within the Guelph camp marked the start of the fourteenth century in Florence, with many of the Whites – Dante among them – being exiled in 1302. Worse was to come. In 1325 the army of Lucca under **Castruccio Castracani** defeated the Florentines and was about to overwhelm the city when the death of their leader took the momentum out of the campaign. Then in 1339 the Bardi and Peruzzi banks – Florence's largest – both collapsed, mainly owing to the bad debts of Edward III of England. The ultimate catastrophe came in 1348, when the **Black Death** destroyed as many as half the city's population.

However, even though the epidemic hit Florence so badly that it was generally referred to as the Florentine Plague, its effects were devastating throughout the region and thus did nothing to reverse the economic – and thus political – supremacy of the city. Florence had subsumed Pistoia in 1329 and gained Prato in the 1350s. In 1406 it took control of Pisa and thus gained a long-coveted sea port.

The early Medici

A crucial episode in the liberation of Florence from the influence of the papacy was the so-called **War of the Eight Saints** in 1375–78, which brought the city into direct territorial conflict with Pope Gregory XI. This not only signalled the dissolution of the old Guelph alliance, but had immense repercussions for the internal politics of Florence. The increased taxation and other economic hardships of the war provoked an uprising of the industrial day-labourers, the **Ciompi**, on whom the wool and cloth factories depended. Their short-lived revolt resulted in the formation of three new guilds and direct representation for the workers for the first time. However, the prospect of increased proletarian presence in the machinery of state provoked a consolidation of the city's oligarchs, and in 1382 an alliance of the city's Guelph party and the **Popolo Grasso** (the wealthiest merchants) took control of the *Signoria* away from the guilds, a situation that lasted for four decades.

Not all of Florence's most prosperous citizens aligned themselves with the *Popolo Grasso*, and the foremost of the well-off mavericks were the **Medici**, a family from the agricultural Mugello region whose fortune had been made by the banking prowess of Giovanni Bicci de' Medici. The political rise of his son, **Cosimo de' Medici**, was to some extent due to his family's sympathies with the *Popolo Minuto*, as the members of the disenfranchised lesser guilds were known. With the increase in public discontent at the autocratic rule of the *Signoria*, Cosimo came to be seen as the figurehead of the more democratically inclined sector of the upper class.

Cosimo il Vecchio – as he came to be known – rarely held office himself, preferring to exercise power through backstage manipulation and adroit investment. His extreme generosity to charities and religious foundations in Florence was no doubt motivated in part by genuine piety, but clearly did no harm as a public relations exercise – even if it didn't impress the contemporary who recorded that his munificence was due to the fact that "he knew his money had not been over-well acquired".

Dante, Boccaccio and Giotto in the first half of the fourteenth century had established the **literary and artistic ascendancy** of Florence, laying the foundations of Italian humanism with their emphasis on the importance of the vernacular and the dignity of humanity. Florence's reputation as the most innovative cultural centre in Europe was strengthened during the fifteenth century, to a large extent through Medici patronage. Cosimo commissioned work from Donatello, Michelozzo and a host of other Florentine artists. His grandson **Lorenzo the Magnificent** (who succeeded Piero il Gottoso – the Gouty) continued this literary patronage, promoting the study of the classics in the Platonic academy that used to meet at the Medici villas. Other Medici were to fund projects by most of the seminal figures of the Florentine Renaissance.

Lorenzo's status as the de facto ruler of Florence was even more secure than that of Cosimo il Vecchio, but it did meet one stiff challenge. While many of Florence's financial dynasties were content to advise and support the Medici, others – notably the mighty **Strozzi** clan – were resentful of the power now wielded by their fellow businessmen. In 1478, these tensions gave rise to the **Pazzi Conspiracy** (see p.28), when the disgruntled Pazzi family conspired to assassinate Lorenzo and his brother Giuliano; Lorenzo survived, the conspirators were executed and the proud merchant clan was broken.

The Wars of Italy

Before Lorenzo's death in 1492, the Medici bank failed, and in 1494 Lorenzo's son Piero was obliged to flee following his surrender to the invading French army of Charles VIII. This invasion was the commencement of a bloody half-century dominated by the so-called **Wars of Italy**. After the departure of Charles's troops, Florence for a while was virtually under the control of the inspirational monk **Girolamo Savonarola**, but his career was brief (see p.132). After he was executed as a heretic in 1498, the city continued to function as a republic, but in 1512, following Florence's defeat by the Spanish and papal armies, the Medici returned, in the person of the vicious **Giuliano, duke of Nemours**.

Giuliano's successors – his equally unattractive nephew **Lorenzo, duke of Urbino**, and **Giulio**, illegitimate son of Lorenzo the Magnificent's brother – were in effect just the mouthpieces of **Giovanni de' Medici** (the duke of Nemours' brother), who in 1519 became **Pope Leo X**. Similarly, when Giulio became **Pope Clement VII**, he was really the absentee ruler of Florence, where the family presence was maintained by the ghastly Ippolito (illegitimate son of the duke of Nemours) and **Alessandro** (illegitimate son of the duke of Urbino).

The Medici were again evicted from Florence in the wake of Charles V's pillage of Rome in 1527. Three years later the pendulum swung the other way – after a siege by the combined papal and imperial forces, Florence capitulated and was obliged to receive Alessandro, who was proclaimed **duke of Florence**, the first of the Medici to bear the title of ruler.

The later Medici

After the assassination of Alessandro in 1537, power passed to another **Cosimo**, not a direct heir but rather a descendant of Cosimo il Vecchio's brother. The emperor Charles V, now related to the Medici through the marriage of his daughter to Alessandro, gave his assent to the succession. Yet this seemingly pliable young man had the clear intention of maintaining Florence's role as the regional powerbroker, and proved immensely skilful at judging just how far he could push the city's autonomy without provoking the imperial policy-makers.

Having finally extinguished the Strozzi faction at the battle of **Montemurlo**, Cosimo went on to buy the territory of Siena from the Habsburgs in 1557, giving Florence control of all of Tuscany with the solitary exception of Lucca. Imperial and papal approval of Cosimo's rule was sealed in 1570, when he was allowed to take the title **Cosimo I, grand duke of Tuscany**. In European terms Tuscany was a second-rank power, but by comparison with other states on the peninsula it was in a very comfortable position, and during Cosimo's reign there would have been little perception that Florence was drifting inexorably towards the margins of European politics. It was Cosimo who built the Uffizi, extended and overhauled the Palazzo Vecchio, installed the Medici in the Palazzo Pitti, had the magnificent Ponte Santa Trìnita constructed across the Arno and commissioned much of the sculpture around the Piazza della Signoria.

The decline of Florence

Cosimo's descendants were to remain in power until 1737, and aspects of their rule continued the city's intellectual tradition – the Medici were among Galileo's strongest supporters, for example. Yet it was a story of almost continual if initially gentle economic decline, as bad harvests and recurrent epidemics worsened the gloom created by the shift of European trading patterns in favour of northern Europe. The half-century reign of **Ferdinando II** had scarcely begun when the market for Florence's woollen goods collapsed in the 1630s, and the city's banks simultaneously went into a terminal slump. The last two male Medici, the insanely pious **Cosimo III** and the drunken pederast **Gian Gastone**, were fitting symbols of the moribund Florentine state.

Under the terms of a treaty signed by Gian Gastone's sister, Anna Maria de' Medici, Florence passed in 1737 to the **House of Lorraine**, cousins of the Austrian Habsburgs. The first Lorraine prince, the future Francis I of Austria, was a more enlightened ruler than the last Medici had been and his successors presided over a placid and generally untroubled region, doing much to improve the condition of Tuscany's agricultural land and rationalize its production methods. Austrian rule lasted until the coming of the French in 1799, an interlude that ended with the fall of **Napoleon**, who had made his sister – Elisa Baciocchi – grand duchess of Tuscany. After this, the Lorraine dynasty was brought back, remaining in residence until the last of the line, **Leopold II**, abdicated in 1859. Absorbed into the united Italian state in the following year, Florence became the **capital of the Kingdom of Italy** in 1865, a position it held until 1871.

Fascism and war

Italy's unpopular entry into World War I cost thousands of Florentine and Tuscan lives, and the economic disruption that followed was exploited by the regime of Benito **Mussolini**. His fascist state of the 1920s did effect various improvements in the region's infrastructure, but his alliance with Hitler's Germany was to prove a calamity. In 1943, the Allied landing at Monte Cassino was followed by a campaign to sweep the occupying German forces out of the peninsula. Florence was wrecked by the retreating German army, who bombed all the bridges except the Ponte Vecchio and blew up much of the medieval city near the banks of the Arno. As elsewhere in Italy, loyalties were split: wartime Florence was both an ideological centre for the resistance and home to some of Italy's most ardent Nazi collaborators. The city produced one of the strangest paradoxes of the time: a fascist sympathizer in charge of the British Institute and a German consul who did so much to protect suspected partisans that he was granted the freedom of the city after the war.

Postwar Florence

Florence has rarely occupied centre-stage in post-war Italy. The one notable exception was after the great **flood** of 1966, when the Arno burst its banks, killing 35 Florentines and destroying or damaging countless works of art. Today Florence is a prosperous city, thanks to industrial development in the Arno valley and the production of, among other things, textiles, leather goods and jewellery. **Tourism**, however, plays an uncomfortably large part in balancing the books. The latest and most ambitious attempt to break the city's ever-increasing dependence on its visitors is **"Firenze Nuova"**, a development to the northwest of the city where people will work, live and play, leaving Florence to develop as a cultural and small-scale commercial city.

Artists and architects

Alberti, Leon Battista
(1404–72). Born illegitimately to
a Florentine exile, probably in
Genoa, Alberti was educated in
Padua and Bologna. One of the
most complete personifications
of the Renaissance ideal of universal genius, he was above all
a writer and theorist: his *De Re
Aedificatoria* (1452) was the first
architectural treatise of the
Renaissance, and he also wrote
a tract on the art of painting,
Della Pittura, dedicated to his
friend Brunelleschi. His theory
of harmonic proportions in
musical and visual forms was
first put into practise in the
facade of Santa Maria Novella,
while his archeological interest
in classical architecture found
expression in the Palazzo

Rucellai, his first independent
project. Even more closely
linked to his researches into the
style of antiquity is the miniature
temple built for the Rucellai
family in the church of San
Pancrazio. His other buildings
are in Mantua and Rimini.

Ammannati, Bartolomeo
(1511–92). A Florentine sculp-
tor-architect, much indebted to
Michelangelo, Ammannati is
best known for his additions
and amendments to the Palazzo
Pitti and for the graceful Ponte
San Trìnita (though in all likelihood this was largely designed
by Michelangelo). He created
the fountain in the Piazza della
Signoria, with some assistance
from his pupil Giambologna,
and the Bargello contains some

of his pieces made for the Bóboli gardens.

Andrea del Sarto (1486–1530). The dominant artist in Florence at the time of Michelangelo and Raphael's ascendancy in Rome. His strengths are not those associated with Florentine draughtsmanship, being more Venetian in his emphasis on delicacy of colour and the primacy of light. He made his name with frescoes for two Florentine churches in the San Marco district – the Scalzo and Santissima Annunziata. For a period in the 1510s he was in France, and the received wisdom is that his talent did not develop after that. However, two of his other major works in Florence date from after his return – the *Last Supper* in San Salvi and the *Madonna del Sacco* in the cloister of the Annunziata. His major easel painting is the *Madonna of the Harpies* in the Uffizi.

Arnolfo di Cambio (c. 1245–1302). Pupil of Nicola Pisano, with whom he worked on sculptural projects in Bologna, Siena and Perugia before going to Rome in 1277. The most important of his independent sculptures are the pieces in Florence's Museo dell'Opera del Duomo and the *Tomb of Cardinal de Braye* in San Domenico in Orvieto. The latter defined the format of wall tombs for the next century, showing the deceased lying on a coffin below the Madonna and Child, set within an elaborate architectural framework. However, Arnolfo is best known as the architect of Florence's Duomo and Palazzo Vecchio, and various fortifications in central Tuscany, including the fortress at Poppi.

Bandinelli, Baccio (1493–1560). Born in Florence, Bandinelli trained as a goldsmith, sculptor and painter. He perceived himself as an equal talent to Michelangelo and to Cellini, his most vocal critic. Despite manifest shortcomings as a sculptor, he was given prestigious commissions by Cosimo I, the most conspicuous of which is the *Hercules and Cacus* outside the Palazzo Vecchio. Other pieces by him are in the Bargello.

Botticelli, Sandro. See p.67.

Bronzino, Agnolo (1503–72). The adopted son of Pontormo,

Bronzino became the court painter to Cosimo I. He frescoed parts of the Palazzo Vecchio for Eleanor of Toledo, but his reputation rests on his glacially elegant portraits, whose surface brilliance makes no discrimination between the faces of the subjects and their apparel.

Brunelleschi, Filippo

(1377–1446). Trained as a sculptor and goldsmith, Brunelleschi abandoned this career after his failure in the competition for the Florence Baptistery doors. The main product of this period is his contribution to the *St James* altarpiece in Pistoia. He then devoted himself to the study of the building techniques of the Classical era, travelling to Rome with Donatello in 1402. In 1417 he submitted his design for the dome of Florence's Duomo, and all his subsequent work was in the city – San Lorenzo, the Spedale degli Innocenti, Cappella Pazzi (Santa Croce) and Santo Spirito. Unlike the other great architect of this period, Alberti, his work is based on no theoretical premise, but rather on an empiricist's admiration for the buildings of Rome. And unlike Alberti he oversaw every stage of construction, even devising machinery that would permit the raising of the innovative structures he had planned.

Castagno, Andrea del

(c. 1421–57). The early years of Castagno's life are mysterious, but around 1440 he painted the portraits of some executed rebels in the Bargello, a job that earned him the nickname "Andrea of the Hanged Men". In 1442 he was working in Venice, but a couple of years later he was back in Florence, creating stained glass for the Duomo and frescoes for Sant'Apollonia. His taut sinewy style is to a large extent derived from the sculpture of his contemporary, Donatello, an affinity that is especially clear in his frescoes for Santissima Annunziata. Other major works in Florence include the series of *Famous Men and Women* in the Uffizi and the portrait of *Niccolò da Tolentino* in the Duomo – his last piece.

Cellini, Benvenuto

(1500–71). Cellini began his career in Rome, where he fought in the siege of the city by the imperial army in 1527. His sculpture is greatly influenced by Michelangelo, as is evident in his most famous large-scale piece, the *Perseus* in the Loggia della Signoria. His other masterpiece in Florence is the heroic *Bust of Cosimo I* in the Bargello. Cellini was an even more accomplished goldsmith and jeweller, creating some exquisite pieces for Francis I, by whom he was employed in the 1530s and 1540s. He also wrote a racy *Autobiography*, a fascinating insight into the artistic world of sixteenth-century Italy and France.

Cimabue (c.1240–1302). Though celebrated by Dante as the foremost painter of the generation before Giotto, very little is known about Cimabue – in fact, the only work that is definitely by him is the mosaic in Pisa's Duomo. He is generally given credit for the softening of the hieratic Byzantine style of religious art, a tendency carried further by his putative pupil, Giotto. Some works can be attributed to him with more confidence than others – the shortlist would include the *Maestà* in the Uffizi and the crucifixes in Santa Croce.

Desiderio da Settignano (c. 1428–64). Desiderio continued the low-relief technique pioneered by Donatello in the panel for the Orsanmichele *St George*, and carved the tomb of Carlo Marsuppini in Santa Croce, Florence. Better known for his exquisite busts of women and children – a good selection of which are on show in the Bargello.

Donatello (c. 1386–1466). A pupil of Ghiberti, Donatello assisted in the casting of the first set of Florence Baptistery doors in 1403, then worked for Nanni di Banco on the Duomo. His early marble *David* (Bargello) is still Gothic in its form, but a new departure is evident in his heroic *St Mark* for Orsanmichele (1411) – possibly produced after a study of the sculpture of ancient Rome. Four years later he began the intense series of prophets for the Campanile, and at the same time produced the *St George* for Orsanmichele – the epitome of early Renaissance humanism, featuring a relief that is the very first application of rigorous perspective in Western art.

In the mid-1520s Donatello started a partnership with Michelozzo, with whom he created the tomb of Pope John XXIII in the Florence Baptistery, a refinement of the genre initiated by Arnolfo di Cambio. He went to Rome in 1431, possibly with Brunelleschi, and it was probably on his return that he made the classical bronze *David* (Bargello), one of the first nude statues of the Renaissance period. Also at this time he made the *cantoria* to be placed opposite the one already made by Luca della Robbia in Florence's Duomo, the pulpit for Prato cathedral (with Michelozzo) and the decorations for the old sacristy in Florence's church of San Lorenzo – the parish church of his great patrons, the Medici.

After a period in Padua – where he created the first bronze equestrian statue since Roman times – he returned to Florence, where his last works show an extraordinary harshness and angularity. The main sculptures from this period are the *Judith and Holofernes* (Palazzo Vecchio), the *Magdalene* (Museo dell'Opera del Duomo) and the two bronze pulpits for San Lorenzo.

Fra' Angelico. See p.134.

Fra' Bartolommeo (c. 1474–1517). Fra' Bartolommeo's earliest known work is the Raphael-influenced *Last Judgement* painted for the San Marco monastery in Florence in 1499. The following year he became a monk there, then in 1504 became head of the workshop, a post previously occupied by Fra' Angelico. In 1514 he was in Rome, but according to Vasari was discouraged by Raphael's fame. The works he later produced in Florence had an influence on High Renaissance art, with their repression of elaborate backgrounds and anecdotal detail, concentrating instead on expression and gesture.

Gaddi, Taddeo (d.1366). According to tradition, Taddeo Gaddi worked with Giotto for 24 years, and throughout his life barely wavered from the precepts of his master's style. His first major independent work is the cycle for the Cappella Baroncelli in Santa Croce, Florence. Other works by him are in Florence's Uffizi, Accademia, Bargello and Museo Horne.

Agnolo Gaddi (d.1396). Taddeo's son Agnolo continued his father's Giottoesque style; his major projects were for Santa Croce in Florence and the duomo of nearby Prato.

Gentile da Fabriano (c. 1370–1427). Chief exponent of the International Gothic style in Italy, Gentile da Fabriano came to Florence in 1422, when he painted the gorgeous *Adoration of the Magi*, now in the Uffizi. In 1425 he went on to Siena and Orvieto, where the intellectual climate was perhaps more conducive than that in the Florence of Masaccio; he finished his career in Rome.

Ghiberti, Lorenzo (1378–1455). Trained as a goldsmith, painter and sculptor, Ghiberti concentrated on the last discipline almost exclusively after winning the competition to design the doors for Florence's Baptistery. His first set of doors are to a large extent derived from Andrea Pisano's earlier Gothic panels for the building, yet his workshop was a virtual acade-

my for the seminal figures of the early Florentine Renaissance – Donatello and Uccello among them. The commission took around twenty years to complete, during which time he also worked on the Siena Baptistery and the church of Orsanmichele in Florence, where his *Baptist* and *St Matthew* show the influence of Classical statuary. This classicism reached its peak in the second set of doors for Florence's Baptistery, taking Donatello's innovations to a new pitch of perfection. The panels occupied much of the rest of his life but in his final years he wrote his *Commentarii*, the main source of information on fourteenth-century art in Florence and Siena, and the first autobiography by an artist.

Ghirlandaio, Domenico (1449–94). The most accomplished fresco artist of his generation, Ghirlandaio was the teacher of Michelangelo. After a short period working on the Sistine Chapel with Botticelli, he came back to Florence, where his cycles in Santa Trìnita and Santa Maria Novella provide some of the most absorbing documentary images of the time, being filled with contemporary portraits and vivid anecdotal details.

Giambologna (1529–1608). Born in northern France, Giambologna – Jean de Boulogne – arrived in Italy in the mid-1550s, becoming the most influential Florentine sculptor after Michelangelo's death. Having helped Ammannati on the fountain for the Piazza della Signoria, he went on to produce a succession of pieces that typify the Mannerist predilection for sculptures with multiple viewpoints – such as the *Rape of the Sabines* (Loggia della Signoria) and the *Mercury* (Bargello).

Giotto di Bondone (1266–1337). It was with Giotto's great fresco cycles that religious art shifted from being a straightforward act of devotion to the dramatic presentation of incident. His unerring eye for the significant gesture, his ability to encapsulate moments of extreme emotion and his technical command of figure modelling and spatial depth brought him early recognition as the greatest artist of his generation.

Vasari tells that as a young man in Cimabue's workshop, Giotto painted a fly on the nose of a portrait his master as working on. It was so lifelike that Cimabue "tried several times to brush it off with his hand".

In all probability his first major cycle was the *Life of St Francis* in the upper church at Assisi, though the extent to which his assistants carried out his designs is still disputed. The Arena chapel in Padua is certainly by him, as are large parts of the Bardi and Peruzzi chapels in Santa Croce in Florence. Of his attributed panel paintings, the Uffizi *Maestà* is the only one universally accepted.

Leonardo da Vinci (1452–1519). Leonardo trained as a painter under Verrocchio; drawings of landscapes and drapery have survived from the 1470s, but the first completed picture is the *Annunciation* in the Uffizi. The sketch of the *Adoration of the Magi*, also in the Uffizi, dates from 1481, at which time there was no precedent for its fusion of geometric form and dynamic action. Two years later he was in the employment of Lodovico Sforza of Milan, remaining there for sixteen years. During this second phase of his career he produced the *Lady with the Ermine* (Kraków), the fresco of the *Last Supper* and – probably – the two versions of *The Virgin of the Rocks*, the fullest demonstrations to date of his so-called *sfumato*, a blurring of tones from light to dark.

When the French took Milan in 1499 Leonardo returned to Florence, where he was commissioned to paint a fresco of the *Battle of Anghiari* in the main hall of the Palazzo Ducale, alongside his detested rival Michelangelo. Only a fragment of the fresco was completed, and the innovative technique that Leonardo had employed resulted in its speedy disintegration. His cartoons for the *Madonna and Child with St Anne* (Louvre and National Gallery, London) also date from this period, as does the most famous of all his paintings, the Louvre's *Mona Lisa*, the portrait of the wife of a Florentine merchant. In 1506 he went back to Milan, thence to Rome and finally, in 1517, to France. Military and scientific work occupied much of this last period – the

only painting to have survived is the *St John*, also in the Louvre.

Lippi, Filippo (c. 1406–69). In 1421 Filippo Lippi was placed in the monastery of the Carmine in Florence, just at the time Masaccio was beginning work on the Cappella Brancacci there. His early works all bear the stamp of Masaccio, but by the 1530s he was becoming interested in the representation of movement and a more luxuriant surface detail. The frescoes in the cathedral at Prato, executed in the 1550s, show his highly personal, almost hedonistic vision, as do his panel paintings of wistful Madonnas in patrician interiors or soft landscapes – many of them executed for the Medici. His last work, the *Life of the Virgin* fresco cycle in Spoleto, was probably largely executed by assistants.

Lippi, Filippino (1457/8–1504) Filippino completed his father Filippo's work in Spoleto – aged about 12 – then travelled to Florence, where his first major commission was the completion of Masaccio's frescoes in Santa Maria del Carmine's Cappella Brancacci (c. 1484). At around

LIPPI

this time he also painted the *Vision of St Bernard* for the Badia Fiorentina, which shows an affinity with Botticelli, with whom he is known to have worked. His later researches in Rome led him to develop a self-consciously antique style – seen at its most ambitious in Santa Maria Novella.

Masaccio (1401–28). Born just outside Florence, Masaccio entered the city's painters' guild in 1422. His first large commission, an altarpiece for the Carmelites of Pisa (the central panel is now in the National Gallery in London), shows a massive grandeur at odds with the then popular International Gothic style. His masterpieces – the *Trinity* fresco in Santa Maria Novella and the fresco cycle in Santa Maria del Carmine's Cappella Brancacci – were produced in the last three years of his life, the latter in collaboration with Masolino. With the architecture of Brunelleschi and the sculpture of Donatello, the Brancacci frescoes are the most important achievements of the early Renaissance.

Masolino da Panicale (1383–1447). Masolino was employed in Ghiberti's workshop for the production of the first set of Baptistery doors, and the semi-Gothic early style of Ghiberti conditioned much of his subsequent work. His other great influence was the younger Masaccio, with whom he worked on the Brancacci chapel.

Michelangelo Buonarroti. See p.117.

Michelozzo di Bartolommeo (1396–1472). Born in Florence, Michelozzo worked in Ghiberti's studio and collaborated with Donatello before turning exclusively to architecture. His main patrons were the Medici, for whom he altered the villa at Careggi and built the Palazzo Medici. The latter was a prototype for patrician mansions in the city, with its rusticated lower storey, smooth upper facade, overhanging cornice and inner courtyard. He later designed the Villa Medici at Fiesole for the family, and for Cosimo de' Medici he added the light and airy library to the monastery of San Marco. In the Alberti-influenced tribune for the church of Santissima Annunziata, Michelozzo produced the first centrally planned church design to be built in the Renaissance period.

Monaco, Lorenzo (1372–1425). A Sienese artist, Lorenzo Monaco joined the Camaldolese monastery in Florence, for which he painted the *Coronation of the Virgin*, now in the Uffizi. This and his other earlier works are fairly conventional Sienese-style altarpieces, with two-dimensional figures on gold backgrounds. However, his late *Adoration of the Magi* (Uffizi), with its fastidious detailing and landscape backdrop, anticipates the arrival of Gentile da Fabriano and fully fledged International Gothic.

Nanni di Banco (c. 1384–1421). A Florentine sculptor who began his career as an assistant to his father on the Florence Duomo, Nanni was an exact contemporary of Donatello, with whom he shared some early commissions – Donatello's first *David* was ordered at the same time as an *Isaiah* from Nanni. The finest works produced in his short life are his niche sculptures at Orsanmichele (especially the *Four Saints*) and the relief above the Duomo's Porta della Mandorla.

Orcagna, Andrea (c. 1308–68). Architect-sculptor-painter, Orcagna was a dominant figure in the period following the death of Giotto, whose emphasis on spatial depth he rejected – as shown in his only authenticated panel painting, the Strozzi altarpiece in Santa Maria Novella. Damaged frescoes can be seen in Santa Croce and Santo Spirito, but Florence's principal work by Orcagna is the massive tabernacle in Orsanmichele. Orcagna's brothers, Nardo and Jacopo di Cione, were the most influential painters in Florence at the close of the fourteenth century – the frescoes in the Strozzi chapel are by Nardo.

Piero di Cosimo (c. 1462–1521). One of the more enigmatic figures of the High Renaissance, Piero di Cosimo shared Leonardo's scholarly interest in the natural world but turned his knowledge to the production of allusive mythological paintings. There are pictures by him in the Uffizi, Palazzo Pitti, Museo degli Innocenti and Museo Horne.

Pisano, Andrea (c. 1290–1348). Nothing is known of Andrea

Pisano's life until 1330, when he was given the commission to make a new set of doors for the Florence Baptistery. He then succeeded Giotto as master mason of the Campanile; the set of reliefs he produced for it are the only other works definitely by him (now in the Museo dell'Opera del Duomo). In 1347 he became the supervisor of Orvieto's Duomo, a post later held by his sculptor son, Nino.

Pisano, Nicola (c. 1220–84). Born in the southern Italian kingdom of the emperor Frederick II, Nicola Pisano was the first great classicizing sculptor in pre-Renaissance Italy; the pulpit in Pisa's Baptistery (1260), his first masterpiece, shows the influence of Roman figures. Five years later he produced the pulpit for the Duomo in Siena, with the assistance of his son Giovanni (c. 1248–1314) and Arnolfo di Cambio. The Museo dell'Opera del Duomo in Siena has some fine large-scale figures by Giovanni, while its counterpart in Pisa contains a large collection of work by both the Pisani.

Pollaiuolo, Antonio del (c. 1432–98) and Piero del (c. 1441–96). Though their Florence workshop turned out engravings, jewellery and embroideries, the Pollaiuolo brothers were known mainly for their advances in oil-painting technique and for their anatomical researches, which bore fruit in paintings and small-scale bronze sculptures. The influences of Donatello and Castagno (Piero's teacher) are evident in their dramatic, often violent work, which is especially well represented in the Bargello. The Uffizi's collection of paintings suggests that Antonio was by far the more skilled artist.

Pontormo, Jacopo. See p.180.

Raphael (1483–1520). With Leonardo and Michelangelo, Raphael Sanzio forms the triumvirate whose works define the essence of the High Renaissance. Born in Urbino, he joined Perugino's workshop sometime around 1494 and within five years was receiving commissions independently of his master. From 1505 to 1508 he was in Florence, where he absorbed the compositional and tonal innovations of Leonardo; many of the pictures he produced at that time are now in the Palazzo Pitti. He then went to Rome, where Pope Julius II set him to work on the papal apartments (the *Stanze*). Michelangelo's Sistine ceiling was largely instrumental in modulating Raphael's style from its earlier lyrical grace into something more monumental, but all the works from this more rugged later period are in Rome.

Robbia, Luca della (1400–82). Luca began as a sculptor in conventional materials, his earliest achievement being the marble *cantoria* (choir gallery) now in the Museo dell'Opera del Duomo in Florence, typifying the cheerful tone of most of his work. Thirty years later he made the sacristy doors for this city's Duomo, but by then he had devised a technique for applying durable potter's glaze to clay sculpture and most of his energies were given to the art of glazed terracotta. His distinctive blue, white and yellow compositions are seen at their best in the Pazzi chapel in Santa Croce and the Bargello. Andrea della Robbia (1435–1525) continued the profitable terracotta business started by Luca, his uncle. His best work is at the Spedale degli Innocenti in Florence and at the monastery of La Verna.

Rossellino, Bernardo (1409–64). An architect-sculptor, Rossellino worked with Alberti and carried out his plans for the Palazzo Rucellai in Florence. His major architectural commission was Pius II's new town of Pienza. As a sculptor he's best known for the monument to Leonardo Bruni in Santa Croce. His brother and pupil Antonio (1427–79) produced the tomb of the Cardinal of Portugal in Florence's San Miniato al Monte, and a number of excellent portrait busts (Bargello).

Rosso Fiorentino (1494–1540). Like Pontormo, Rosso Fiorentino was a pupil of Andrea del Sarto, but went on to develop a far more aggressive, acidic style than his colleague and friend. His early *Deposition* in Volterra (1521) and the roughly contemporaneous *Moses Defending the Daughters of Jethro* (Uffizi) are typical of his extreme foreshortening and tense deployment of figures.

ROBBIA–ROSSO FIORENTINO

Spinello Aretino (active 1370s–1410). Probably born in Arezzo, Spinello studied in Florence, possibly under Agnolo Gaddi. He harks back to the monumental style of Giotto – thus, paradoxically, paving the way for the most radical painter of the next generation, Masaccio. His main works are in Florence's church of San Miniato al Monte and Santa Caterina d'Antella, just south of the city.

Uccello, Paolo. See p.158.

Vasari, Giorgio (1511–74). Born in Arezzo, Vasari trained with Luca Signorelli and Andrea del Sarto. He became the leading artistic impresario of his day, working for the papacy in Rome and for the Medici in Florence, where he supervised (and partly executed) the redecoration of the Palazzo Vecchio. His own house in Arezzo is perhaps the most impressive display of his limited pictorial talents. He also designed the Uffizi gallery and oversaw a number of other architectural projects. He is now chiefly famous for his Tuscan-biased *Lives of the Most Excellent Painters, Sculptors and Architects* (see p.356).

Veneziano, Domenico (1404–61). Despite the name, Domenico Veneziano was probably born in Florence, though his preoccupation with the way in which colour alters in different light is more typically Venetian. From 1439 to 1445 he was working in Florence with Piero della Francesca on a fresco cycle that has now perished. Only a dozen surviving works can be attributed to him with any degree of certainty and only two signed pieces by him are left – one of them is the central panel of the so-called *St Lucy Altar* in the Uffizi.

Verrocchio, Andrea del (c. 1435–88). A Florentine painter, sculptor and goldsmith, Verrocchio was possibly a pupil of Donatello's and certainly his successor as the city's leading sculptor. A highly accomplished if sometimes over-facile craftsman, he ran one of Florence's busiest workshops, whose employees included the young Leonardo da Vinci. In Florence his work can be seen in the Uffizi, Bargello, San Lorenzo, Santo Spirito, Orsanmichele and Museo dell'Opera del Duomo.

Books

ountless **books** have been written on Florence across many centuries. Many more concerned with Italy or Tuscany in general have touched on the city. We have concentrated on titles which relate more or less exclusively to the city, or to cultural matters such as the Renaissance in which the city has played a prominent role. Most of the books recommended below are currently in print, and those that aren't shouldn't be too difficult to track down in secondhand stores. Wherever a book is in print, the UK publisher is given first in each listing, followed by the publisher in the US, unless the title is available in one country only, in which case we have specified the country concerned. If the same publisher produces the book in the UK and US, the publisher is simply named once.

General

Harold Acton, *Florence: A Traveller's Companion* (Constable, UK). A wide-reaching anthology of literary and other musings on Florence across the centuries.

Harold Acton, *The Last Medici* (Cardinal, UK). Elegant biography of the least elegant member of the dynasty, the perpetually wine-sodden Gian Gastone.

Gene A. Brucker, *Renaissance Florence* (University of California). Concentrating on the years 1380–1450, this brilliant study of Florence at its cultural zenith uses masses of archival material to fill in the social, economic and political background.

Eric Cochrane, *Florence in the Forgotten Centuries 1527–1800* (University of Chicago Press). Massively erudite account of the twilight centuries of Florence; intimidating in its detail, it's unrivalled in its coverage of the years when the city's scientists were more famous than its painters.

J.R. Hale, *Florence and the Medici* (Thames & Hudson, UK). Scholarly yet lively, this covers the full span of the Medici story from the foundation of the family fortune to the calamitous eighteenth century.

Christopher Hibbert, *The Rise and Fall of the Medici* (Penguin/Morrow). More anecdotal than Hale's book, this is a gripping read, full of heroic successes and squalid failures.

Christopher Hibbert, *Florence: The Biography of a City*

(Viking/Norton). Yet another excellent Hibbert production, packed with illuminating anecdotes and fascinating illustrations – unlike most books on the city, it's as interesting on the political history as on the artistic achievements, and doesn't grind to a standstill with the fall of the Medici.

Mary Hollingsworth, *Patronage in Renaissance Italy* (John Murray, UK). The first comprehensive English-language study of the relationship between artist and patron in *quattrocento* Italy's city-states. A salutary corrective to the mythology of self-inspired Renaissance genius.

George Holmes, *Florence, Rome and the Origins of the Renaissance* (Oxford University Press). Magnificent portrait of the world of Dante and Giotto, with especially compelling sections on the impact of St Francis and the role of the papacy in the political and cultural life of central Italy.

Francis King, *A Literary Companion to Florence* (John Murray). King's book is livelier and more analytical than Acton's *A Traveller's Companion* (see p.353), with amusing essays on visitors to Florence over the centuries and an area-by-area run down of what they've had to say about the city.

Mary McCarthy, *The Stones of Florence* (Penguin/Harvest). Written in the mid-1960s, *Stones* is a mix of high-class reporting on the contemporary city and historical anecdotes.

Mark Phillips, *The Memoir of Marco Parenti* (Heinemann/University of Princeton). The journal of a Florentine patrician, evoking the backroom politics and financial wheeler-dealing of fifteenth-century Florence.

Art and architecture

Charles Avery, *Florentine Renaissance Sculpture* (John Murray). Serviceable introduction to the milieu of Donatello and Michelangelo.

Vincent Cronin, *The Florentine Renaissance* and *The Flowering of the Renaissance* (both Pimlico, UK). Concise and gripping narrative of Italian art's golden years – the first volume covers the fifteenth century, the second switches the focus to sixteenth-century Rome and Venice.

J.R. Hale (ed), *Concise Encyclopaedia of the Italian Renaissance* (Thames & Hudson, UK). Exemplary reference book, many of whose summaries are as informative as essays twice their length; covers individual artists, movements, cities, philosophical concepts, the lot.

Frederick Hartt, *History of Italian Renaissance Art* (Thames & Hudson/Abrams). If one book on this vast subject can be said to be indispensable, this is it. The price might seem daunting, but in view of its comprehensiveness and the range of its illustrations, it's actually a bargain.

Ross King, *Brunelleschi's Dome* (Pimlico, UK). Tells one of architecture's greatest tales: the invention and construction of Florence's great dome by Filippo Brunelleschi. Gives an excellent sense of the fervid atmosphere of the time, and is surprisingly difficult to put down.

Michael Levey, *Early Renaissance* (Penguin). Precise and fluently written account, and well illustrated; probably the best introduction to the subject. Levey's *High Renaissance* (Penguin) continues the story in the same style.

Anna Maria Massinelli and **Filippo Tuena**, *Treasures of the Medici* (Thames & Hudson/Vendome). Illustrated inventory of the Medici family's collection of jewellery, vases and other *objets d'art*, published to celebrate the five-hundredth anniversary of the death of Lorenzo the Magnificent, perhaps the clan's most compulsive collector.

Peter Murray, *The Architecture of the Italian Renaissance* (Thames & Hudson/Schocken). Useful both as a gazetteer of the main monuments and as a synopsis of the underlying concepts, from the Romanesque to Palladio.

John Shearman, *Mannerism* (Penguin). Shearman's brief discussion analyses the complex, self-conscious art of sixteenth-century Mannerism without oversimplifying or becoming pedantic.

Giorgio Vasari, *Lives of the Artists* (Penguin, 2 vols). Abridgement of the sixteenth-century artist's classic work on his predecessors and contemporaries. Includes essays on Giotto, Brunelleschi, Leonardo and Michelangelo. The first real work of art history, and still among the most penetrating books you can read on Italian Renaissance art.

Individual artists

The Complete Paintings series: *Botticelli*, *Leonardo da Vinci*, *Piero della Francesca*

(Penguin). Paperback picture books, reproducing every painting in black and white, plus several colour plates. Also gives detailed analysis of dates, authenticity and a host of other art-historical issues.

James A. Ackerman, *The Architecture of Michelangelo* (Penguin/University of Chicago). If you come out of the Sagrestia Nuova in Florence wondering why people make such a fuss about Michelangelo's buildings, Ackerman's book will make you see it with fresh eyes.

Umberto Baldini and **Ornella Casazza**, *The Brancacci Chapel* (Thames & Hudson/Abrams). Written by the chief restorers of the Brancacci frescoes by Masaccio, Masolino and Filippino Lippi, this luscious book is illustrated with magnificent life-size reproductions of the freshly cleaned masterpieces.

Bonnie Bennett and **David Wilkins**, *Donatello* (Phaidon/Moyer Bell). Worthy homage to one of the most influential figures in the history of Western art.

Kenneth Clark, *Leonardo da Vinci* (Penguin). Rather old-fashioned in its reverential connoisseurship, but still highly recommended.

Bruce Cole, *Giotto and Florentine Painting 1280–1375* (Harper Row/HarperCollins). Excellent introduction to the art of Giotto and his immediate successors.

Ludwig Goldscheider, *Michelangelo: Paintings, Sculpture, Architecture* (Phaidon). Virtually all monochrome reproductions, but a good pictorial survey of Michelangelo's output, covering everything except the drawings.

William Hood, *Fra Angelico at San Marco* (Yale University Press). Maintaining this imprint's reputation for elegantly produced, scholarly yet accessible art books, Hood's socio-aesthetic study of the panel paintings and frescoes of Fra' Angelico is unsurpassed in its scope. A book to read after you've made your first acquaintance with the pictures.

BOOKS ON INDIVIDUAL ARTISTS

Literature

Giovanni Boccaccio, *The Decameron* (Penguin). Set in the plague-racked Florence of 1348, Boccaccio's assembly of one hundred short stories is a fascinating social record as well as a constantly diverting and often smutty comedy.

Benvenuto Cellini, *Autobiography* (Penguin). Shamelessly egocentric record of the travails and triumphs of the sculptor and goldsmith; one of the freshest literary productions of its time.

Dante Alighieri, *The Divine Comedy* (Oxford University Press, 3 vols). No work in any other language bears comparison with Dante's poetic exegesis of the moral scheme of God's creation – in late medieval Italy it was venerated both as a book of almost scriptural authority and as the ultimate refinement of the vernacular Tuscan language. The OUP edition is clear, and has the original text facing the English version. One of the better translations, Laurence Binyon's, is

printed in full in the *Portable Dante* (Penguin).

George Eliot, *Romola* (Penguin). One of the great unread nineteenth-century novels; a rich quasi-Shakespearean romance about love, ambition and betrayal. Set in Savonarola's Florence, with cameo portraits of many of the leading figures of the time, it's also a meticulously researched evocation of the city.

Niccolà Machiavelli, *The Prince* (Penguin). A treatise on statecraft which did less to form the political thought of Italy than foreigners' perceptions of the country; yet there was far more to Machiavelli than realpolitik, as is shown by the selection in Penguin's anthology *The Portable Machiavelli*.

Petrarch (Francesco Petrarca), *Selections from the Canzoniere* (Oxford University Press). Preoccupied with secular love and worldly fame, Petrarch is often described as the first modern poet. This slim selection of some of the Italian language's greatest lyrics at least hints at what is lost in translation.

Magdalen Nabb, *Death in Springtime*, *Death in Autumn*, and many other titles (Collins, UK). Florence is the locale for many of Nabb's brilliant thrillers, based on a good knowledge of the city's low life… and the Sardinian shepherds who dabble in a spot of kidnapping in the hills.

LITERATURE

Artistic and architectural terms

AMBO A simple pulpit, popular in Italian medieval churches.

APSE Semicircular recess at the altar end of a church.

BADIA Abbey.

BALDACCHINO A canopy on columns, usually over an altar.

BATTISTERO Baptistery.

CAMPANILE Bell-tower, sometimes detached, of a church.

CAMPO Square.

CAMPOSANTO Cemetery.

CANTORIA Choir loft.

CAPITAL Top of a column.

CAPPELLA Chapel.

CARTOON Preparatory drawing on paper for a painting.

CENACOLO Last Supper.

CHANCEL Part of a church containing the altar.

CHIESA Church.

CHIOSTRO Cloister.

CIBORIUM Baldacchino, or the vessel for the communion bread.

CORNICE The top section of a classical facade.

CRYPT Burial place in a church, usually under the choir.

CUPOLA Dome.

DIPTYCH Twin-panelled painting.

DUOMO Cathedral.

FRESCO Wall-painting technique in which the paint is applied to wet plaster for a more permanent finish.

INTARSIA Inlaid stone or wood.

LOGGIA Roofed gallery or balcony.

LUNETTE Semicircular space in vault or ceiling.

MAESTÀ Madonna and Child enthroned.

NAVE Central space in a church, usually flanked by aisles.

PALAZZO Palace, mansion, or block of flats.

PALAZZO DEL PODESTÀ Magistrate's palace.

PALAZZO DEL POPOLO, PALAZZO PUBBLICO, PALAZZO COMUNALE Town hall.

PIETÀ Image of the Virgin mourning the dead Christ.

PIETRA DURA Inlay of hard or semiprecious stones.

POLYPTYCH Painting on several joined panels.

PORTA Gate.

PORTICO Covered entrance to a building.

PREDELLA Small panel below the main scenes of an altarpiece.

RELIQUARY Receptacle for a saint's relics, usually bones.

SGRAFFITO Decoration created by scratching a layer of plaster.

SINOPIA Sketch for a fresco, applied to the wall.

STUCCO Plaster made from water, lime, sand and powdered marble, used for decorative work.

TONDO Round painting or relief.

TRIPTYCH Painting on three joined panels.

TROMPE L'OEIL Work of art employing tricks of perspective.

INDEX

Don't bury your head in the sand!

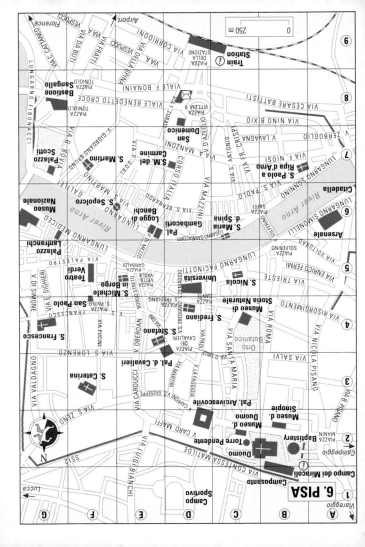

6. PISA

Viareggio

SS12 Lucca

Florence

Airport

Campo dei Miracoli

Camposanto

Duomo

Baptistery

Torre Pendente

Museo d. Sinopie

Museo d. Duomo

PIAZZA MANIN

VIA CONTESSA MATILDE

VIA CARD. MAFFI

Pal. Arcivescovile

S. Caterina

Pal. d. Cavalieri

PIAZZA DEI CAVALIERI

S. Francesco

S. Stefano

Museo di Storia Naturale

S. Frediano

Università

S. Michele in Borgo

Teatro Verdi

San Paolo

Palazzo Lanfranchi

River Arno

Loggia di Banchi

Pal. Gambacorti

S. Maria d. Spina

Museo Nazionale

S. Sepolcro

Palazzo Scotti

S. Martino

S.M. del Carmine

San Domenico

S. Paolo a Ripa d'Arno

Bastione Sangallo

Train Station

PIAZZA DELLA STAZIONE

PIAZZA VITT. EM. II

Citadella

Arsenale

River Arno

LUNGARNO PACINOTTI

LUNGARNO MEDICEO

LUNGARNO MEDICEO

LUNGARNO SIMONELLI

LUNGARNO SONNINO

VIA S. PAOLO

VIA ENRICO FERMI

VIA NICOLA PISANO

VIA B. PISANO

VIA RISORGIMENTO

VIA TRIESTE

VIA ROMA

VIA SANTA MARIA

Orto Botanico

VIA SALVI

VIA CESARE BATTISTI

VIA NINO BIXIO

V. ZERBOGLIO

VIALE BONAINI

VIALE F. BUONARROTI

VIALE BENEDETTO CROCE

PIAZZA TONIOLO

CORSO ITALIA

VIA S. MARTINO

VIA MAZZINI

VIA S. BERNARDO

VIA DI MEZZO

V. PALESTRO

V. DI SIMONE

VIA E. SIGHIERI

V. DI BUTI

VIA DA BUTI

VIA DELLA FAGGIOLA

VIA CORRIDONI

VIA VESPUCCI

VIA DA FRATTI

VIA VESPUCCI

VIA G. BOVIO

GALILEI

VIA S. MARIA

VIA CARDUCCI

VIA S. GIUSEPPE

VIA LUIGI BIANCHI

VIA VALDAGNO

VIA S. ZENO

VIA S. LORENZO

VIA FUCINI

VIA CONTRO

V. OBERDAN

VIA S. FREDIANO

VIA SANTA MARIA

PIAZZA DANTE

VIA GARIBALDI

BORGO STRETTO

Campo Sportivo

N

0 250 m

LUNGARNO FIBONACCI

VIA C. CATTANEO

VIA G. MANZONI

VIA DERNA

VIA FR. CRISPI

VIA S. ANTONIO

VIA LAVAGNA

VIA F. NIOSI

PIAZZA SAFFI

PIAZZA GAMBACORTI

PIAZZA SOLFERINO

PIAZZA VETTOVAGLIE

PIAZZA S. PAOLO

PIAZZA S. FREDIANO

PIAZZA CAIROLI

V. GIORDANO BRUNO

V. D'AZEGLIO

A | B | C | D | E | F | G

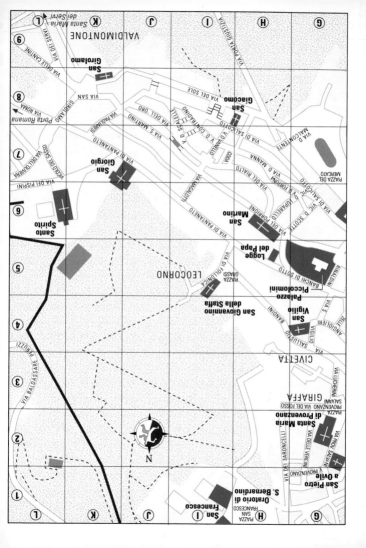

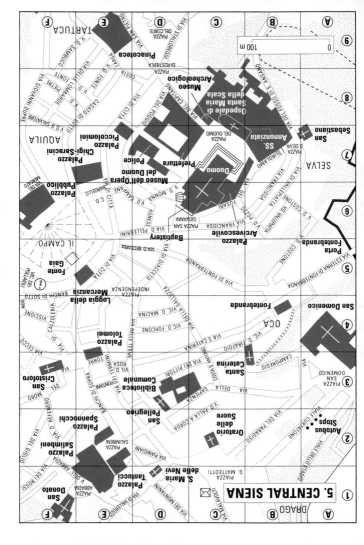

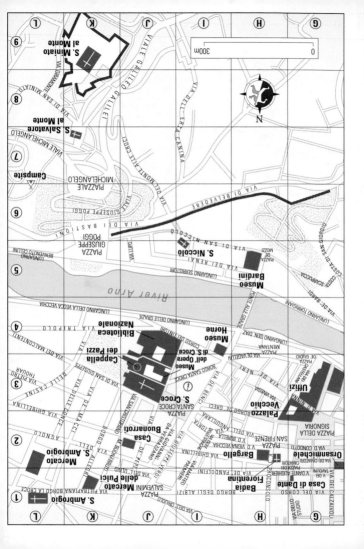

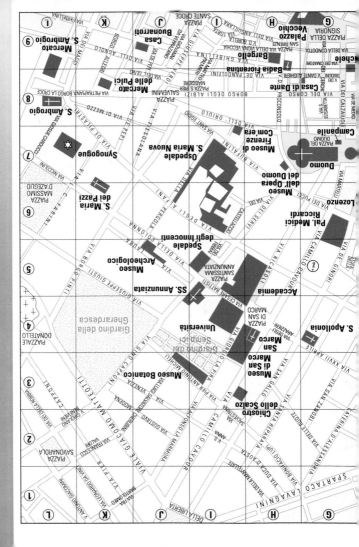

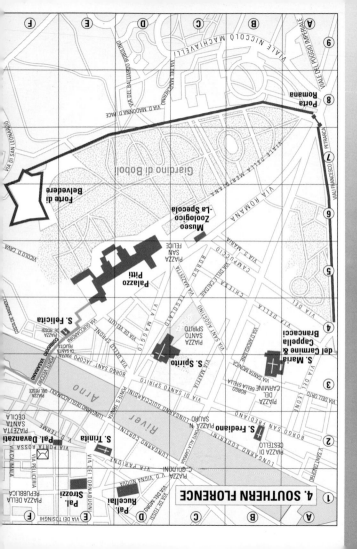